Marrying Anita

A Quest for Love in the New India

Anita Jain

BLOOMSBURY

First published in Great Britain 2008

Copyright © 2008 by Anita Jain

The moral right of the author has been asserted

No part of this book may be used or reproduced in any manner whatsoever without written permission from the Publisher except in the case of brief quotations embodied in critical articles or reviews

Some of the names, locations and details of events in this book have been changed to protect the privacy of persons involved

Bloomsbury Publishing Plc
36 Soho Square
London W1D 3QY

www.bloomsbury.com

Bloomsbury Publishing, London, New York and Berlin

A CIP catalogue record is available from the British Library

ISBN   978 0 7475 8367 7
10 9 8 7 6 5 4 3 2 1

Typeset by Hewer Text UK Ltd, Edinburgh
Printed in Great Britain by Clays Ltd, St Ives plc

The paper this book is printed on is certified by the © Forest Stewardship Council 1996 A.C. (FSC). It is ancient-forest friendly. The printer holds FSC chain of custody SGS-COC-2061 for my mother and father

You can tell the condition of a nation
by looking at the status of its women.

—*Jawaharlal Nehru, first prime minister of India*

Prologue

When I ask my father why he left India, he trots out the same two childhood hardship stories, which in their baroque absurdity bear the tincture of caricature. The one about the banana I've heard every few months since my own childhood, usually provoked when I, or someone else in close proximity, is eating a banana. "I never ate a whole banana when I was growing up. When I was small, we would cut the banana into eight pieces, one for each of us, seven brothers and one sister. *Beta*, you don't know how lucky you are to be eating the full banana," he would say, shaking his head mournfully.

The other, about the comb, is relatively new, and by that I mean my father started telling it to me fifteen instead of twenty-five years ago. For some reason, I have the impression that it is more beloved than even his banana story, because he launches into it with especial plangency. He tells me, his hands waving about for emphasis, "*Beti*, you don't know how tough it was for us growing up. We had one comb between us seven brothers and one sister. And the comb only had two teeth. Two teeth, can you imagine?" In its abject plainspokenness and stark imagery, the story of the comb is far more tragic than the banana story. What could be sadder than a comb with two teeth?

The image of my father and his siblings running the useless, broken comb through their unruly hair, day after day, morning after morning, before school or before work in an empty simulation of what others might be doing with a perfectly functioning comb, undoes something in me. They undergo the pretense not because they hope it will tame their locks but because they know the act of using the comb is what separates them from the real poor of India, the filthy and gray-dusty children of the sweeper who cleans their latrine. Although ineffectual, the gesture brings them ever closer to respectability, to wealth, to a destiny where combs actually detangle and slick back and give shape to a stubborn head of hair.

My line of questioning about why my father left India has become more persistent, forcing him to come up with ever more byzantine tales of indigence. I see him struggling, but sometimes he rises to the occasion and remembers one that could proudly share a shelf with, if not the comb story, then surely the one about the banana. A few years ago, he told me that he was the first of his friends and colleagues to buy a car. He'd found a job as the head of a technical training institute in Kanpur, one of India's "small" towns that is actually quite large, situated in the middle of the great dust-swept state of Uttar Pradesh, a territory in the northern plains dense with people and spare of opportunity—then and now. Like most people he knew, he got around on a scooter. But more and more people were driving cars on India's bare-bones roads, and my father thought having one, not unlike the skeletal comb, would mark yet another advance in the world, carve more distance from his rough-and-tumble upbringing. The car would be physical evidence that hard work and education could add up to something in a country as hopeless and haphazard and relentlessly hot as India.

Although my frugal father will skimp on necessities or comforts others would consider basic—clothes and food, for instance—he's always been fascinated by technology and hates the idea that he might not be in the know. My father's not a techie, he's just an early adopter. I was the last girl I knew to get

Guess jeans, but my family was the first on our block to get a microwave, then a soon-obsolete Beta videotape player, then a Texas Instruments computer. Scraping together all his savings, my father went to the shop in Kanpur and bought a 1939 Ford. It was 1971, and the car cost 1,200 rupees, just under $200 at the time.

He drove it home, proudly called out my mother, and then took her for a spin. After their drive, he parked it on the curb and he and my mother went into their flat to have dinner and retire for the evening. The next morning, he was filled with excitement to drive the vehicle—a whole car!—to work. He couldn't wait to show his colleagues his shiny new (or at least new to him) white Ford. When he stepped out into the sunshine, he saw that it wasn't there.

Shortly after that, he left for America. He was thirty-three years old.

During the summer of 2005, a few months before I turned thirty-three, I moved to India, reversing the migration pattern of my father and nearly a hundred of my relatives, and of many, many others, from a country incorrigibly retrograde, immobilized in amber. In the decade before I returned, the nation had embarked on a makeover, having finally—finally!—cast an envious glance at the so-called tiger economies of Southeast Asian countries such as Thailand and Malaysia. That summer, the stock market was on a rampage, jumping a hundred points a day for weeks on end. India, with its double-digit annual growth rate, was mentioned in the same breath as the economic powerhouse of China. The country's top Bollywood stars, Sushmita Sen and Aishwarya Rai, were making a leap to the big-time neon lights of Hollywood. Fashion designers around the world were looking toward India for inspiration, popularizing long tunics and calf-length peasant skirts. Indian couturiers in their own right were watching models strut their inventions down catwalks in New York and Paris. After decades of being ignored, modern Indian artists could now see their paintings sell in heated auctions at Sotheby's and Christie's in New York and London for six or even seven figures. In 2005, three paintings by contemporary Indian artists crossed the one-million-dollar mark. Before that, the highest amount fetched for a canvas of modern Indian art had been just over $300,000.

And then there was the ongoing technology boom. The United States underwent its boom-and-bust hi-tech cycle, but India had no such tentative pas de deux with technology. It was an out-and-out tango. The rampant practice of software out-sourcing, the vast majority of which ends up on Indian shores, was well documented in the press. Americans learned that people named Prakash and Priti, who went by Peter and Peggy at work, were handling their credit card or technical support queries for U.S. companies from call centers in Bangalore. As more U.S. companies began outsourcing an increasing amount of their business activity, some of which had been handled by skilled workers in the United States, the news stories took on a more alarmist tone—about how Americans were losing their jobs to Prakash and Priti, Rakesh and Sanjay, Shanti and Deepika as corporations tried to cut costs.

I had fled New York, a great glossy and effectual city that seemed to offer a haven to everybody but me, for New Delhi, the sweaty, bureaucratic, and oddly welcoming capital of India. I had been to Delhi before, numerous times in fact, but this time it was different. There was a palpable buzz in the air. Restaurants packed with patrons popped up in every nook and down every grimy alley, no longer restricted to the luxury hotels as they had been for decades. Thai, Italian, Greek. And the bars. Delhi was now laying claim to proper watering holes where the country's like-minded could congregate over a beer or a vodka–Red Bull. Yes, many of these places were still far out of reach for the average Indian, but one couldn't help but notice: Delhi was beginning to look like a city.

Historians will tell you Delhi has been home to nine distinct cities through the ages, the remnants of which are scattered everywhere, like seeds from a flower: a poet's tomb fifty paces from my front door, an old fort not far past the Sundar Nagar market. But I will tell you that there are ten cities of Delhi and I live in the last, one with restaurants where one can order mushroom-and-goat-cheese farfalle, use wireless broadband, and go to nightclubs where girls in spaghetti-strap tank tops gyrate to the latest hip-hop-influenced Bollywood hit.

The waves whipping through India sent Delhi into the modern age. Previous avatars of Delhi had announced themselves with a newfangled type of Indo-Islamic cupola or the wide, orderly streets designed under the British raj. This one arrived atop the juggernaut of globalization, which never travels far without its handmaiden of technology, and nobody knew where it would lead.

That wasn't why I left New York City and came to India, though I'd heard intriguing tales of this new New Delhi. I came for different reasons, reasons that were far more resonant with the never-budging India of time past. I came to find a husband.

Part One

Chapter One

One Friday evening in July, I was padding around my summer sublet, a dorm room in graduate student housing at Columbia University, when Patricia called. Patricia was a friend from London who, like me, had recently moved to New York City. I'd returned to the United States after spending seven years overseas as a foreign journalist.

"Hey, my friend Rupert's having a birthday party down at a bar in the East Village. He's an English journo, and I'm sure his friends will be fun. Do you want to come?" Patricia asked.

I'd just been mulling over which old college friend to call up and ask to accompany me to a movie. But after a few weeks in the city, I'd realized that I couldn't rely solely on my old college friends for a social life. Over the years that I'd been away, they'd formed their own tight-knit circles, and I'd been gone so long that they'd forget to include me in their weekend plans. When they did include me, as frequently happens after a protracted absence, I often felt I couldn't relate to what they were talking about.

Patricia's proposition seemed far more enticing. During my years overseas, I'd spent many an evening out with British journalists. In my experience, they were big drinkers, rapacious conversationalists, and entirely unpredictable.

"What time and where?" I replied.

That summer was inordinately steamy, nearly Delhi-esque in its climes. I tossed on some jeans and a tank top and some low-heeled sandals and walked outside into the moist dusk. I laugh now, but back then, a few months before I turned thirty, the evening was laden with promise, almost clinging to me along with the thick air. As I zoomed downtown on the 1 train from 116th Street, I likened myself to so many who came before me to conquer New York and make it their home.

I arrived the summer of 2002 jobless and with limited resources, having left a fairly senior position at a news service in London in the middle of the worst media downturn the world has ever seen, exacerbated by the September 11 attacks less than a year earlier. I was homesick and, as per the zeitgeist of my generation, dissatisfied. I wanted to do something different.

New York City had always beckoned from afar. Nearly all of my closest friends from college had moved there when I went overseas after graduation. I'd grown up in an antiseptic suburb of northern California and wanted to see the world. I happened to know there was one, having been born in India and visited on numerous occasions. But after spending my twenties in far-flung places like Singapore and Mexico City, New York began to call to me. There was no denying the allure of the city's frenetic energy and its center-of-the-universe appeal. I'd always suspected I would live there one day, when I was ready. I just happened to become ready when the precarious house of cards from which New York drew both its recent prosperity and its glamour came tumbling down.

The dot-com economy had been exposed as little more than a pyramid scheme. The era for baby-faced, pimply pioneers and the sage, forward-looking venture capitalists who threw money at them was over. Several of my friends who had earlier been employed at online media outlets were now searching for jobs with print publications, which, of course, were nearly impossible to come by. The collapse of the Internet bubble had a ripple effect on the whole economy, but the media industry was hit the worst. People were bemoaning the demise of magazines, like *Mademoiselle*, that had been around for decades.

So here I was in the inaugural years of the twenty-first century with a not-too-shabby résumé in hand. I had exchanged my flat in central London for my Columbia dorm room, which I had sublet from a friend of a friend. As I headed downtown that night, I was relieved that I'd finally found a job, if not my dream job, after several months of looking. That and the prospect of a night out filled me with hope.

I arrived at a small bar on Fifth Street in the East Village and took a seat next to Patricia at a long wooden table. She introduced me to her friend Rupert and his girlfriend, seated across from us. A friend of Rupert's who was visiting from London, named Guy, came back to the table with drinks and took a seat next to me. Guy, also a journalist, immediately began regaling me with exotic tales of travel, managing to keep me entertained for the next half hour.

Two more British men walked into the bar. Journalists again, the one who knew Rupert was named Philip, and he was visiting from Africa. He'd brought along a colleague of his who worked for the same newspaper in New York, Simon.

As I was sipping my second glass of Sancerre, Philip had sidled up next to me. He had shaggy blond hair that fell in hanks on both sides of his head and a wolflike face that gave him a hungry appearance. I much preferred the looks of the friend who accompanied him and who, like me, didn't know any of the others now assembled at the table. Simon was bigger; one could even describe him as pear shaped, but it was a heft that gave him gravitas. He had the pleasant, clean-cut look of a mild-mannered man, a type I'd developed a soft spot for over the years. (One of my favorite sayings about the opposite sex is "Men should be seen, not heard.") When Philip mentioned that Simon had worked in Spain and Italy, and spoke fluent Spanish and Italian, I felt something spike in my chest.

A few months earlier, I had left my Spanish boyfriend in his hometown of Santander, a city by the sea perched on rolling hills, like San Francisco. Jose Luis, with his Roman nose and Grecian-bust head of curls, was as kind and trustworthy as a man could be, but our backgrounds were too different, and I could not envision a future. He was a chef; I was a journalist. Our conversations foundered, if not in the chasm between our unshared interests, then certainly in the yawning canyon dividing Spanish and English. Neither of us had managed to master the other's native tongue.

While Philip chatted away to me in one ear, my gaze alighted on Simon, who had yet to say a word all evening. The quiet, confident type, I thought. The kind who does not need to trumpet his ruggedness or sophistication.

I addressed a question to Simon: "So you were in Spain and Italy? When did you move to New York?"

"Yes, I was based in Rome last. I moved to New York six months ago," he said.

"How do you like it?" I asked, quickly adding that I'd just moved here as well—cleverly establishing our camaraderie.

"New York is all right. Where did you move from? Your accent is American," he said.

"I grew up in the U.S., in California. Then I went overseas. I was just working in London and then traveling for a few months in Spain," I answered, pleased when I noticed that his face seemed to register our commonalities.

"And you're a journalist?" Simon asked.

"I am, but an unemployed one," I said.

Simon smiled, waiting for more information.

"Well, actually, I just got a job, which I'm starting next week. It's at this Zionist rag—and no, I don't mean the *New York Times*," I said cheekily, knowing my British audience would appreciate the sentiment, as European rhetoric tends toward a softer approach on the Middle East conflict. I was about to start working at a recently launched daily newspaper that promoted an aggressively pro-Israel ideology.

Simon's smile grew wider, and then he began chuckling. Philip, who'd been edged out of the conversation, laughed as well, though I don't think my quip quite registered with him. Guy had disappeared earlier but returned when we were enjoying the laugh. He tried to draw me back into conversation. Then it hit me: these three men were *competing* for my attention.

You know those moments when through some karmic commingling or cosmic beneficence, all the elements of an evening come together? That night, I was just drunk enough to feel charged and confident without overdoing it. And the attention I was receiving from Philip, Simon, and Guy was enough to fuel a fairly steady stream of quick-witted conversation. I'm sure a benign smirk rested on my face the entire evening.

Patricia came over to me. "We're all leaving for a place in Soho," she said.

"Oh, okay," I said, noticing that everybody in our group was paying for their drinks and rising from their seats. My drinks had been taken care of by my admirers and I didn't leave a cent.

I left the bar with Philip and Simon flanking me like guards on either side. The three of us began walking down the street and rounded the corner at the next avenue—was it Avenue B? Halfway down the next block, one of the guys noticed that no one from the group in the bar was following us.

"Weren't they right behind us?" Philip asked.

"I thought they were," Simon said. "Well, why don't we call them?"

I kept my mouth shut, as I'd clearly been paying no attention to anyone but the men who were paying attention to me.

I dialed the number Philip provided for Rupert and handed the phone over to him. Rupert told Philip the group had cabbed it downtown to the Lower East Side and gave him directions to the new bar. All three of us were newcomers to New York. Simon and I had lived there only a few months, and Philip was visiting. We all looked at each other and shrugged.

"Aw, fuck it, let's just keep walking," Philip said, voicing the idea we all had in mind—to uncover the city's nocturnal wonders on our own.

That evening, we prowled the East Village, entering every bar in the vicinity—the wood-paneled dives, where we stood up or sat on stools at the counter; the red-upholstered lounge with sofas; the intimate, sparse, dark and narrow bar with leather couches. We were all very drunk, and though I was aware—or at least I am now—that alcohol and the prospect of sex do loosen a man's tongue, it did nothing to diminish the woozy effect their fusillade of compliments induced in me.

At one of the first bars we dropped into, where we sat arrayed in separate sofa chairs, Philip leaned forward and said, "You know, you have beautiful eyes."

"Why, thank you," I said, giggling.

Now it was Simon's turn. "Well, I think your hair is quite lovely."

"Really, do you? Well, I think both of you are pleasant-looking people as well," I said.

The three of us erupted into laughter. This was as much about them as it was about me, in that way that men competing for a woman are in fact asserting their masculine prowess more than trying to impress their catch. By this point, I'd learned that both had girlfriends in another city.

I am never the best-looking woman in a room—in New York, or in London, or, as I would later learn, in Delhi. I am most certainly not the thinnest, and I'm almost always the shortest. But having grown up small and Indian in California, I had early on learned that I would have to develop more rarified qualities to distinguish myself from other girls. I was abysmal at sports (the only B I ever received in high school was in physical education) and was embarrassingly good at my studies. I got an A+ in calculus, but compensated by getting a C in what they called "citizenship," meaning that I was too often found whispering in the aisles and passing notes back and forth with my friends during class.

It would probably have been easier to turn my academic achievement into an advantage had I grown up in a place like New York or New Delhi. But I'd grown up in northern California, populated as far as the eye can see with the athletic, golden hued, and freckled. Back then, there were only two or three other Indian students in my entire high school. If I was ever going to get any male attention that didn't include trying to copy my exam answers, I had to develop character, and I mean that in both senses of the word, which perhaps is a rare combination. A loud, goofy laugh, an insouciance, and—I must confess—a certain manic quality have often led others to describe me as a "character," while I'd like to believe I'm also in possession of what people traditionally think of as qualities defining good character: honesty (to a pathological degree, at times), loyalty, steadfastness. Perhaps I flatter myself.

But I digress. Back to the East Village that sticky July night. The bars were closing down and we were ejected from a place at 4 A.M., but we didn't want to end our revelry. Not surprisingly, when a man offered to sell us some marijuana a few blocks from the bar from which we had just emerged, we bought it and jumped the fence at Tompkins Square Park right across the street, which had closed for the night. We rolled a joint and I had a few drags, which made me slightly steadier on my feet. Yet I was still giddy from the evening—how could I not be?—and I did cartwheels on the grass.

A guard came over and we tried to hide our spliff, but he wanted to smoke as well. He was from Haiti and his name was Jean-Michel. The evening had attained fantastical proportions.

Philip, though, was getting antsy and wanted to go home— and me to go with him.

"Look, they've put me up in this really nice hotel. You can sleep in the other bed. I won't touch you, I promise. I'll take you for breakfast in the morning," he pleaded.

"No, I don't think it would be a good idea," I said.

"Please, I promise I won't touch you," he beseeched.

Not wanting our easy rapport to turn ugly, I looked up at Simon. "Will you make sure I get home okay?"

He nodded yes, telling Philip, "Hey, come on, mate, leave her alone."

Simon and I jumped into a cab, leaving Philip swearing and wobbling on the street as we sped uptown. I felt ashamed that I was living in a dorm room and prepared Simon for the sight in the taxi—"I'm staying in a college dormitory. It's just temporary until I find an apartment." When we got home, I kept him up talking on the couch until light filtered in through the fire escape window. I asked him about his girlfriend in Rome. They'd been together for many years, and the long-distance relationship had been hard on him.

I liked him. I wanted to know things about him, everything about him, even if they excluded me from the picture. I wanted to keep talking. But this is not the reason men with girlfriends end up in another woman's apartment at 6 A.M. Simon suggested we sleep. We went into my room and got into my twin bed. I took off my jeans. Simon did as well. We were both uncomfortable lying stiffly next to each other, he because he felt guilty and I because I actually liked him. I finally nuzzled myself into his arm and he began kissing me.

After a few minutes, Simon piped up, "May I remove your bottom?"

Waves of laughter broke in my belly but did not spill forth from my mouth, afraid as I was of embarrassing him. To this day, my friends can send me into hysterics by saying in their most clipped imitation of a British accent, "May I remove your bottom?"

"Yes, you may," I said in a small voice.

He did, but we were too shy, in addition to guilty, drunk, and fatigued, to do much but touch each other tentatively before we fell asleep.

In the late morning, around 11 A.M., an extremely guilt-ridden Simon woke up and threw on his clothing. I sat up in bed, still wearing my tank top from the night before. I asked him to call me, so that the night, or rather I, wouldn't feel cheap. He hurried out and I went back to sleep.

In the late afternoon, around 5 P.M., I was woken by the sound of my cell phone ringing. When I answered, a man with an English accent said, "Hello, is that Anita?"

Thinking it was Simon, I mumbled into the phone, "Hmm, yeah, just woke up. How are you? Did you get home alright?"

"Anita, this is Guy. Where did you guys end up disappearing to last night? I was waiting for you at the other bar."

I tried to figure out who it was, and then I recalled the third guy, Guy, from the night before.

"Oh, hi. I'm so sorry. We just got lost and carried on. It was quite a big night of drinking," I said, already feeling ashamed for what had transpired.

"That's too bad, because I'm just here for the weekend and then going back to London. In any case, Rupert and I are going out tonight. Would you like to come?"

I begged off that evening, thinking I'd had enough fun, not to mention male attention, for one weekend. Instead, I went out to dinner with Farhad, another friend I'd met in London and who'd transported himself to New York a few months before I did. He was attending a graduate program at Columbia and had hooked me up with my dorm sublet.

We were having dinner in the crowded outdoor area of one of those restaurants along Broadway near the university. Between mouthfuls of pasta, I began relating all of the previous night's high jinks, taking particular glee in drawing out every last detail.

Farhad laughed mirthfully when I was finished and decided to dub the evening the "Night of the Three Blokes."

"Anita dear, you have many fine qualities, and it goes without saying that were I at all interested in women I would certainly find you attractive, but I've never known you to be that much the mankiller," Farhad said.

"Right, thanks," I said.

He continued, unbidden and deep in concentration, trying to explain precisely the effect, or lack of one, I had on men. "You know, you're more of an acquired taste. You're like the Indian girl in *Bend It Like Beckham*—you know, quirky and intense, but not for everybody. No breezy glamourpuss like Keira Knightley. And also, English men hardly paid any attention to you when you were in London."

"Thanks for reminding me, Farhad," I retorted. "Are you done yet?"

After all, it was true. English people always seemed to me far more accessible when you met them outside of England. In London, Farhad, an Iranian man who'd grown up in Japan, and I clung to each other and to our misfit status. Even the Asian Brit culture, with its lingo and icons, seemed so daunting as to be hermetically sealed.

"But you're right, what happened last night has never happened to me before. Maybe my luck's changing. Maybe New York will be different," I said, pausing. "And I really like this Simon guy, but he has a girlfriend in Rome. Should I call him?"

"Absolutely not! Stay away from men with girlfriends," he said, aware that I had a less-than-spotless record in this regard. "Anyway, it doesn't seem like you'll be single for long."

Nothing came of Simon and me, though it would be quite a few months before I was able to forget him. I would return countless times to the East Village over the next three years, though somehow I could never correlate that night with the British journalists with the neighborhood's swarm of NYU students and black-toenailed Goths. Had it really happened? I couldn't even locate the watering holes we'd been to that evening. Much like in those movies where a gullible mark realizes he's been subjected to some elaborate con and the hotels or offices he'd entered as part of the scheme no longer exist or never did, they'd vanished, along with the endless romantic possibilities I'd envisioned for myself that night.

Chapter Two

My parents, living in semiretirement in California, had been waiting for my return to the U.S. for years. Their wayward daughter, who'd been carelessly frolicking in foreign countries without a jot of concern for her future, was finally within striking distance—that is, arranging-to-be-married distance. Their daughter, who seemed not to care that she had let precious marriageable years slip through her fingers, was now only a national long-distance phone call away. She could now be harangued far more frequently and for far less money.

Throughout my twenties, they had tried to arrange introductions with various suitors they'd found through newspaper advertisements in the cities in which I'd lived. In Singapore, I'd met one or two men as they were passing through. In London, also at my parents' behest, I agreed to these meetings more out of a desire to silence my parents than a hope that anything would come of them. Overseas, I was far less susceptible to their long-range attacks. But now it seemed a front had opened up on domestic soil. And my left flank, the one that housed my tender heart, was dangerously vulnerable.

I had always expected to get married. It would not be a stretch to say that "*shaadi*," the word for "marriage" in many Indian languages, is the first word a child in an Indian family understands after *mummy* and *papa*. To an Indian, marriage is a matter of karmic destiny. There are many happy unions in the pantheon of Hindu gods—Shiva and Parvati, Krishna and

Radha, Ram and Sita. Marriage is even enshrined in Hinduism, India's majority religion, as one of the four life stages: child, student, householder (i.e., with spouse and kids), and ascetic. Yes, as a good Hindu, one must get married—even if only to later renounce the marriage and family, give up worldly comforts, and live in the forest, as the fourth stage prescribes. Even the great Buddha was married before he became a wandering mendicant.

My parents wed in an arranged marriage four decades ago and are among the happiest couples I've ever known, bringing to mind Tolstoy's first line of *Anna Karenina*. Substituting the word "couples" for "families," it would read, "Happy couples are all alike; every unhappy couple is unhappy in its own way." It's a truism really, for I suspect every happy couple is similar in that they engage in a lifelong conversation—both metaphorically and literally.

My parents chatter away to each other incessantly, from the moment they awake until they sleep, gossiping about friends and relatives alike and teasing each other about their respective foibles—my father's television addiction and my mother's propensity for relentless nagging—and then laughing it off. (If I have learned anything from my parents, it is this: the grave importance of teasing and being able to be teased, and the near holy need to laugh.)

"What are you doing? You know you're only allowed to watch television from seven to nine in the morning and five to ten at night," my mother will say, while my father is glued to a midday *Oprah*.

"You never let me do anything. I live in a prison," my father will reply, fake-glumly.

"*TV ko bandh karo.* Turn the TV off. And look, the dishwasher hasn't even been unloaded," my mother will say, and then, without any real anger and rolling her eyes, "I give you only one chore, and that even you cannot do!"

They rarely fight—except the Pavlovian bickering triggered by my mother's noticing my father hasn't unloaded the dishwasher—and they do everything together. Bringing a particular Hindu twist to their successful coupledom, my mother said once during one of our family *pujas*, or prayer ceremonies, a few years ago that she would like to be married to my father over and over again in her subsequent lives.

I attribute their successful marriage to two factors that seem to contradict each other—my father's progressive ideas about a woman's status and my mother's agreeable and self-effacing nature. My father is a man who gave his wife full freedom to become an independent-minded woman, but my mother took that freedom, noted it, appreciated it, stored it away, and decided to be entirely dependent on my father. By her own decision, my mother never pursued a career and doesn't drive.

They are inseparable the entire day. They wake up at 6 A.M., do yoga and breathing exercises to a videotape, eat breakfast, perform errands and do the shopping together, eat one large meal around 3 P.M. meant to combine lunch and dinner for dietary reasons, nap, and then sit in the family room of their recently built split-level McMansion in a neo-California suburb that sprang up a year ago. There, in their spacious family room, my father watches television and my mother reads her various health, spiritual, and self-help books and articles, furiously underlining parts that strike her as being of the utmost importance, which she immediately relays to my father.

"*Sunno ji,* listen to this, green tea is very good for the body and has many antioxidants. We should drink it four times a day, this article says."

"*Haan*, okay. I'll buy some tomorrow. We'll start drinking it instead of chai. No more chai," my father will reply absentmindedly without having diverted an iota of his attention away from *Desperate Housewives*.

"This book says we should visualize all of the things we would like to happen in our lives. We must always engage in positive thinking. And you're always thinking too negative too much. This is why you are getting depression all the time," she will say.

"*Haan*, I will start visualizing good things only then. Only best things. I'll start tonight," he'll say, still focused on the television.

"We should visualize nice boy for Anita. I am visualizing and praying all the time, but you are always watching TV. You should also visualize," my mother will say.

Mention of his daughter's marriage will perk up his ears, and for the first time he will turn away from the television and look at my mother.

"What can I do?! I'm trying so hard to find a boy! I've put out so many advertisements in the newspapers. Even I've started looking on the Internet, but she is not doing. That girl is not serious about *shaadi*," he will say, a sad look creeping into his face. He has momentarily forgotten about Eva Longoria's affair with the boy gardener on *Desperate Housewives*.

"We must make her serious about *shaadi*. Anita is not listening. Basically she is not caring about finding boy. I will visualize only good boy for her," my mother will say.

"*Haan!* She is not caring at all about *shaadi*. I will call her right now and ask her what she is doing and why she is waiting. Everybody is doing *shaadi*, and she is not listening to us. Anita doesn't listen to anyone. This is the problem," my father will say, leaping up at a crucial cliffhanger scene to grab his cell phone.

At that moment, I could be sitting in an intimate Soho lounge on a date with a French investment banker, or with a group of girlfriends drinking martinis in some chic new place with chrome and orange accents in Tribeca.

Hearing my phone, I will rush to grab it, fumbling around in my purse as the first few rings elapse, only to have my heart sink when the display panel flashes "Papa" over and over. I will sigh heavily, wait for three or four more rings (hoping it will stop), and then answer, "*Haan*, Papa."

"Listen, Anita. Mummy and I were just talking about you. You are not serious about *shaadi*! You are not caring! You are just going here and there. Always with friends. Now you've come back to America and your age is now getting more, and you must search for a boy. What will you do about *shaadi*?!" Papa will say, clearly agitated as a television commercial blares in the background.

"Papa, can we please talk about this later? I am looking. I'm trying. I promise. I just haven't found anyone," I'll moan, my relaxed post-work mood disintegrating.

And it was true. I *was* looking. I'd been looking all my life, in fact. Romance had always been a top priority for me. Not for me plugging away at work to scale vertiginous professional heights. Certainly I was just as ambitious as the next person, but not at the expense of romance—that first tentative kiss, that gently ribbing e-mail, that delicious moment impregnated with desire when you are with a lover and a bottle of wine and Dusty Springfield is playing off the computer in your apartment and you can't decide which is more urgent and enticing, to talk and spill all your secrets or to lunge at each other.

How to explain, then, why I returned to New York empty-handed despite my energetic efforts at romance over the years and over many cities? It just happened, like it did to all the other women in New York who'd been involved in a string of relationships in their twenties only to find themselves alone soon after hitting thirty.

I returned to New York with no fancy job, no assets, and certainly no life partner. I had watched many of my peers who had also sought their fortunes abroad in journalism, finance, or consulting embark on amorous adventures that had ended in marriage. I had heard numerous stories of rendezvous in exotic locales, Bali or Koh Phi Phi or Paris. Hadn't I also flung myself into the world for this? To meet risk-courting war photographers or city-hopping financiers involved in complex options and swaps transactions, or even bookish magazine editors, bespectacled and bearing copies of Kerouac, Thompson, Mailer, and Amis—both Kingsley and Martin? Making things even worse upon my arrival in New York was that nearly all of my close girlfriends who lived in the city were married.

I could not fault my parents for wanting to see their daughter happily settled—isn't that what all parents want? And, for traditionally minded Indian parents, they had certainly given me a rare amount of freedom during my twenties to find someone of my own choosing to marry. I hadn't, and now, as they saw it, it was time for them to step in.

At the same time, it had always been up to me who I dated, so it seemed desperately retrograde to allow my parents to find someone for me. And I'll admit to being more than a little intrigued about what I would find in New York, a city renowned for its vulturous dating culture.

I had been living in Asia and Europe, where courtship seemed to unfold at a more organic pace. Friends met up routinely in bars or pubs after work, facilitating an environment in which friends of friends could be introduced or brought into the fold. In New York, people seemed to spend endless amounts of time at work and then scurry off to the gym. Later, they would log on to their computers, trying to conjure up a perfect fit in their dark apartments.

Other aspects of the dating culture were even more daunting. In a type of sexual free-for-all, women threw dozens of men up against their bedroom walls in the hope one would stick. I was hardly a prude, but the casualness with which people conducted their sexual lives intimidated me. Even the argot of dating I heard in New York was formidable. At my job at the small fledgling newspaper, I would overhear young women talking about JDate and booty calls, and, worst of all, fuckbuddies, a term that still makes me cringe when I hear it. Nonetheless, I was willing to wade into this indecorous morass to see what I could find.

At first, I retained some principles, such as my conviction that Internet dating turned people into commodities. Moreover, it seemed kind of time consuming. Men spent hours writing the perfectly turned ironic New Yorky profile to get women to write to them, and then when the women met their sharp-witted suitors, they were more tongue-tied than rapier tongued; in fact, these guys wouldn't recognize irony if it came up and introduced itself.

So I went to a lot of parties with my friends from college. I began to realize, however, that after my years overseas, my tastes in men tended somewhat toward the international. I couldn't seem to muster the requisite interest in wholesome boys from Ohio. They were so *earnest*. And the ones who weren't were the Williamsburg hipsters who cobbled together an existence from writing blogs and playing experimental music. They were so aggressively *quirky*. The lack of interest, more often than not, was mutual.

A married friend, Nadia, who'd attended a business school in France, always made a point of inviting me along to her alumni cocktails at some well-appointed downtown bar. Once I met a dashing Lebanese diplomat who'd also come along with friends. We chatted for an hour before he placed his hand on my bottom. I thought it was a bit forward, but then I thought being an acting ambassador to the UN might account for his confidence, as well as my willingness to go along with the overture.

He suggested we go to another bar. It was deep winter, so I interpreted his willingness to leave a cozy, warm place for another as a sign of his interest in me. We put on our heavy woolen coats, tied scarves around our necks, gloved our hands, and stepped out onto a slushy Twentieth Street. I was heading toward a bar I knew down the street when the diplomat turned to me and said in his cultured accent, "Why don't we just jump in a cab and go to my apartment uptown?"

Taken aback, I said, "Well, I'm not so into that idea. Why don't we just step into this place and have a drink?"

In the second bar, we found a dark corner, and the Lebanese diplomat went to the bar to fetch two glasses of red wine. When he returned, I tried to engage him in conversation, saying something pathetically vague like, "So this is fascinating. You're the acting ambassador to the UN?"

"Yeah, it's fine. I just have to vote on issues here and there," he said, his hands roaming down my back and hips.

I noticed his hands were making forays into the breast region. We hadn't even kissed yet. I leaned in for a kiss, but he pecked me on the cheek. His hands continued to familiarize themselves with my body. I decided to take a more direct approach and brought my lips close to his, just short of a full pucker. He pulled away.

"Um, kiss?" I ventured, nodding toward his hands, which were lying on the front of my sweater on my breasts. "Isn't that kind of what we're supposed to do first?"

"I find kissing a bit intimate," he said, diplomatically enough.

"Well, I find this a bit too intimate. I think we should finish our drinks." I swooshed to the opposite end of the sofa. We left a few minutes later. I jumped into a cab. He didn't ask for my number.

I decided to give him diplomatic immunity. Wasn't I over-reaching if I thought I could bag the Lebanese ambassador to the UN? I was as yet uncowed.

At a rooftop party a few months later, I met Alex, a handsome consultant with dark and curly hair. We talked all night, and soon after, I received an e-mail from him inviting me to his apartment for dinner. It was our first real date, and I was flattered—and encouraged—that he was already cooking for me. He lived uptown near Harlem and I took the train from Grand Central after work, stopping off to buy some Argentine wine on the way. He brought out some cheese and opened the wine. Fumes from the vegetarian lasagna he was preparing in accordance with my dietary restrictions wafted out to the living room.

He was a telecom consultant, and since I was reporting on telecommunications at work, I thought it might make an apropos conversation piece.

"So do you think Verizon's move into voice-over-IP will be successful? It really seems it's the future of telecoms," I said, perkily.

"Uh, sure. I guess. It's a big company. It'll survive," he said.

Hmm, talking about Verizon's corporate strategy didn't seem to be setting the mood for romance. By the time dinner was ready, I took a different tack and started cooing over the food. "It's just so good. Where did you learn to cook like this?"

When we'd polished off the wine and lasagna, Alex brought out a tiramisu, and this is when he started talking about his long-distance girlfriend who lived in Tokyo. He also sought my advice on how to ask out the cute girl from the gym, saying he wanted a female perspective on it. Perhaps I shouldn't have talked quite so lengthily about Verizon's aggressive Wi-Fi rollout.

Even this deflating experience didn't dim my optimism about finding romance in New York. What eroded my idealism was the following succession of cads I met, all of whom told me—over dinner or while we were kissing at the end of a boozy night—"I'm not looking for anything serious." If it was spoken at the outset, then it was a perfect "Get out of jail free" card. They could always stop calling or taking my calls because they'd been "honest" with me.

The line so irked me that I began hearing it whispered everywhere, every man—the security guard at my office building, waiters at restaurants, the cashier at the CVS pushing change at me across the counter—silently mouthing the words at me. *I'm not looking for anything serious. I'm not looking for a serious relationship.* How did anyone procreate in this city?

I seemed to have greater luck attracting romantic attention when I left New York. It was during a trip to Argentina that I met Juan Carlos, a black-haired, green-eyed painter—of buildings, not canvases. Within an hour of meeting me, he said he would become a vegetarian as soon as we married, that he'd never felt this way for any woman before— *"nunca en mi vida"*— that I was the mother of his children. Oddly, by the end of the night, he couldn't remember my name.

Nothing fazed Juan Carlos, however. He quickly jotted off a poem explaining his lapse: "I wrote your name in the sand, but a wave came and washed it away. I wrote your name in a tree, but the branch fell. I have written your name in my heart, and time will guard it."

Perhaps, though, I'm giving the impression that I was always being mistreated or rejected. I, too, was picky about who I wanted to enter a relationship with—though I don't recall ever telling anyone "I'm not looking for anything serious."

One Christmas, the ever-helpful Nadia invited me to her stockbroker husband's office party. I didn't remember talking to anyone in particular that evening, but one of her husband's colleagues noticed me and asked Nadia's husband for my number.

When William called, I couldn't place him, but Nadia's husband assured me he was a decent guy and that he was one of the firm's more successful stockbrokers—and since they were paid on commission, this was actually saying something. Something like "He's loaded, *loa-ded*. Like $400,000-a-year loaded." William had made dinner reservations at Sushi Samba near Union Square for Saturday evening. By this point, I'd been so disappointed by the behavior men in New York got away with that I was touched that someone had simply made reservations in my honor.

I didn't recognize William when I arrived at the restaurant fifteen minutes late, but was pleased that he was rather attractive. At some point during dinner, I asked him about his family.

"It's just me and my mother," he said.

"Oh, okay. So where is your father?" I asked.

"My father's not in the picture," he said, in a way that told me not to pursue that line of conversation. He didn't say "My father left us before I was born" or "That's a sore topic," but "My father's not in the picture."

Later, when William told me his mother was a lesbian, I began to think it was entirely possible that his father had been found at a sperm bank. I processed this with careful determination not to let the realization pass across my face. It was only when he told me his mother was adopted that I flinched. I was holding some noodles with my chopsticks and they fell into my lap. Let's see, his mother didn't know who her parents were, and he didn't know who his father was. I was sitting with the Man Who Had No Past.

I looked at William, at his bright blue eyes, his blondish hair, his oddly red-tinted lips. He was like a phoenix rising from the ashes of an unknown civilization. I was too unnerved to see him again.

Dating in New York was steadily grinding me down, like water on a stone rubbing all my edges smooth. Of course, there was the growing acknowledgment of how futile it seemed, and not just for me. Many women I encountered and befriended in New York—most of my colleagues, my landlord's daughter—were facing the same emotionally excruciating uphill battle. But I began to realize something else too, something that caused me no small amount of surprise. And this was that perhaps I, too, was looking for something a bit more like what my parents had enjoyed for so many years. My resistance to my parents' attempts to arrange my marriage began to soften.

Chapter Three

The pressure on me to find a husband started very early. A few days after my first birthday, within months of my family's arrival in the United States, I fell out the window of a three-story building in Baltimore. My mother's greatest concern at the time, after learning that I hadn't been gravely injured, was my marriageability.

"What boy will marry her when he finds out?" she cried, begging my father to never mention my broken arm—from which I've enjoyed a full recovery—to prospective suitors out of fear my dowry would be prohibitively higher. Though technically illegal, the practice of a bride's family giving a handsome dowry to the groom and his family still thrives in India, and the country's newspapers are filled with reports of dowry-related harassment, suicides, and murders. A reasonably well-off family in India can easily spend $100,000 in dowry these days.

Much savvier in the ways of his new country, my father laughed it off. "But there is no dowry in America!" he said.

Fulfilling his parental duty, my father placed matrimonial ads for me every couple of months during my twenties in such immigrant newspapers as *India Abroad*. They read something like, "Match for Jain girl, Harvard-educated journalist, 25, fair, slim." I took it as a personal victory that they didn't include the famous Indian misnomer "homely" to mean domestically inclined. Depending on whether my father was in a magnanimous mood, he would add "Caste no bar," which meant suitors didn't have to belong to Jainism, an offshoot of Hinduism with the world's most severe dietary restrictions. Root vegetables like carrots are verboten.

Despite years of living in the U.S., my father still harbored a prejudice against meat eaters. He would immediately discard responses from those with a "non-veg" diet. There was, however, a special loophole for meat eaters who earned more than $200,000 a year. (As for me, my vegetarianism had lapsed for the duration of my relationship with my Spanish chef boyfriend, Jose, who'd gotten me addicted to chorizo. Once, I was horrified to discover, he'd put a skinned rabbit in my freezer.)

In more traditional arranged marriages—which are still very much alive and well in India—couples may get only one or two meetings before their wedding day. In big Indian cities, in America and elsewhere in the Indian diaspora, a couple may have a few months to get to know each other before they are expected to walk down the aisle, or rather around the fire, as they do seven times, in keeping with Hindu custom.

Although I've long believed that you need no more than six months to assess someone's character, I'd never thought I'd get married the way my brother had. He'd met his wife through a newspaper ad my parents had taken out in *India Abroad.* He's happily married with two young daughters, but he'd never had a girlfriend before his wedding day. My first kiss was at fourteen with Matt from the football squad. Maybe that's where it all started to go wrong.

My father's desultory casting around to see what was out there became much more urgent as time wore on in New York and I was no closer to marriage. It was becoming difficult to overlook my advancing age, thirty-one, and soon, thirty-two—an age for an unmarried woman that makes Indian aunties shudder in horror. It wasn't even like I was divorced, implying that I'd at least tried.

Being a divorced thirty-two-year-old Indian woman has the exact opposite effect that being an unmarried thirty-two-year-old Indian woman does. Instead of clucking around you asking about your matrimonial intentions, all the aunties studiously avoid you, assuming you've all but escaped death from an abusive husband. This, and the fact that the divorcee in question might be cursed, and contact with them might somehow be transferred to the aunties' children, keeps aunties at a safe distance.

My parents' quest for a husband for me eventually led them to a dizzying array of Web sites. Only a couple of months earlier, my father had begun dabbling on the Internet after hearing he could pay his bills and buy and sell stocks online. That's when he tripped onto the marriage sites, and it was as if he'd stumbled across a magic key in a fantasy game that unlocked the door to a world full of untold wonders. Among countless others, there were shaadi.com, indiamatrimony.com, bharatmatrimony.com, and jeevansathi.com—this last of which translates to "life partner" in Hindi. Within these sites were subsites for Indian communities, like punjabimatrimony.com or parsimatrimony .com. At his fingertips were hundreds upon thousands of potential grooms.

In fact, there was a surprising number of people on these sites one wouldn't expect to succumb to such an antiquity. Some of them seemed to be men that I would actually consider meeting. They could have been the guy in the next cubicle, someone's freshman-year roommate at NYU, even the cute guy I ran into at a bar in the Lower East Side last night.

Far from being a novel approach to matrimony, these sites are a natural extension of how things have been done in India for decades. Well before the explosion of the country's famously vibrant press in the fifties, Indians were coupling via matrimonial advertisements in national newspapers ("Match sought for Bengali Brahmin, wheatish complexion," etc.).

My father took to these Web sites like a freshly divorced forty-two-year-old on match.com. He uploaded my profile on several, indicating that only men living in New York City need apply. Unfortunately, in the world of shaadi.com, this meant most of the men lived in New Jersey, commuting to their jobs in software development or IT support in the city.

My father also *wrote* my profile. This may be why some of my dates were surprised to discover I enjoy a glass of wine or two with dinner, and another couple afterward, even though the profile read "I never drink." And Papa would write back to those who appeared promising. Separating the wheat from the chaff is no small task, as anyone who's done any online dating can attest. As my father likes to say, wagging his head, "You get a lot of useless types."

Like most Indians of their generation, and notwithstanding their long stay in the U.S., my parents believe there are only two legitimate professions: doctor and engineer. Yes, they've heard of such newfangled professions as investment banking and law, but oh no, they won't be fooled. Across India can be heard the refrain, "It is good match: they found doctor," and my father expected nothing less for his little girl.

The problem is that while he wanted a doctor or engineer, my heart beat for an aging but rakish foreign correspondent. Nearing fifty, he'd just seen his marriage fall apart, and he mourned its passing by plastering his body with fresh tattoos and picking bar fights. I found it terribly sexy that he rode a Harley, perhaps less so that his apartment was decorated with Wonder Woman paraphernalia. He was on a downward spiral, but perhaps my parents might appreciate that he'd won a Pulitzer prize earlier in his career?

During my parents' frantic search for a husband for their daughter—that two-headed beast of an unmarried thirtysomething woman—I began getting bombarded with odd e-mails that read, "We liked the girl's profile. The boy is in good state job in Mississippi and cannot come to New York. The girl must relocate to Mississippi." The message was signed by Mr. Ramesh Gupta, "the boy's father," and the e-mail wasn't addressed to me. It was to my father. I had been CC'd.

That wasn't as bad as the one I'd received a few weeks earlier that demanded, forgoing any preamble, what the date, time, and location of my birth were. Presumably sent to determine my astrological compatibility with a Hindu suitor, the e-mail was dismayingly abrupt. But I did take heart in the fact that it was addressed only to me.

At least e-mails weren't intrusive. One Sunday, I was woken by a call at nine A.M. A woman with a heavy Indian accent asked for Anita. I have a raspy voice at the best of times, but after a night of "social" smoking, my register is on par with Clint Eastwood's.

So when I croaked, "This is she," the perplexed lady responded, "She or he?" before asking, "What are your qualifications?"

I said I had a B.A. "B.A. only?" she responded.

"What are the boy's qualifications?" I flung back in an androgynous voice.

She smirked: "He is M.D. in Kentucky only."

Still bleary eyed, but with enough presence of mind to use the deferential term for an elder, I grumbled, "Auntie, I will speak to the boy only."

Neither she nor he called back.

Of course, as a woman who'd led a remarkably independent life, I found these missives from the parents of suitors alarming. But then my search for anything resembling affection in the alienating city on my own—it had now been well over a year—wasn't quite working out either. I couldn't even get someone to call me back after a date, let alone marry me. Perhaps if I met some of these suitors directly—the ones my father had been in correspondence with—I might just end up liking one of them. Yes, maybe a little romantic assistance might not hurt. Certainly it was a bit ironic that I expected the men to go through my father, while I circumvented their parents, but I wanted to convince myself as much as possible that I wasn't *really* doing this arranged-marriage thing. Papa was just handling the back end. It distanced me from the process.

Since my father was the point of contact on shaadi.com, he would be contacted by a potential suitor or would contact one himself, they would exchange e-mails, and then my father would make a decision on whether to pass along my e-mail address.

I did have my limits. I hit delete on e-mails with fresh-off-the-boat Indian English, like "Hope e-mail is finding you in pink of health" or "I am looking for life partner for share of joy of life and sorrowful time also." Then there was always that swoon-inducing romantic opener: "I am B. Sc in electrical engineering and also having master's in systems operation."

One of my first setups in New York was with a man named Vivek, who worked in IT in New Jersey, where he'd lived his entire life. He took the train into the city to meet me at Starbucks. He was wearing pants that ended two inches above his ankles.

We spoke briefly about his work before he asked, "What are you looking for in a husband?"

Since this question always leaves me flummoxed—especially when it's asked within the first few minutes of conversation by somebody in high-waters—I mumbled something along the lines of, "I don't know, a connection, I guess. What are you looking for?"

Vivek responded, "Just two things. Someone who's vegetarian and doesn't smoke. That shouldn't be so hard to find, don't you think?"

It's a common online dating complaint that people are nothing like their profiles. Sometimes they could be nothing *but* them.

Another time, I met a very sweet journalist named Manish for lunch in Chinatown. Afterward I was planning to meet my gay friend Farhad in a store. Manish walked me the few blocks into Soho, and I asked him to come in and say hello. Upon meeting Farhad, Manish became extremely animated and even helped my friend choose a sweater. After he left, I asked Farhad what he thought. He gave me a knowing glance, and we both burst into laughter.

As with any singles Web sites geared toward one community, you also got your interlopers. A forty-four-year-old Jewish doctor managed to make my dad's first cut: he *was* a doctor. Mark said he believed Indians and Jews shared similar values, like family and education. I didn't necessarily have a problem with his search for an Indian wife. (Isn't it when they dislike us for our skin color that we're supposed to get upset?) But when I met him for dinner, he seemed a decade older than he was, which made me feel like I was a decade younger.

My father's screening method was hardly foolproof. Once, he was particularly taken with a suitor who claimed to be a brain surgeon at Johns Hopkins and friends with a famous Bollywood actress, Madhuri Dixit. I was suspicious, but I agreed to speak to the fellow. Within seconds, his shaky command of English and yokel line of questioning—"You are liking dancing? I am too much liking dancing"—told me this man was as much as a brain surgeon as I was Madhuri Dixit. When I refused to talk to him again, my father called me up to say, "Don't you think we would make sure his story checked out before marrying you off?"

Sometimes, though, we would get close, really close. In my last year in the city, I was put in touch with an Indian-American consultant living in Bombay named Sameer. I liked the fact that he'd grown up in America but had returned to India to work. I too sometimes threw around the idea of trying to find a job in India, seeing as the country was undergoing massive change.

During every summer break in college, I found myself back in India, trying to learn as much as I could about the country of my birth. I'd even worked as a journalist in New Delhi in 1995 when the country had just started to dismantle its dirigiste economy.

Sameer and I had great conversations on the phone—among other things, he had interesting views on how people our age were becoming more sexually liberated in Indian cities—and I began envisioning myself draped in the finest silk saris. Sameer had sent a picture, and while he wasn't Saif Ali Khan, he wasn't bad. My father kept telling me he wanted it all "wrapped up" by February—it was only Christmas!

Back for a break in New York, Sameer kindly came to see me in Fort Greene, the Brooklyn neighborhood where I was then living. At a French bistro across the street from my apartment, he leaned over the table and said, "You know, your father really shouldn't send out those photos of you. They don't do justice to your beauty."

Sameer was generous, good natured, engaging, seemingly besotted with me, on an expat salary—and also on the Atkins diet to lose fifty pounds. My Bombay dreams went up in smoke.

In this, I guess I was like every other woman in New York, complaining a man was too ambitious or not ambitious enough, too eager or not eager enough, too skinny or too fat. But they were finicky, too. These men, in their bid to fit in on Wall Street or on the golf course, wanted a wife who was eminently presentable—to their boss, friends, and family. They wanted a woman to be sophisticated enough to have a martini, and not a Diet Coke, at an office party, but not, god forbid, "sophisticated" enough to have three. Sometimes I worried that I was a bit too sophisticated for most Indian men.

What I had come to appreciate about Indian men was their clarity of intent. I'd never heard from an Indian man, or at least not the ones I'd met on shaadi.com, "I don't think I'm ready for a relationship right now."

Indian men also seemed to share my belief that Westerners made the progression toward marriage unnecessarily agonizing. I recall one Indian lawyer friend telling me he thought it was absurd how a couple in America could date for years and still not know if they wanted to get married.

With other forms of dating, the options seemed limitless. The long kiss in the bar with someone I'd never met could have been just that, an exchange that has a value and meaning of its own that can't be quantified. Ditto for the one-night stand. (Try explaining that one to my parents.) The not-knowing-where-something-is-headed can be wildly exciting. It can also be soul crushing.

Indians of my mother's generation—in fact, my mother herself—like to say of arranged marriage, "It's not that there isn't love. It's just that it comes after marriage." Maybe I didn't buy it entirely. But after a decade of Juan Carloses, and affairs with married men, and Craigslist flirtations, and emotionally bankrupt boyfriends, and (oddly, the most painful of all) the guys who just never call, it no longer seemed like the most outlandish possibility.

Some of my single friends in New York would say they weren't convinced marriage is what they really wanted. I didn't really buy that, either. And no modern woman wanted to close the door on any of her options—no matter how traditional—too hastily.

My friend Radhika, an unmarried thirty-seven-year-old photographer, used to hate going to her cousins' weddings, where the aunties never asked her about the famines in Africa or the political conflict in Cambodia she'd covered. Instead it was, "Why aren't you married? What are your intentions?" As much as she dreaded this, they've stopped asking, and for Radhika, that's even worse. "It's like they've written me off," she says.

During a trip to India while living in New York, I was made to eat dinner at the children's table—they sent out for Domino's pizza and Pepsis—because as an unmarried woman, I didn't fit in with the adults. As much as I resented my exile, I realized that maybe I didn't want to be eating *dal* and *sabzi* and drinking rum with the grown-ups. Maybe that would have meant they'd given up on me, that they viewed me not as a yet-to-be-married girl but as an unmarriageable woman who'd ruined her youth by being too choosy and strong headed.

This way, the aunties could still swing by the kids' table as I was sucking on a Pepsi and chucking a young cousin on the chin, and ask me, "When are you getting married? What are your intentions?"

And I could say, "Auntie, do you have a boy in mind?"

Chapter Four

It was in New York that I began thinking that something was wrong—deeply, heart-wrenchingly wrong—with the Western dating system. I would come home after an evening of swapping New York "war stories" with girlfriends, in which we regaled each other with horrific dates or detailed every phone call and e-mail exchange from a short-lived fling in order to decipher why our intended had unceremoniously disappeared. Most of these evenings ended up with one or another of us whining about our loneliness and wondering when it would end, to be comforted by yet another in our gaggle that we should just get on with our own lives and not worry about men, and that soon enough, when we were least expecting it, love would walk in through the front door or sit next to us on a flight.

The next week we would switch roles and the whiner would offer warm words of advice and hand-holding to the comforter. I heartily participated in all of these discussions, more often than not as the one plunged in despair when I first arrived in New York, and later, hardened and somewhat resigned, as the one extending succor.

After months of these cocktail-drenched evenings, two fleeting thoughts slipped across my mind, which later would take on shape and bulk and eventually morph into full-blown arguments. The first of these took hold when a friend was complaining how a man she'd met at a party two weeks ago had seemed very interested and had taken her number but had not called since. And today she'd discovered that a colleague she had a crush on had a girlfriend. Two leads that had seemed promising just last week had fallen through, which in New York is enough to induce a midmonth slump.

I bit my lower lip and, ever helpful, said, "What about that guy you were talking about last month, the one you made out with at that bar in Soho?"

"Oh yeah, him. He's too young. I can tell he's not interested in something serious," my friend said.

"Okay, well what about that guy Jason who's really into you and asking you out all the time? I think he's kind of cute," I offered hopefully.

"Eew," she said.

"Okay, what about going online? I know you're not really that into it, but . . . I don't know. It just seems like there's no other way to meet somebody," I said, the first tendrils of my seedling thought stretching their tiny arms.

"I tried it. I only met freaks. I was just wasting my time," she moaned. "I just don't know where I'll meet someone."

Then the petals of my thought opened to reveal its essence. Yes indeed. Where are we in the West supposed to meet someone we'd like to marry, or at least be committed to? If we graduate from university without having found someone, we assume we'll meet someone over the next few years. But where exactly?

In many workplaces, romantic relationships are frowned upon, and people are often averse to dating someone in the office for fear it will end badly and they will still have to see their ex-lover on a daily basis. We are told that it's best to meet friends of friends. We all think this is a brilliant idea, until we realize that we've already met all of our friends' friends . . . two years ago.

Then of course, there's the online route. Although the popularity of online dating in the last few years has somewhat reduced the stigma of having had to resort to the Internet to find a date, it's hardly a preferred method. Having found a girlfriend or boyfriend from an Internet site still seems the refuge of the desperate and socially isolated. And then there's the nagging little fact that many of us *have* tried online dating to no avail.

So then what?

This is when I found myself saying to my friend, "You're right. I don't know where you'll find someone, short of bumping into him on the street."

From that point on, I became mildly obsessed with the inadequacies of the Western dating system, or rather lack of it. Where exactly are we supposed to meet someone to marry?

For years, I never questioned the Western dating system. The tenets on which it rests seemed perfectly sound: after meeting a man or woman through work or friends, one gets to know him or her, and if one likes what one sees, one continues to deepen the commitment, which sometimes leads to marriage. What surprises me now is how much this system leaves to chance encounter, to a kind of fate or fortune. For a decidedly unmystical society that seems to have the answer for everything else—the best medical care, cutting-edge technology, superhighways, and space shuttles—it seems odd that people are left to their own resources, casting around for another lonely soul, for what is arguably the most important decision of their lives.

If the institution of marriage is present in every society that we know of, from Lapps in northern Sweden to aborigines, and nearly all cultures promote marriage as the foundation of society, isn't it odd, then, that there is very little provision for how it is supposed to occur in the West? I puzzled over this gap and eventually arrived at a "the emperor has no clothes" conclusion.

It was so obvious no organized system for marriage existed in the West that people simply failed to blame the obvious for why they couldn't find someone to marry. They were told by their therapists and their friends that it was because they were too neurotic, too unhappy, had to work on themselves before they could be happy with someone else, or that they wanted it too badly. People are told to blame themselves, and they do: they try to lose weight, they develop new interests, they get a nose job. We wonder what's wrong with us when really we should wonder whether there isn't a better way of doing things. It is a curious misplacement for a self-congratulatory culture in which people are constantly trying to shift blame *away* from themselves.

Once I began questioning the efficacy of the Western dating system in resulting in marriage, I started wondering why it is that wanting to be committed to someone else is too often associated with weakness in the West. I noticed that when people were happily self-sufficient, they liked to preach how they weren't looking for a serious commitment and didn't have time for one. It was only when they were dissatisfied that they began to think of marriage or commitment as a solution. But how many people *are* happily self-sufficient?

Does marriage have to be a salve to loneliness to have value? Isn't it valuable to begin with? In the West, the modern ideal is to be independent, on one's own, and to be able to make the *choice* to live with another human being, to welcome someone else as a bonus to one's existence—if and when one is ready.

Couldn't one be a perfectly sound person who leads a far more purposeful life once engaged in a harmonious symbiosis with another human being? I certainly think so. Moreover, why do we have to be "perfectly sound" before we can meet someone? Why can't we be desperately alone and unhappy and become much more balanced or healthy after getting involved with someone?

We've all seen this happen with friends—"God, Peter seems so much happier now that he's going out with Jessica. He's not drinking as much." Conventional wisdom frequently tells us that we're happier when we give to others and focus less on ourselves, so it seems rather a glaring void that there is no institutionalized system of finding a mate in Western culture these days.

To admit to others that I yearned for a long-term commitment or marriage—which is basically to say that I wanted to be able to think about someone else for a change—sounded regressive as soon as it emerged from my mouth. It was atavistic in nature, a throwback to a time when women couldn't financially support themselves. It was a piece of treacherous anathema in the age of strong, independent working women.

Of course, marriages were more or less arranged in Western cultures according to one's social status and wealth until the twentieth century, which ushered in a freewheeling era that allowed people to choose their own mates. However, no system stepped in to replace the practice of arranged marriage once it fell by the wayside, leaving a lot of young men and women lonely and frustrated. In the West, people are so resolutely convinced that they alone are equipped to choose their own mates that they readily give up their right to happiness in favor of self-determination.

In India, where marriages are routinely arranged by parents and extended family, marriage is not a choice. It just *is*. There is simply no concept of living a life alone. It happens here and there, but as a mistake, an unintentional slippage in society. In the West, people do it all the time, even relish it, saying things like, "I would rather live alone than with the wrong person." But spend ten minutes with most of these people and it becomes apparent that they are lonely.

I must confess that there was a third idea churning through my head, one considerably less broad and analytical, not to mention altogether more banal. And this thought was completely mortifying, yet enough within the realm of possibility that it kept my eyes pinned back and staring at the ceiling on more than a few sleepless nights. The bogeyman: namely that if I stayed in New York any longer I would end up growing old alone, "treating" myself to brunch every Sunday and the occasional Broadway show.

In my three years in New York, I hadn't come close to even having one romantic relationship. Dating felt like an absurd cat-and-mouse game, where people were more concerned about what they could get away with than with settling down—"Can I keep dating other men? Do I have to give up my fuckbuddy if I actually like this woman that I'm dating?"

My dilemma was driven home one gorgeous Saturday in late May, one of the first days of the year with a limpid royal-blue sky and an undoubtedly summery climate. In short, the kind of day when everybody floods to Central Park for the first picnic of the season.

My friend Nadia, the one who gamely took it upon herself to introduce me to every available single man she encountered in New York, had invited me to a picnic. In addition to Nadia and her husband, there were a few other married couples and six or seven of us single thirtysomething women, all in flowery print dresses, which I suspected we were all wearing for the first time that spring. I recalled Nadia looking radiant, a few months pregnant with her first child. She'd brought three types of cheese—Brie, Gouda, and Emmentaler—and crackers, strawberries, grapes, a pasta salad with artichokes and tomatoes, and a few bottles of chilled white wine. I had shown up empty-handed and hungover from a late night out with some girlfriends, in which we ended up talking about . . . guess what?

The ever-resourceful Nadia was talking to some of the others, her back to me, and I watched how the sun glinted off of her black, shiny hair. Her husband caressed her head for a few seconds while he said something into her ear. She let out a deeply felt laugh. I noticed the slight bump under her dress. And then I looked up at the sky, the dazzling, mocking clear blue sky. Lording over me, the firmament teased me, "See how happy you could be on a day like this? But you are not, because Kurt/Joe/Mark did not call you back after your date last week. How are you ever going to have a bump under your flower-print dress and a man to caress your head if no one even calls you after going out on a date with you?"

I made initial attempts at conversation with some of the others at the picnic, but I eventually fell silent, because in my belly, a heaviness had taken root. I couldn't form words, and when I did, they came out all shaky and strange, as if I were speaking English as a second language. That was when I started crying, right in the middle of the picnic. Not sobbing gustily, or even audibly. But if you'd been looking at me, you'd have noticed a small torrent of tears gush down both sides of my face. Someone did, one of the husbands sitting on my right. He saw me with my plainly damp cheeks and, without saying a word, handed me his sunglasses.

I thought I should say something by way of explanation. He wasn't asking for one, but it seemed the proper thing to do. "I'm sorry, I'm just emotional today. It's . . . it's just that dating in New York is so hard. I'm not sure I can do it anymore."

His naked eyes squinting into the sun, he nodded and half smiled sympathetically, not sure, of course, what I was really getting at. It took about another ten minutes to compose myself

behind his sunglasses. I finally got up, handed back the sunglasses, said my good-byes, and walked through the throngs of
picnickers. It was only four P.M. and they would be there for at
least another two hours before carrying on to another venue,
perhaps some sidewalk café where they would continue to drink
wine into the early hours of the next morning. As I walked to the
street and then to the subway station, my sobs were no longer
soundless. They were loud, sniffling, and phlegmy. I was
hyperventilating.

When I emerged from the train in my neighborhood in
Brooklyn some three quarters of an hour later, it was still
contemptuously brilliant outside. All the cafés on my street
were crowded with merrymakers. That day, I literally ran home
in tears.

I had become precisely the kind of woman I was determined not
to become before I'd come to New York: that proverbial single
thirtysomething female propped up at the bar waiting for her
ship to come in. Despairing of another summer of Sunday
brunches with the stodgy and unresponsive company of the *New
York Times*, I knew I had to leave New York, but where could I
go?

I suspected I would encounter the same kind of never-ending
carousel of dates in other U.S. cities I would consider living in,
like Los Angeles or San Francisco. Certainly single girlfriends I
knew living in those cities had provided ample evidence of this.
And in European cities I would have to learn a new language, not
to mention compete with Monica Bellucci look-alikes who
spoke four or five languages and could stand for hours in
stilettos.

I recalled the experience of a friend of mine who'd met her
current husband while covering the U.S. invasion of Afghanistan

in late 2001. She was one of the only women there amid hordes of male photographers, journalists, and other adventure seekers.

"I remember going to this one party in Kabul. There were like fifty men and two women. Every man there chatted me up," she said. "They were literally stepping on each other to fetch me drinks."

Should I go to Kabul or even Baghdad? But I'd been mostly a financial reporter, writing about companies and stock markets; I'd never really covered war before. Despite the advantageous statistics, it seemed a bit drastic to move to a war zone to find love.

That was when I began to think of going to India. There are more men in India than women, around 930 women to every 1,000 men according to recent census data, the vast discrepancy a disturbing result of infanticide and sex-segregated abortion. And yet, it would work to my advantage, comparing favorably, of course, with the proportion of women to men in New York, which is always cited as something obscene like seven to one. This last figure may be an urban myth, but certainly it bore itself out anecdotally. Most parties I attended in New York featured thirty women and two men.

Statistics may be inappropriate evidence in an emotional argument, but they often are a last bastion of hope. When I would moan about ending up alone, Farhad would routinely shut me up with, "You won't end up alone. Few people actually do. Take solace in cold, hard statistics." And miraculously, I would. Sometimes this statistical advantage was all I could cling to when I would wake up with a jolt in the middle of the night, clutching my skipping heart.

In one of his e-mails citing the statistical unlikelihood of my ending up alone, Farhad also added, "Anyway, we are going to grow old together, gin bottle in one hand, fag in the other, cackling at the married suburbanites as we stir up a storm in major global cities well into our 70s. Who needs a man when you can grow old and bitter with a flaming faggot by your side?"

Leave it to Farhad to describe the most horrifying scenario I could conceive of.

So I figured my options were simply more plentiful in India. I could go in for a strict arranged marriage, an "assisted" marriage, or I could merely date in a pool far more oriented toward marriage than the one I was dealing with in New York City.

I knew that arranged marriage certainly was no longer as entrenched in India as it was just a generation ago, losing its grip among a modern and urbanized segment of society. Outside of the major metropolitan cities, people still readily submitted to the practice. In cities like Delhi and Bombay, the vast majority of marriages were still arranged, but I'd also heard that a culture of dating and sleeping around was gaining ground. Nonetheless, in India, a desire to be married wasn't at loggerheads with the advances for which feminists had struggled. Even arranged marriage was acceptable in circles one would think had moved far beyond tradition. Bollywood megastar Madhuri Dixit left her career in 1999, when she was the highest-paid actress in the country's history, to marry a nonresident Indian surgeon from Los Angeles. Her parents arranged the union and the couple reportedly only met once before deciding to get married. Likewise, Aishwarya Rai, who was poised to make a transition from a successful Bollywood career to one in Hollywood, damaged her chances for superstardom when she chose to get married to the son of Indian film legend Amitabh Bachchan in 2007. She adopted her husband's last name and moved in with her in-laws.

As I sat on my couch drinking coffee before heading out to the subway in the morning, or in my midtown office struggling to focus on a story I had to submit by the end of the day, I noticed my mind wandering more and more to the idea of going to India. Something else beckoned me from there as well, or rather someone else.

I'd been in touch by e-mail with a man I'd met on a trip to India two years earlier for my friend Seema's wedding. Mustafa Rafiq Ali was a journalist with a newspaper based in Kashmir, and what had started out as a friendly correspondence recently had taken on a more flirtatious tone. Old-world charm never fails to endear a man to me, and Mustafa had it in abundance. I'd discovered through friends that he descended from a long line of Sufi saints, or *pirs*. Sufis practice a more mystical and tolerant form of Islam, and *pirs* serve as guides to the community. In India, shrines of these *pirs*, or *dargahs*, are daily thronged by worshippers.

To my eyes, Mustafa's life was enveloped in a haze of romance, mystery, and danger—this last owing to an ongoing insurgency in Kashmir that has claimed tens of thousands of lives. The frequency of our e-mails had increased of late, and was it wrong to hope our friendship might take a romantic turn, one befitting my perhaps dramatized notion of his life? Certainly my chances with him would be much better if I were in India instead of New York City.

Of course, the idea I could really end up with him was far-fetched, not least because he was Muslim, which would no doubt cause a ruckus within both our families. And certainly, Mustafa never led me to believe our flirtation would take us anywhere, but perhaps you can understand what a vivid imagi-nation and a lackluster love life can do to one's hopes, parti-cularly from the vantage point of what now seemed a very drab cubicle somewhere above midtown Manhattan?

People commonly go to India to find themselves or to find god, but I went to India to find a husband. I would give myself a year, what I figured was ample time in such a marriage-oriented society. In my mind, my decision also overturned two conventions, which, in the lexicon of the West, could be seen as nothing less than *empowering*. The first convention is that of an Indian man who has grown up in the West going back to the motherland to find a traditional, virginal, "simple" bride. The second is that of a South Asian woman being dragged back by her parents—one hears of this more in the U.K. among Pakistanis and Bangladeshis—to be married off, more often than not to a domineering and narrow-minded groom who restricts the freedoms she's enjoyed in the West. I willingly—and willfully—returned to find a modern Indian husband on my own terms.

Going to India to find a husband also raised other considerations. I wondered if I would be able to find someone modern enough in his thinking to be comfortable with a wife having a great deal of her own agency, not just in terms of making decisions for the household but in having a full life outside the marriage—one that included going out with friends, drinking, and smoking. A woman who has had sex in the past—and not just with those two long-term boyfriends. I wasn't sure what I would find, but I owed it to myself to try.

Chapter Five

It would take a year from the heartbreaking picnic on that beautiful day in Central Park for me to set my plans in motion and eventually move to Delhi. While still in New York, I began looking around for some freelance writing gigs and luckily managed to line up some steady work in Delhi with a U.K. newspaper.

In the months preceding my departure from New York, I learned more about the country's booming growth, which appeared to be having a dramatic effect on young people in Delhi and other metropolises. Nearly half of the population of India is under thirty, a staggering statistic. I was curious about what I would find in this country in flux moving rapidly from rigid tradition to modernity, from poverty to gilt-edged prosperity. Would men take relationships more seriously than they did in New York? Would they treat me like an outsider? Like a foreigner or an Indian?

As I pondered my own fears, I thought of my father's oddly parallel reverse journey more than three decades earlier, from Delhi to New York. Papa and I were the same age when we uprooted our lives to pursue a perhaps better future in another country. Retracing my father's steps the other way made me feel traitorous, as if I were not grateful for the comfortable life he gave us in America. Moreover, I worried that it belittled my father's own decision. Were his sacrifices worthless if I ended up in India anyway?

My father began angling to leave India after he'd graduated from university in the sixties. He may have hailed from a background of grinding poverty, but he happened to be in possession of a good head for mathematics. (This is something I had inherited from him, until, it seems, my freshman year at university, when my genetic knack for numbers and cosines and derivatives was sacrificed at the altar of the lesser god of the liberal arts.)

He opted, in a manner of speaking, for a career in engineering. One could hardly call it a decision, since most young men in India in those days who didn't go into the family business defaulted into engineering. In the heavily regulated economy back then, there were precious few companies to join, and one usually had to have connections to get a position in one of them. Along with tens of millions of his countrymen and a handful of women, my father sat for the entrance exams to attend Roorkee University, then the country's leading college of engineering. He got in on his second try.

With a degree from the country's top college in engineering, Papa assumed he would be rewarded with steady and prestigious employment. In the sixties, many people of my father's generation in other parts of the world broadened their horizons in a variety of ways. They questioned authority for the first time, they learned about a world they had not known existed outside their borders, they dabbled in hallucinogenic drugs, they slept around, or they simply began working at a well-remunerated job in an unprecedented era of prosperity and opportunity. Upon emerging from university in 1961, my father, however, was slapped with the full centripetal force of India's despair. He bounced from one dust-coated sepia-toned northern Indian town to the next, working as a lecturer or a principal at small colleges or technical institutes. Rohtak, Etah, Mainpuri, Baraut,

Kanpur. They were all the same. These nowhere places reeked with the stench of hopelessness. Unruly students who didn't care enough to attend class were matched in apathy only by their teachers, who couldn't be bothered to teach them. Papa lived on paltry sums of money—a couple hundred rupees a month, the equivalent at the time of about $50.

He was fresh out of college and terribly idealistic. He wanted to see change, to effect change, even if it was in a poky town where time appeared to have stopped. Arriving as the new principal of a technical institute in Mainpuri (or was it Baraut? The towns blend together in my father's mind), he was dismayed by the lackadaisical attitude of the instructors, who were often absent from their scheduled lectures. The students may have appeared no better than common thugs, but they deserved an education at least. He decided to take action and did something unprecedented in the annals of this particular institute: He sent memos issuing warnings to his staff, including to several department heads.

One department head was so troubled by this strange chimera of a document that had been sent to him—the likes of which he could never have imagined possible—that he went to throw himself into a nearby canal. Apparently colleagues held him back from jumping to his death, but the memo had so thoroughly shattered the man's worldview that he was said to have gone mad and was never the same again.

In the one or two stints during which my father actually worked as an engineer instead of at a university, he was appalled at the way money greased the palms of anyone with even a veneer of power. As a subdivision officer for the Uttar Pradesh state electricity board, my father was responsible for certain electricity cable projects. After a month or two, he discovered his clerk, who handled the documents for procuring equipment on my father's behalf, had been taking bribes from suppliers, saying they'd been demanded by my father. Enraged, my father transferred the clerk to another district, since terminating his employment was impossible. For this, my father was later dressed down by his own boss, who had come to enjoy the clerk's largesse in the form of lavish meals whenever he visited from his post in a nearby town.

Hope lay elsewhere, but not there. Perhaps in England, which had left its imperial imprint—not to mention its imprimatur, India being the empire's crown jewel, its quickest study—on the nation in its parliamentary democracy, civil institutions, and rule of law. Or maybe in America, presided over by a boyishly handsome man named Kennedy. There were other countries, too, hundreds of them in fact. Though not necessarily English speaking, they had to be better than this, he thought. Yes, hope lay anywhere but there.

It wasn't just financial destitution and lack of opportunity that led my father to search for a different life. He also had a sense of adventure and youthful wanderlust about him, one that led him to draft letters to the embassies of 150 countries— Mexico, Spain, the Netherlands, Afghanistan—inquiring whether they needed any engineers. Each embassy wrote back, after some time and in careful English, that no, they did not need engineers at the time, but he was welcome to follow the proper immigration channels.

And on occasion, his request to immigrate was honored. Once, while on a trip to Delhi from one of his nowhere towns, he wandered into the Canadian embassy. In the lobby for visa applicants, he saw an old *sardarji*, *dhoti* wound around his legs, white beard flowing, topped off by a proud turban like the proverbial cherry. In fact, as he looked around the room, he noticed it was a sea of turbans—light blue, yellow, maroon, white, black, lavender even—all heading for Ontario, Toronto, Vancouver.

My father asked the old Sikh in Hindi, "Where is everyone going?"

"To Canada," the reply in Punjabi came.

"What will you do there? Do you even speak English?" my father asked sniffily, though my father's own English left much room for improvement.

"You don't have to. My son lives there. I will stay with him. Everybody is going now," the man said.

Heeding the words, Papa carefully filled out an application he found on a nearby counter then and there, and after a brief wait, a young, bespectacled white man called his name. The man met my father in the lobby and reached out to shake his hand. My father had encountered few *goras* before, but he knew better than to shake hands with an underling. He kept his hands firmly by his sides. He would, of course, greet the immigration officer properly. The young Canadian led him to an office, sat behind the desk, and began my father's visa interview. It was to be my father's first experience with the West's more egalitarian approach to humanity. Despite my father's poor show of courtesy, he would soon receive a letter saying his application to immigrate to Canada had been granted. Having applied on a lark, he couldn't scrounge up the fare for the flight, and so he remained in India.

A few years later, in the late 1960s, my newly married father applied for an immigration visa to England, which had been flooded by immigrants from the Indian subcontinent in the wake of its departure as imperial ruler. Many of these new visitors worked as laborers, assuming tasks locals no longer deigned to perform. Papa's visa was approved, and this time, my father was able to dun relatives and friends for enough

money for the airfare. A week before he was to depart, the
mother of the woman he'd married just under a year ago—my
grandmother—threw a fit. She began wailing that if her daughter, one of six, were to leave India, she would die right then and
there. Papa stayed put.

As the decade wore on, Papa became increasingly desperate.
He was now living in Delhi and working as a part-time lecturer
at various polytechnic colleges. None of them would make him
permanent staff, and his salary arrived erratically, sometimes
after five or six months in a lump sum. And when it did arrive,
the couple thousand rupees just covered the basics—rent, food,
petrol for the scooter.

When my mother became pregnant with my brother in 1970,
insomnia began to plague my father. He would toss and turn all
night, wracking his brains to come up with new ways to support
his growing family. My father was a born entrepreneur, but
moneymaking opportunities were few then in a state-run India
inimical to entrepreneurship. Lying back on his pillow, eyes
pinned open to the peeling ceiling (much like mine were during
those sleepless nights in New York when I feared a life of certain
spinsterhood), he would envisage himself mailing reams of
documents, standing in long queue after queue, waiting for
meaningless stamps of approval for yet another dead-end low-
paying government job.

On one of those nights he had what he describes as a heart
attack, which most certainly was nothing more serious than a fit
of panic (I've clearly inherited a flair for the dramatic from Papa
along with my knack for math). The next morning he went to
the U.S. embassy, which at the time had remarkably lax
immigration laws compared to what they are now. Then, the
U.S. allowed some Indian professionals, such as doctors, engineers, and pharmacists, into the country under what was called

the "third preference." Today the U.S. doesn't grant immigration visas to Indians who aren't sponsored by family members already living in the U.S. Others must arrive on student, work, or marriage visas. Visitor visas for Indian men of a certain age are routinely rejected for fear they will stay on and work illegally in the U.S.

My father filled out reams of forms and went home to my mother. Three months later, he received a letter saying his immigration visa had been approved. The visa was good for four months and would expire on June 26, 1972. His mother-in-law had recently passed away and no longer presented a hurdle to his dreams of emigration. Also, his own father, to whom he'd been very close, had died in recent months, making his decision to leave that much easier.

He had four months to come up with money for a plane ticket for himself—his wife and six-month-old son would follow after he'd settled in and found a job—and a $1,000 draft check, which was required by the U.S. government if no friends or family members agreed to extend their financial support.

Former classmates and cousins he had written asking if they would vouch for him—not lend him money but simply say they would support him if he could not look after himself—had replied to his entreaties with various profuse apologies. He would have to arrange for the draft check, it seemed. The official exchange rate at the time was 7.5 rupees to the dollar. But it wasn't as simple as collecting 7,500 rupees and exchanging them for dollars. It was impossible to convert rupees into dollars in India legally, as the government wished to avoid depleting its foreign currency reserves. In fact, this transaction became possible only in the early 2000s.

So, under the impossibly labyrinthine system, my father had to gather 7,500 rupees for the check and put another 7,500 rupees in a trust in an Indian bank until he was able to send the $1,000 in actual U.S. dollars back to the Reserve Bank of India. While he managed to raise the initial 7,500 rupees from his own savings and various handouts from family members, he would have to ask someone else to agree to put the second lump of money under trust for a few months until he could earn it back in the U.S.

One wealthy friend agreed to do it for him, seeing as it would only require shifting a small portion of his savings to a separate account until my father made good on his promise to the central bank. Somehow, though, the friend never got around to going down to his bank and executing the simple transaction. Near-daily visits to his friend's house only turned up more reassurances with no action. Time on my father's four-month visa was running out, and his paperwork was nowhere near completion. Finally, my father's sister agreed to assist him in the banking sleight of hand.

With this sorted out, he now had to cobble together another 2,500 rupees for the one-way plane ticket. He sold his scooter for 2,200 rupees, but he was still short 300 rupees. He certainly couldn't continue to ask his family members for cash, even if it was a relatively measly amount. It seemed entirely unfair that 300 rupees, or the equivalent of 40 dollars at the time, would keep him from his dreams.

Then an unforeseen and miraculous thing happened. On April 3, 1972, U.S. president Richard Nixon devalued the dollar, having only months earlier delinked the dollar from the gold standard. The dollar fell to 7.2 rupees instead of 7.5. Now my father would only have to exchange 7,200 rupees for the $1,000 draft check, benefiting him by exactly 300 rupees and opening the door to America.

Boarding an airplane for the first time, my father flew out of New Delhi's international airport, heading to John F. Kennedy

International Airport, with a week remaining on his visa. He had only eight dollars in his pocket. He would have to make do with that until he could access his $1,000 draft check in a few weeks' time.

I thought about my father's harrowing journey as I sat in my Premium Economy seat on British Airways flying eastward from JFK to the airport from which he departed India. Other than being redubbed Indira Gandhi International Airport, it had seen precious few other changes in the intervening three decades.

Of course, I was in a much stronger position than he was when he left for America, but his fears and hopes must have been much like mine. Would he find what he was looking for? Would I?

Ironically enough, it was my father's own self-taught views on women that had given me hope that I would be able to find a husband in India liberal enough in mind-set and outlook to handle me. My father is neither an intellectual nor a sophisticate, as he likes to remind me often enough. How often have I seen him belching after dinner, rubbing his bare belly and clad just in his undershorts, saying, "Ah, *beti*, I am a simple man. Just give me *dal* and *chapati* and I have eaten like a king!"

Having retired from a career in engineering he never really chose, he turned his formidable faculties to what really interested him, business, and acquired a mini-empire of low-income duplexes in the suburbs of northern California. His success followed years of failed moneymaking schemes, like the defective pantyhose vending machine he purchased a few years after his arrival in the States, and later a roach-infested flophouse in Las Vegas.

My father's interests tend toward daytime talk shows and his latest cash-generating shenanigans, which at this moment is day trading. But while he may not be highbrow in his pursuits or refined in his habits, a distinct nobility of mind and dignity of character underlie his ideas and actions regarding gender relations.

Disgusted with the poor treatment of women he observed growing up in 1940s India, my father became an ardent feminist. He was hardly poised to become one, born into a lower-middle-class family of seven brothers and one sister in Meerut, an industrial town two hours outside of Delhi. It was a town earlier immortalized in history as the one whose hotheads gave India its first insurrection against imperial rule, the 1857 mutiny against the British. Although my paternal grandfather ensured that all his children received a proper education—all of them went on to study engineering—I suspect the Hindi-language public schools my father and his siblings attended may have given short shrift to ideas stemming from the Enlightenment such as equality, justice, and liberty. Given a background destined to turn a man into a brute, or at least one not especially attuned to his feminine side, my father managed to chart a personal philosophy predicated on the belief that women are equal to men and should be treated so accordingly, every day, in every conversation.

As in many language other than English, there are several ways to say "you" in Hindi. (The English language is veritably impoverished when it comes to the second-person pronoun, our default for the second-person plural across the vast English-speaking world being the inelegant "you guys.") There is the formal "*aap*" that is used for elders and unfamiliar people, the familiar "*tum*" used with friends and siblings, and beneath that, the somewhat rough-hewn "*tu*," which can be deployed with affection, as parents do with their children or between close friends, but can also be crude, unrefined, and imperious when directed at servants or underlings.

My mother, in accordance with her generation and small-town middle-class manners, was expected to address my father with the formal "*aap*." In my mother's era, it was also considered disrespectful for a woman to utter her husband's name, as in, "Rajiv, dinner's ready!" or "Amit, what a day I had today," or even when referring to him in the third person ("Ashok and I would like our son to be a doctor."). To this day, I have never heard my mother mouth my father's name, Naresh. When calling out to him, she says, "Listen up!" or "Do you hear?" When referring to him in conversation with other Indians, she just uses "he." To avoid confusing non-Indians who would not understand her delicacy, she will say "My husband." As a childish prank, I used to try to trick her and get her to voice his name by asking her the correct pronunciation or employing some other ruse, but she would always manage to get around repeating his name.

In every conversation in the forty years my parents have been married, my father also addresses my mother as "*aap*" and has similarly never uttered her name, Santosh. When conversing with others, he will refer to her as "she" much as she does with him. I've never actually seen any other Indian man do this. Other uncles address their wives with the middle form "*tum*," or even the boorish "*tu*," while most often wives reply with "*aap*." I've also seen many couples of my parents' generation, having perhaps established a good rapport or being from a more modern background, address each other equally with "*tum*" as well as refer to each other by name. Indeed this is what modern couples do now and what I would expect to do when speaking Hindi with a partner. If my father had simply done what most men of his generation did and employed the middle form of "you," it hardly would mark him as a discourteous or ill-mannered husband, and I daresay many men in the West would do the same. But my father believed that if women were equal to men, then certainly one should start at the beginning, as it were: linguistic parity.

I still marvel at the depth of principle and reserve of restraint that would keep a man from ever letting his wife's name slip, even after forty years. For a woman, of course, it's hardly unusual to fathom that she would continue to use the respectful form when addressing her husband, seeing as females in all societies have been inculcated to behave in a manner that is seen as befitting their gender. But for a man in a traditional society, it is nothing short of extraordinary.

There's a story my father likes to tell that reveals a lot about his character. After his search for the perfect bride took him to some two hundred homes (okay, this may compromise his sterling feminist credentials, but let's assume he was exaggerating for effect), he finally met my mother over tea and snacks in her home in Ghaziabad, a dust-drenched town bordering Delhi. The meeting was brief and my mother, eyes downcast, didn't say a word the entire time, but my father was impressed by her beauty and her large and soulful eyes—which he noticed the one time he managed to catch her gaze—and conveyed as much to my mother's family.

Though not cash rich, my mother's family was respectable and proud, her father a senior government official who had been in jail repeatedly for his violent agitation against the British colonial regime. In prison, powdered glass was often mixed into his meals, causing my grandfather to suffer from stomach problems for the rest of his life. My mother and several of her siblings were born during his stints in jail, and since my grandfather handled the paperwork, they aren't aware of their actual birth dates. My mother's official birth date is August 2, 1944, but she could have been born months earlier or later.

My maternal grandmother, cursed with six daughters, was nonetheless fiercely protective of all of them, and my mother was one of her favorites, being just a bit pluckier than the others. So when my father expressed interest in marrying my mother, my grandmother leveled with him: "My daughter doesn't cook."

My father, exhausted by his long search and clearly besotted with my mother, said, "That's okay. We'll go out to eat."

Sensing that she'd landed a pliant husband for her daughter, my grandmother couldn't help but push the matter further. She said, "And she can't even make *chai*." It was a prime example of "clearing up domestic chore issues early on," a longtime favorite principle of both my parents, who are always telling me, "Make sure you tell your husband first thing that he will do half the cooking and half the cleaning, or else later you'll be stuck doing it all."

Good naturedly, my father replied with, "That's okay. I can make *chai*."

And he did, for a while, until my mother decided she'd established her position in the household. He even took her out for dinner every night for the first two weeks after they wed, which to me is even more bizarre, since eating out back then was very rare and my father had little disposable income. It was one of the rare instances in which his passion for money was overruled by something else—in this case, his love and respect for my mother.

I thought of all these things as I tried to focus on the Hindi film *Swades*, playing on the personal screen in front of me on my BA flight. The movie was about a man, played by Shah Rukh Khan, who spends years in America as a NASA scientist before returning to live in the Indian village in which he grew up.

The plane hit the tarmac, and immediately the unbearable summer of India infiltrated the sturdy exterior of the Boeing. In the ramp to the gate the smells hit—the odor of a country's baking earth and the airport's distinct mothballed mustiness.

My friend Seema, an old family friend, and her husband, Ashok, arrived to pick me up from the airport and took me to their home in Gurgaon, where I would stay for the next two months until I found my own place in New Delhi.

We sat down for dinner around midnight, and by candlelight, since the electricity had gone out in their new flat, which had been built the previous year as Gurgaon, a satellite city outside of Delhi, underwent a property boom. (I knew from experience that the power could be out for several long minutes or, god forbid, several hours.) I watched as Seema heaped her husband's plate with rice and *dal*, then mine, then her own, before taking her seat. Bewildered from the long flight, I couldn't make much conversation that first dinner. Nor could I eat much, but I knew better than to leave food on my plate and forced down mouthfuls.

It was the first time I was properly meeting Seema's husband. I had met him at their wedding, but you don't actually get to speak to the bride and groom at Indian weddings. I didn't know what he would make of me—was I a freewheeling American or, at the end of the day, just a simple girl from Meerut?

That first night, I slept without an air conditioner, for which Seema and Ashok apologized repeatedly. They'd meant to install it in the guest bedroom before I arrived but had left it to the last minute, and the workmen had dropped and damaged it when they came to fit it earlier that afternoon. They would return tomorrow with another.

Seema sat with me on the bed in the guest room for a few minutes after dinner while I tried to orient myself in my new surroundings.

"I'm so sorry about the AC, but it's just tonight you'll have to sleep with the fan. Will you be okay?" she asked.

"Yes, I'll be completely fine," I said, lying, stun-gunned as I was from the 120-degree heat. I felt like I was perched on the sun's surface, and I'd just arrived from New York, where a heat wave the previous week had sent summer temperatures soaring. "I'm just exhausted. I'm sure I'll just collapse. Thank you so much for letting me stay."

"What are you talking about? You're like family," Seema said.

There was something else I wanted to say, but I didn't know how. It had been so long since I'd seen Seema, and since I'd always been closer to her older sister Poonam, I didn't know how to broach a personal topic, to break through the formality of the situation.

"Seema, do you . . . do you think everything will be okay?" I asked warily.

"What do you mean? Of course everything will be okay," she said.

"No, I mean, will I be able to live here as an independent woman, you know, set up a home and find friends?" I pressed on sheepishly. When I'd lived in Delhi in 1995 for just under a year, I'd stayed with my aunt and uncle and didn't have to deal with servants, and buying furniture, and gas bills, and other domestic minutiae.

"Yes, yes, that's what I'm here for. I'll help you with everything," she said.

"And, also, do you think . . . do you think an Indian man will want to marry me? You know, I guess I'm not very traditional," I confessed in a rush.

"You see those moths circling that light up there? They will be gone by tomorrow morning. That's what your worries will be like—here right now, gone tomorrow," she said, giving me a warm smile.

I smiled and hugged her. Seema left the room, and I changed into a T-shirt and shorts, though even this felt like too much clothing. If I had been in my apartment in New York, I would have stripped down completely, but I was in India now, and I certainly didn't want the sixteen-year-old servant boy Gopal, or Seema or Ashok, to walk in on me naked. That would be inappropriate, to say the least.

I watched the moths flutter near the light over the bed. A few moments later, I turned off the light. But I couldn't sleep despite the long journey. It was easy enough for Seema to say everything would be okay, but she was married and had both of her and her husband's parents to rely on. I'd lived in foreign countries before, but Singapore and England, even Mexico, seemed far more straightforward than India.

India was a chaotic, turbulent country that, though in the midst of a massive economic and social upheaval, was still not a place that single women could reside very easily, even in metropolises, defined as they were by their fathers or their husbands. Of course, I'd read media story after story about the vibrant and modern New India, but was it true? And more important, would I be too modern, too forward, too American for an Indian man? Didn't I see Seema prepare Ashok's plate before sitting down for dinner? I'm sure I could learn to do that. Yes, yes, of course I could, I thought to myself, before interrupting my thought process with "Hey, wait a minute, why can't my husband prepare *my* plate? Bastard! Who does he think I am? I'm not his servant!"

Oh, god, I'll never survive here. I tossed and turned, torturing myself with these thoughts. I wondered whether I would find a man with my father's own progressive ideas, which seemed a far easier prospect in the India I had moved to than it was in his era. Papa, of course, had taken a much larger risk than I had, and his life in a new country must have seemed far more uncertain from his perspective when he had emigrated there so many years earlier than mine did now. I was sleeping in my own bed in the home of a family friend, and I had steady work lined up, unlike my father.

How petty my concerns seemed when compared with his. At least I'd been on my own in several countries and I'd been to India before. Moreover, the India of today was not the one he had left. It was integrated into the global economy, and Indians were by now familiar with Western culture and mores, thanks to cable television, outsourcing, and the Internet. I comforted myself with these thoughts. Maybe things wouldn't be too bad.

I drifted off to sleep just as the eerie early morning light filtered in through the window.

Part Two

Chapter Six

We are sitting on the floor of the drawing room in Vijay's immaculate, tiny flat in Delhi's Greater Kailash neighborhood. In fact, it is the only room in the top-floor *barsati*, though a spacious wraparound balcony more than makes up for what the flat lacks in breadth indoors. Jimi Hendrix casts his dreamy gaze down at me from his perch on a three-foot-tall poster on the wall. He holds a joint aslant in the left corner of his mouth, and a nimbus of smoke rises toward the nimbus of his hair. Judging from the soporific look in his eyes, the joint is producing the desired effect. I too hold a joint of what Vijay is telling me is grade-A Manali hash. And it too is having the desired effect.

It's been a couple of weeks since I arrived in Delhi, and a young woman I've recently met, Nandini, has asked me to join her and her friends at the city's hottest club, a dancing extravaganza spread out over three floors. The place, called Elevate, is in a mall in Noida, one of the Indian capital's satellite suburbs.

Space in New Delhi has grown tight over the years, unable to contain the country's rampaging growth. While Delhi's landscape looks much the same as it did when I lived here ten years ago, the two outlying boomtown suburbs, Noida and Gurgaon, have borne the brunt of India's dizzying economic expansion, hosting the majority of India's call center industry—itself a byword for the country's technology revolution.

Residential housing has colonized these new suburbs. Middle-class houses, luxury high-rises, and gated estates grow like

ragweed, fueling an exodus from the crowded metropolis.
Whereas there's only one modern mall within city limits, Ansal
Plaza, dozens of three- and four-story malls have sprung up in
Noida and Gurgaon. Every weekend, they are packed to the
rafters with young canoodling couples and families with tots in
tow, ordering lattes and catching the latest Bollywood flick at the
plush PVR cinema. Restaurateurs and nightclub entrepreneurs
have caught on to the trend, and now Delhi's night owls leave
the city for these hip new restaurants, clubs, and bars in a curious
reversal of the weekend invasion of Manhattan by the so-called
bridge-and-tunnel crowd from New Jersey and Long Island.

Nandini is the sister of a man who'd contacted me on
shaadi.com just a few weeks before I left New York. Since I
was leaving and he lived a couple hours outside of the city, we
never managed to meet before my departure for Delhi, but he
suggested over e-mail that I look up his sister, whom he wrote is
"going through similar stuff with men." (I would meet him for
the first time some eighteen months later at his wedding in
Jaipur.) I didn't have many friends in Delhi and certainly didn't
know any single women, so I got in touch with Nandini soon
after I arrived.

Ten years younger than me, Nandini grew up in Kanpur, a
fairly large manufacturing town in the heart of Uttar Pradesh,
the same state my parents are from. Despite never having been
there, I imagine it is as raucous, cacophonous, chaotic, and
middle class as the other U.P. towns I've visited.

Over the next few months, Nandini and I will become close,
swapping details of our dates and dalliances and commiserating
over near misses. I find Nandini's mind-set to be remarkably
similar to mine, and maybe one peculiar to the modern India.
While we are both ultimately looking to get married, minor
detours in the interest of romance, sex, and fun are permitted. As

a corollary, it would be unthinkable for either of us to ever enter a marriage without taking the car out for a test drive, as it were.

This night of my introduction to Delhi's nightlife, Nandini and her best friend, roommate, and occasional lover, Anil, pick me up from a Barista café (part of a Starbucks-style chain in India) in south Delhi, and we head to their friend Vijay's house, where we drink before heading to Elevate. I learn that this is a common thing to do as drinks in bars and clubs are prohibitively expensive, far out of proportion with the country's meager salaries. Clubgoers might earn what they consider a handsome sum of $200 a month in a job at a call center, but one night of drinking could easily run them upward of $50.

Anil and Nandini have both worked with Vijay and describe him as a "cool" guy who works in the Internet industry and manages a rock band. Still, I am not prepared for Vijay's long, kinky hair, Lennon glasses, goatee, and beanpole figure. Vijay looks more a member of a rock band than its manager. We file into the drawing room and arrange ourselves on the floor, while Vijay fetches drinks.

Here we are, Nandini, Anil, Vijay, and I, sipping on our cokes with Old Monk rum, India's answer to Bacardi, and eating Chinese take-away on the floor. It hasn't taken me long to come face to face with the New India. This is it, more or less. Though I'd heard about the "youthquake" phenomenon in India's major cities, in which young people in recent years have embraced a culture of drinking, clubbing, and taking party drugs, I hadn't expected to encounter it so soon or so easily.

Certainly drinking alcohol had long been a set piece of urban Indian culture, with men socializing and bonding over whiskey or rum before a heavy dinner was laid out at midnight or even later. But in this New India, women heartily join in with the men, knocking back drinks and smoking hash with nearly as much alacrity. Indeed, I would later notice far less of a stigma attached to a woman partying in Delhi than in the Indian diasporas of London or New York, where far stricter norms are imposed on a woman's behavior, perhaps owing to the immigrant focus on overachievement and the time capsule effect created by Indian immigrants leaving the motherland decades ago.

As I look around Vijay's flat, I think to myself that I should fit in just fine here. This crowd is hardly a far cry from the types of people I've kept company with in other cities. I notice the only furniture in the room is a desk, home to a computer outfitted with speakers, from which emanates the Pink Floyd–influenced crooning of a Delhi rock band that Vijay manages. In addition to managing the band, named Moksha, Vijay helps run the Internet operations at one of the country's largest newspapers. Anil is involved in launching the Internet division for a new television channel and also writes two blogs, one on computers and another one, on the side, about his personal life. Both men hail from tiny towns in Kerala, the southern state renowned for its long-standing communist government, its phenomenal 99 percent literacy rate, and its lush and picturesque countryside.

Both Vijay, in his early thirties, and Anil, in his mid-twenties, tell me they arrived in Delhi soon after they graduated from university down south. For young men like Vijay and Anil— bright, English-speaking, interested in the new world that the Internet had opened up for them—there are only two places to go in India, Delhi or Bombay, if they don't want to go overseas the way Vijay's brother or Anil's best friend had. Though they hadn't known each other until Anil worked under Vijay at the Internet division, they tell a similar story.

I'm curious about the men's motivations and how different or similar they are to the Indian men that have come before them, like my father.

"Why did you leave Kerala? Isn't it really nice there?" I ask.

"There wasn't much for me to do there," Vijay answers.

When I ask Anil, he says, "Same reason. My town was tiny and I wanted to get out and go to the big city. Bombay is more finance oriented. Delhi's more the media hub," he replies.

Despite being one of India's most functional states, sleepy Kerala held little in the way of New World enterprise. It seems that they left for the same thing my father had longed for as he traversed the dust bowl of northern India, stuck at one dead-end job after another, more than thirty years earlier.

"If if I'd stayed in Kerala, I would have joined my father at the small-town newspaper that he edits, and that would have been it," Vijay says.

"I would have probably worked as a teacher, or maybe some small-time engineer," says Anil.

The hash is just starting to play with my thoughts, and I say, half under my breath, "It's so easy to get trapped in time in India."

I look at these two men in front of me, in T-shirts and jeans, sprawled on the floor with their legs akimbo eating chicken Manchurian. They are a different breed from the men I've met in New York who left India after graduating from college and came to make it in the U.S., but I can't seem to place why they strike me as so different. Then it hits me: these two are comfortable in their own skin. When the Internet burst upon the world around 1995, for once, India wasn't far behind. Vijay and Anil wore the easy confidence of men who are in the thick of things, not aspiring to belong or striving to succeed.

Lost in my stoned reverie, I envision Vijay and Anil fronting a mob of engineering students as they burst through riot fences, which stand in for the labyrinthine restrictions India's socialist government has long imposed on industry. The country has already squandered too many of its years behind a socialistic veil, and this mutinous army of Indian geeks rises up and shouts, "No!" NO! We will no longer allow our world-class education—and indeed, India's science education is peerless—to languish on decades-old blueprints of electricity grids. NO! We will not build another power plant in the hinterland so that most of the electricity can be siphoned off by corrupt bureaucrats. NO! We will not make minor adjustments to a fifty-year-old model of an automobile. NO! We will not lay another Mesozoic-era telephone cable. (Haven't you heard of bloody cell phones?) No, no, NO!

I see this crazed rabble leap upon the newfangled vision dubbed the World Wide Web. First they begin using a program called e-mail that allows them to write to cousins and aunties settled abroad. Then they find interactive games on the Internet that they can play in real time with friends living in nearby cities. Next they begin looking around just a bit—"surfing," as it will soon be called—for information on bands like Nirvana, whose music they've heard somewhere. They soon stumble on chat rooms where people who are also interested in Nirvana are talking about other music. Have they heard of Smashing Pumpkins or maybe Pearl Jam?

Before long, this rebel militia of Indian brainiacs sniffs out other chat rooms, places where they can talk to members of the opposite sex. Sometimes, they become close to young women in places like the Ukraine and Germany. And oh, how nice these women are! And so open, so different from Indian women, who won't talk to you at college and always walk around in groups. And it is so much easier to share their deepest, darkest feelings on the computer. That they are lonely, that they have never been kissed, that they long to sleep next to a woman, breathing in the smell of her hair and skin. They've never been close to a woman before, a woman who is not one of the various snoring aunties they'd shared a bed with growing up.

India cries "YES!" to the Internet, and its self-imposed socialist exile from the world ends. The country joins the global economy and finally gets to enjoy the perks of having access to the latest trends, like the Internet. It is as if India has rejected the ascetic heritage that produced Buddha and Lord Mahavira—the sage responsible for the spread of my religion, Jainism—and unlike them, returned from the forest and reentered society.

As I'm watching Nandini, Anil, and Vijay talk and joke, passing a cigarette between them or swigging from the same bottle, I find myself feeling envious. Propped up against pillows on the floor, they have an unstudied sensuality that the West has not taught me. They are part of something, this New India, that I can never fully claim as my own, for I have grown up in America—a country to which I could also never lay full claim either. Moving from one lower-middle-class neighborhood in California or Las Vegas to another, I always felt removed from the other kids with the grape Kool-Aid stains around their mouths and their homes with the wet-dog smells. Perhaps it was a superiority I felt back then; we always had fresh fruit in our kitchen—mangoes and cantaloupes, even—and my mother kept our home immaculate. What would I have felt growing up in India? I will never know.

Nandini asks me a question, and I realize that somehow during my stupor we've made our way to Anil's Maruti Zen. The spliff is still going around in the car and somebody has thought to bring the rum and Coke as well. We are zipping down a sleek highway to Noida, perhaps one not so different from the first highway my father must have encountered in America after landing at JFK airport. I smile happily and look out the window.

To get to Elevate, we take a glass elevator to the top floor of the mall. After being patted down by security, Anil and Vijay pay for our tickets and we enter the club, which is pounding—in every sense. The music, the walls, the people, my head. Nandini and Anil find their friends, and soon we are surrounded by young men and women, who mostly are wearing glittery tank tops, tight jeans, and high heels. Not a sari in sight. I find out later that "ethnic" clothing is actually banned from the club. I never discover whether this is because the flowy fabric of *kurta*s and *dupatta*s inhibits getting down and shaking that ass, or because it distracts from the Western ethos of the club. In any case, the ethos is working.

Vijay hands me a rum and Coke and we dance for a while. They are playing a song I've come to love since my arrival in India. I hear "Kajra Re" everywhere—on television, at the mall, on the radio. It's an eight-minute song that has so many distinct parts that it sounds like eight different tunes.

"I love this music!" I scream over the song to Vijay, whose hair is flailing around in his face as he dances.

"I don't really like this music. I mean, I hate it, actually," he says.

I'm taken aback, since it's not evident from the way he's dancing. "What? But it's so fun to dance to! Why don't you like it?" I ask, yelling into his ear.

"I prefer Western music. This stuff is so poppy and it's all the same," Vijay says. "You know, Hindi music is for people who aren't really into music."

True, Bollywood music in the past had been garish and tinny, but it has improved tremendously in the last few years. Artists were incorporating elements of hip-hop, house, and electronic beats into traditional *filmi* music, making it not only more complex and aesthetic, but surprisingly danceable.

I recall how a decade ago, in 1995, when I'd lived in India as a young journalist, it was not considered cool to like Bollywood music, which was no more masterful than other sappy pop. Old classics from Mohammad Rafi or Mukesh were okay to hum along to, but you certainly would not be grooving to "Tujhe dekha to," featured in *Dilwale Dulhaniya Le Jayenge*, perhaps the most mawkish Bollywood film ever made—and that is saying something in India. In fact, Bollywood music has acquired enough cachet that Saturday nights at the club are devoted exclusively to Hindi numbers. Friday nights are reserved for electronica, the other music wave that has engulfed the country.

We've been dancing for an hour, and I notice Vijay is starting to flag. After all, he is a rock devotee to the core, favoring the ballads of Dire Straits and the Doors and the guitar riffs of Jimi Hendrix. We decide to sit down for a while on one of the velvet divans that line the sides of the club. People walk by us carrying a lethal-looking concoction in a three-foot-tall fluorescent vessel.

"So you're a Jain, right? So is my ex-wife. She was also from the north," he mentions a few minutes into our conversation.

"You were married before?" I say, shocked.

The only divorced people I'd known of in India were aunts of mine who'd been subjected to the worst kind of physical and mental abuse. I'd understood from my parents that people in India stayed married under any and all conditions and only used divorce as a last resort. Whenever I mention to my parents that a friend or acquaintance is getting a divorce, they expect to hear that the husband flies into violent rages or is a ferocious alcoholic. When I say, "Oh, they just didn't get along" or "They fell out of love," they insist, "But that's no reason to get divorced."

Vijay, with his gentle manner and soft voice, seems an unlikely wife beater—though his dancing style definitely leaned toward maniacal moshing. Perhaps he'd had an alcohol or a drug problem? Why else would a woman openly will herself into the life of a stigmatized divorcee in India, shunned by society and never to be remarried? Well, it turns out that while Vijay might have enjoyed the delights of Manali more than his wife would have liked, this wasn't the deal-breaker.

"Why did you get divorced?" I ask.

"I don't know," he says. "I guess we were just different. She was really career oriented and I think she got tired of my being so laid-back."

I might have been talking to a guy in an East Village bar in New York.

I'm still digesting the idea that Vijay seems to have gotten divorced for such a trifling reason as differing temperaments when our conversation is interrupted by a young turbaned man. Amarjeet is the bass guitarist for Moksha, the band that Vijay manages. Soon we're joined by other members of the band. There's TJ, a handsome and jovial guy trailed by a line of skimpily dressed women who can't be older than twenty. Vijay tells me this is to be expected. TJ, a very talented acoustic guitarist, is the envy of his fellow band members, attracting women to him like flies. I also meet Ajay, the drummer and the most preppy looking of the lot, and the electric guitarist, Ravi, who goes by his last name, Nair.

The long night of drinking and smoking hash is beginning to hit me, and things are blurring together—these faces, this band, this club, these tiny skirts revealing long swaths of bare leg. I realize that nobody's asking me the usual questions—whether I'm married, or what my parents do, or which towns they're from. Nobody even seems that interested in my life in America or that I've just arrived from New York City. They simply want to know if I want another drink or cigarette.

Looking at these men in the band, all of them sporting shoulder-length hair except for clean-cut Ajay and Amarjeet—whose long hair is hidden under a turban—I think to myself how they could be from anywhere. Indeed, I've met countless young men like them in Spain, Indonesia, Mexico. Shaggy-headed, pot-smoking, guitar-strumming rock junkies who pay more allegiance to the Rolling Stones than they do to country, creed, or religion. Looking up at these men from my seat, I decide they all belong to a nation called Hendrixstan, a country that has been invaded by enemy forces and its population forced to disperse all over the world, creating this diaspora of "Hey man"–greeting, high-fiving males, living among us but really patriots for another cause.

"Anita, it's almost five o'clock. I think we should leave," Vijay says in my ear. He stands up first and offers me his hand. I shakily rise and he supports me as we head off to find Anil and Nandini, who are remarkably still on the dance floor. We leave as day is breaking. I get a sinking feeling in my stomach.

Despite a lifetime of keeping bruising late nights, I've developed a strong visceral reaction to staying up until dawn. And whatever vestigial interest in this vampiric behavior I had was cured by a few months in Spain in my late twenties. Encroaching lambent early morning light has always made my stomach turn and my body clock screech in horror, "What have you done to me?" Even the wretched waking up at dawn to catch a plane or train is preferable to extending an evening into daylight. Nandini seems to have read my mind. When the guys suggest getting some omelettes at the Ambassador Hotel or *paranthas* at a *dhaba*, Nandini says in Hindi, "If I see the sun come up, I'll go crazy."

We drive back to Vijay's flat and polish off the remaining Chinese food. Nandini and Anil return to their flat. It'll take nearly an hour to get home to Seema's place in Gurgaon, and I don't have the energy to take a taxi. I decide to stay over at Vijay's place. He unrolls the bedding that we earlier used as cushions for our backs on his tiny floor. What will India's modern avatar reveal next? I've fallen asleep before I can think of an answer.

Chapter Seven

I've been in India for more than a month and have yet to find a place of my own. I'm still staying with Seema and Ashok in Gurgaon, and every day, as I travel to my office in Delhi, I take my place among the thousands of commuters making the same journey.

Depending on the vagaries of Indian traffic, my trip can take anywhere from forty minutes to an hour and a half. Every day, I pass a freeway under construction that, when completed, will cut the commuting time from Gurgaon to Delhi by half. Despite the hundreds of thousands of people who will benefit from this highway and the millions of dollars saved on work time and gasoline, the government is already a year behind on delivering the project, and it's nowhere near completion.

On most days I hitch a ride into the city with Seema, who works as a camerawoman at a national television station, one of the country's few females working in the field. A large roundabout near the house has yet to be paved, despite the presence of numerous sweaty, dark-skinned laborers apparently hard at work. Seema, a gentle soul with a gift for curses that sound like poetry, always swears under her breath when we pass the bumpy *gol chakkar*.

"Bloody road. What have they been doing for weeks? Wish these workers would get their heads out of their asses and do some work," she mutters as we jiggle up and down. "You know, Anita, Indian men should have three arms, one devoted exclusively to scratching their balls."

Listening to Seema's ongoing commentary on traffic and road conditions has become my morning entertainment. But these comments are rather mild, aimed as they are at mere incompetence. She reserves her more colorful remarks for lechers. Just that weekend, we'd gone shopping and she'd caught a man leering at us. In the most eloquent Hindi, she shouted at him, "I'll tear your eyes out and play marbles with them." Another time, irked at the insolence of another man, she cried out, "I'll rip the hair from your pubis and attach it to your upper lip."

So-called "eve teasing" is a common phenomenon in India, perhaps due to the disconnect created by the relative visibility of women in the public sphere—as opposed to in certain parts of the Islamic world—even as gender relations are still largely circumscribed. Men see, but they are not allowed to touch, leading to pent-up frustration.

Somewhere along our commute, we invariably get stuck behind a herd of goats branded with large pink crosses, followed by a spindly-legged goatherd with a walking stick. Here Seema's curses get louder.

At some point, we will invariably slow down to swerve around the cows milling about the road. Sometimes it seems as if cows around the world have heard through the bovine grapevine of a legendary place called India, where they can roam free—in fields, in streets, in marketplaces, anywhere they want to go. Unlike the life of containment and slaughter they face everywhere else in the world, in this neverland, not even a hair on their head can be touched. Indeed, in India, they are rumored to be *holy*.

"The cows must be whispering to each other in Australia, 'Hey, I just got a letter from my cousin Jane, who's finally made it to India. She says it's this amazing place where they go anywhere they want,'" I tell Seema.

Seema laughs. "Yes, Indians are so tolerant of everything. It's the only thing that makes this country work. Can you imagine if people were up in arms about everything all the time like they are in the West? It would be chaos," she says, as we idle in a traffic jam caused by an errant truck trying to merge with the jumble of scooters, autorickshaws, boxy Marutis, and sleeker Hondas.

Ah yes, the famous Indian patience. I'd heard the argument before and only half believed it. To me, Indian patience seems responsible both for India's ongoing existence as well as its underdevelopment. People might be frustrated enough to curse but not furious enough to demand change. I think of the unlikely circumstance of an intersection lying unfinished for weeks in the U.S. Local residents would have gathered a committee, written a letter to city officials, and appointed members to follow up until it was finished.

I'm learning quite a bit from these morning drives with Seema. To me, she embodies the Indian paradox—or rather, that everything in India is a paradox. The oft-repeated saying goes, "Whatever can be said about India that is true, the opposite is also true." For instance, the average annual income in India is $500. But also consider that the booming economy mints thousands of new millionaires each year. India is a sexually repressed country, but one that emerged from the same civilization that gave the world the *Kama Sutra*, the ancient Hindu version of *The Joy of Sex*, and temple art depicting scenes of bestiality and orgies.

Seema is one of the ballsiest women I've ever met. Married for just two years, she spends half the month away from her husband on television shoots, often in other countries, like China or Iran. A consummate tomboy from childhood, she performs a job usually reserved for men, which involves lugging around large amounts of heavy camera equipment on her five-foot-two-inch frame. She's also a conscientious wife and daughter-in-law, visiting her husband's family a few times a week. And, most interesting to me, she'd had an arranged marriage.

One morning, she tells me about her decision to marry Ashok. She'd never had a boyfriend before she was married and had always assumed her parents would find someone for her. She'd agreed to meet Ashok for the first time at a Barista café. The world-traveling, accomplished twenty-eight-year-old woman found herself turning demure, much like Indian women are expected to do at these marital introductions in order to appear docile and malleable—an *adjusting* wife.

"I looked down at my hands. He asked me all the questions," she explains. "I was too nervous to say anything."

"You're kidding," I say, squinting at her disbelievingly. This is not the Seema I've come to know.

"No, I'm serious. I'd never been alone before with a man who wasn't a family member or a colleague," she says. "I couldn't think of anything to say."

"So what did you think of him?"

"I thought he seemed nice, presentable. I didn't have a problem with him. So when I went home, I told my parents that he was fine and I would marry him. He did the same."

"I can't believe that meeting him once was enough," I say, shaking my head.

"Well, when we left the café, I walked behind him and noticed he had a cute ass."

Not everything was done according to tradition, however. She also told her parents she wanted a yearlong engagement period so that she could continue to enjoy her unmarried life a little longer before the onslaught of festivities and then various family obligations. She also wanted to get to know Ashok better.

Although both sets of parents would allow the betrothed couple to see each other on occasion, maybe once a month, they were discouraged from meeting often. But the two secretly met up each day of their engagement—even if it was a stolen twenty minutes, sharing a cigarette on their way home after work.

In an Indian twist on the old saw that "familiarity breeds contempt," parents fear their children will have nothing to discover in their spouses once they are married if they know each other too well beforehand. In the very institution of arranged marriage is embedded the idea of discovery, of excavation, of falling in love with another—to whom one is also committed forever. In an arranged marriage, whatever is revealed—an annoying tic, a nasty habit—must be accepted and assimilated. It is an entirely different process of discovery if there is a way out, an escape hatch.

One night at dinner, after Seema serves both of us before taking her seat, Ashok tells me why he too had always expected to have an arranged marriage despite the fact that his parents had had a love marriage three decades prior. They had eloped under great duress. His mother, a Brahmin of the highest subcaste, had fallen in love with Ashok's father, who was from one of the lower castes and also a student of her father, a university professor. Despite being a man of learning, Ashok's maternal grandfather would not sanction the union, and the two were forced to run away together. Both sides of their family disowned them, and they raised their three sons in isolation for many years before reestablishing contact with family members.

"My parents are very happy together, but I always wanted an arranged marriage," he says.

"Why, though, if your parents didn't have one?" I ask.

"It just seemed so romantic. My mother's father, after he started speaking to us, used to describe arranged marriage as the most romantic of enterprises," he says. "He would talk about the magic of discovering something new about one's spouse as well as the opposite sex, each day, every day—at least for a few years. He would tell me how he rushed home from work after he first got married with a spring in his step to see his young wife. That's when I decided to have an arranged marriage."

And indeed, Ashok and Seema's marriage seems very strong. They usually drive into Delhi together every day, if not in the same car, then one following the other. And they try to do the same in the evening, coordinating their departures from work, though Ashok often works late. Ashok doesn't begrudge Seema her frequent overnight trips, and Seema doesn't complain about her husband's long hours. They make certain to eat dinner together every night, even if it's close to midnight when Ashok returns. On weekends, they visit each other's respective families together.

The Indian system of arranged marriage, it seems, is like a net, catching those for whom premarital sexual or romantic experience is not a high priority. In the West, a person's lack of initiation into the rituals of dating and sex at an early age can hold him or her back from finding a lover later in life. "I would never go out with him. I don't think he's ever had a girlfriend," we whisper to each other.

Seema and Ashok's is a fairly traditional arranged marriage in the sense that both sets of parents met each other before the couple did, and then the two agreed to marry after their first meeting. However, even today, in the vast majority of arranged marriages across India, couples hardly get the chance Seema and Ashok did to spend time with each other. Indeed, most of my cousins in Meerut and Ghaziabad only met their spouses once, in the presence of their parents, before marrying. Certainly I wouldn't marry someone I met once, but I could see agreeing to marry someone before I got to know them—*in principle*. Isn't that kind of what we do anyway when we immediately project a future with a man upon meeting him for the first time?

Observing Seema and Ashok's togetherness brings my aloneness into stark relief. I've already orchestrated a transcontinental migration by myself, and now I have to look for a place to call my own in anarchic Delhi. How much nicer it would be to go through the process of finding a flat and settling into it with someone by my side. I will only later discover how very true this is.

With rent being relatively more manageable in Delhi than it is in New York, I assume it won't be long before I am ensconced in my own flat in a centrally located neighborhood. For once, I can afford a place with some space, an exciting development after my cramped quarters in New York and London. In my mind's eye, I decorate my Delhi flat in the opium-den-cum-*nawabi* style—all low-lying divans, cushions, and throw pillows.

I contact a real estate agent provided by my office. At first I look in the posh expatriate enclaves of Jor Bagh and Golf Links. My agent Rajesh, a smooth-talking Punjabi with a Mitsubishi Lancer, and his meek sidekick, Gagan, who speaks only in Hindi, show me apartments that are indeed spacious, with dark, cavernous rooms. They seem ideal for a French diplomat with three kids in tow, but I'd be lonely in them. Also, they're far too expensive, and the neighborhoods themselves seem a touch sleepy and staid for my taste.

Insulated from the grimy chaos of the city, these leafy, well-groomed areas are populated with expatriates working as diplomats, senior business executives, and journalists. They live side-by-side with upper-middle-class Indians, many of them Punjabi families who'd come to Delhi after Partition. Delhi is known for the type of expat who *falls in love* with India and tries to extend his allotted stint, but mostly what he's in love with is the grand lifestyle and the cheap domestic help.

I decide to target different neighborhoods with more activity and shopping. Rajesh has tired of showing me places after realizing his commission will be smaller than anticipated and leaves me to Gagan. I tell Gagan to look for a place in Defence Colony, a vast middle-class area where many of the country's military personnel have found homes after retiring. It's also inhabited by a mix of Indian families and professional couples, as well as younger expats on a less generous package.

Gagan dutifully arranges for me to see a few flats. I find one I like, a two-bedroom place with a nice balcony that is sufficiently well lit and in good condition. Gagan sets up an appointment with the owner the following day at the apartment, where I tell her I'm interested. I bring along Seema for good measure. The owner looks me up and down.

"Are you married?" she asks.

"No, not yet," I say.

"You'll be living here alone?" she asks.

"Yes," I reply.

"Are you from India?" she asks.

"Well, my parents are, but I grew up in America and I have a U.S. passport," I say, knowing that expatriates are viewed favorably by landlords.

She nods solemnly, still scrutinizing me. She doesn't seem eager to rent to me, but I can't make out why.

"I work for a foreign newspaper and can bring verification papers from my office," I say quickly.

This doesn't sway her indecision. Turning to Gagan, she tells him, "I need to check with my husband. I'll get back to you tomorrow."

When I call Gagan the next day, he says the owner can't rent the place to me.

"Well, why not?" I ask, crestfallen.

"I don't know. She's not renting it out now," he says.

"But I don't understand what the problem is. She met me, and I can verify all my details."

"Yes, I know, but these things happen," he says, sounding eager to get off the phone.

"But why? What happened? I've looked at so many places. I just don't understand," I plead.

Hearing the angst in my voice, Gagan at last decides to enlighten me. "Sometimes they don't like to rent to single women. And also, they don't like Indians either."

"What? But I'm not Indian! I mean, I am Indian, but I have a U.S. passport," I cry.

"Yes, but you're Indian. Your parents are Indians. People like to rent to foreigners," Gagan says.

I'm familiar with this self-directed racism. In part it owes something to the colonial hangover—the idea that whites make better tenants, better friends, or better lovers, just *because*. But there's another reason too. Indians in nicer neighborhoods prefer to rent to foreigners because they will eventually leave the country. Indian tenants, however, have developed a reputation, deserved or not, for overstaying their lease and refusing to vacate the premises, knowing that it will take years for the notoriously backed-up Indian courts to enforce the lease.

But it isn't the racism that troubles me. I've come to expect this. In fact, earlier that week, one landlord slammed the door on me when I went to see a place, saying, "I'm very sorry, but I don't rent to Indians." Of course, she also belonged to this pariah Indian community. It's more this business of being a woman on my own that irks me.

"Gagan, what do you mean they don't like that I'm a single woman?" I say.

"They say, '*Woh akeli ladki hai. Hum akeli ladki ko flat rent par nahin denge.* She's a single woman. We won't rent the flat to a single woman,'" Gagan says by way of explanation, but not explaining a thing.

"But in New York and London, landlords prefer single female tenants to men or couples. They consider them neat and quiet, easier to deal with than men," I say hopefully.

"I'll call you tomorrow with some more places to show," Gagan says, concluding the conversation.

I put down the phone, knowing in the same way we do when a former lover says something similar that it's the last time I'll hear from him.

Much by chance, a few days later, I come across an explanation for this strange practice of refusing to rent to single women in a newspaper article. Apparently, it's a uniquely Delhi phenomenon. In Bombay and Bangalore, many young professional women live on their own. It seems Delhi landlords fear single women will entertain male company at home, thus bringing disrepute on the house. Even more unbelievably, homeowners suspect young women who can afford a place of their own to be involved in prostitution. In other words, landlords in Delhi are afraid their homes will be turned into virtual *and* literal brothels. This schizophrenic attitude affords another example of the rampant fear of female sexuality in India.

I find a new property agent in the balding and pear-shaped form of Mr. Khan, who, though in his mid-forties, looks older, a lifetime of excessive consumption of mutton *biryani* and Old Monk having taken its toll. I explain to Mr. Khan that I've been looking for a month and haven't found anything and am tiring of my long commute from Gurgaon. I also lay out the difficulties I've had renting as a single woman.

"Not to worry, Anita. I am here now and I will find you a home and hearth soon enough," he says, trying to sound like a dashing white knight swooping in and rescuing me but coming off as more of a benevolent uncle.

Mr. Khan picks me up from my office in his Honda City and we drive to Defence Colony, where's he lined up three or four apartments for me to see. I quickly learn Mr. Khan is an avid talker.

"You know, Anita, I'm having too many problems with my in-laws. My wife's mother and brother, they will not let my wife have any of the nest egg from her late father. I'm driving to Jaipur every weekend for this problem only," he tells me.

"I'm really sorry to hear that, Mr. Khan. Families shouldn't fight over money." I nod my head in sympathy.

"Yes, in my salad days, I would never think people can behave like this only with their own daughter or sister. But you live and learn. What to do," he says, mopping sweat from his forehead with a handkerchief.

Mr. Khan is one of those people who seem distinctly out of step with the current times. He claims to be a descendant of the *nawab* of Rampur, and indeed, the dissipation of the latter years of the Mughal era suits Mr. Khan's air of fallen nobility and maudlin charm. I could better envision him at a *mujra*, sprawled across a silk-covered bolster, pulling at a hookah, and watching a nautch girl perform her sensual dance, than as a property dealer in modern-day Delhi. Mr. Khan seems defeated in his current incarnation as provider to a wife, two teenage daughters, and a young son.

Knowing my "circumstances," I assume he's only showing me flats for which he has spoken to the landlord about my being a single Indian woman—that is, prostitute—beforehand. Mr. Khan is working so hard to find me a place that it isn't long before I see another flat in Defence Colony that is acceptable. Like the first that I fell for, it's neither too big nor too small, is in decent shape, and receives good sunlight. I tell the landlord, a sweet-looking elderly gentleman, that I'm interested in renting, and he seems pleased. Mr. Khan tells me papers will be drawn up the following day, and we both shake hands with the landlord before leaving.

But when Mr. Khan calls the next day on my cell phone, he has bad news.

"Anita, I am very sorry to tell you this, but the landlord has changed his mind. A thousand mea culpas. Delhi is very bad for this, you know," Mr. Khan says in his most apologetic tone.

Even though I'm now somewhat prepared for the turn of events, it still comes as a heavy blow.

"But, Mr. Khan, I thought you told all the landlords that I was a single woman before you showed me the place! I can't believe this has happened again," I say, now imagining my plight as similar to that of civil-rights-era African-Americans trying to move into white neighborhoods.

"I *did* tell the landlord, Anita. But apparently, he told his daughter later that he wanted to rent to you, and she rejected the idea. She said single women were too much trouble," he says.

Apoplectic with fury, I scream into the phone, "But she's a woman! She's probably around my age too. I can't believe this country," I cry.

"Don't worry, Anita. I will find you a place under god's oath. It is my responsibility only. I will run from pillar to post, but I will not rest until you have a flat. Delhi is very bad for women, you know. I will call you back tomorrow morning with more places," he says.

And he does. Mr. Khan is indefatigable in his search. We see ten, fifteen, twenty more rentals together. None of them are quite right. I must confess to straying once or twice and seeing some flats with other agents. I just want to see what else is out there, but in the end I know I'll come back to Mr. Khan.

Finally, some two weeks later, he says to me, "Anita, I think I've shown you all the available flats in Defence Colony."

"Oh. Huh. Have you?" I say. "What do we do now?"

"Well, I have a few in Nizamuddin I've lined up, but after that, I don't know what we're going to do." He pauses. "I'll pick you up in an hour."

"Okay," I say, dejected. It appears as if even Mr. Khan is giving up on me.

Nizamuddin is an upscale older neighborhood, divided by a major road into eastern and western parts. It is slightly more posh than Defence Colony but not on the same level as Jor Bagh and Golf Links. Mughal-era monuments are strewn around Nizamuddin East, principally Humayun's Tomb, the grand mausoleum erected for the medieval emperor upon his death. Nizamuddin West contains the *dargah* for the Sufi saint Nizamuddin Auliya, which is surrounded by an old Delhi-style warren of filthy *galis* and crowded alleyways.

Mr. Khan has selected three rentals for me to visit. The first two are dingy and run-down, and even though my situation is desperate, I still believe that having the right apartment is key to my new life in Delhi. My heart is beginning to sink as we pull up to the last flat on his list. After this, I don't know what I will do. I'd like to think Mr. Khan will stick by me until we find something. We've become a team of sorts, battling the dark forces of Indian racism and sexism. I've become fond of him, and besides, I know he desperately needs my commission since his wife won't be getting her inheritance.

We walk up the two flights of stairs to the second floor and pause before the door. I suck in my breath and close my eyes. "Please let this one work out," I whisper to myself.

We step into a clean, airy, and recently renovated apartment with a living room balcony offset by sliding French doors and opening onto a tree-lined street. I start to feel better immediately. We mount another flight of stairs to see the terrace, which comes with the flat. A grassy patch covers one side, and from here, there's a view of the pearly white dome of Humayun's Tomb. It's around five o'clock, and patches of pink are showing in the gray-white sky. I walk to the other end of the terrace, which overlooks the smaller tomb of the court poet Khan-e-Khana.

I look over at Mr. Khan triumphantly. "I'll take it," I say.

Walking from the other side of the terrace toward me in his slow, waddling gait, Mr. Khan wipes his pate with a handkerchief and, grinning back at me, says, "See, Anita, I told you I would find you a place."

This time, the landlord is well aware of my unimaginable condition of being a single professional woman and decides to rent to me anyway. Perhaps it's not too dissimilar to my other search—finding a husband. If you look persistently enough, without either lowering your standards or admitting defeat when you get turned down on occasion, you'll eventually find the perfect one—and who knows, it might even come with a bonus terrace and an enchanting view.

Chapter Eight

I've a couple of weeks left in Gurgaon with Seema and Ashok before I can move to my new place in Delhi, and by this time, we've developed a familiar routine. I'm usually home before they arrive together from work, one driving in front of the other, at nine or ten in the evening. When they return, Gopal sets the table and brings out the dishes that he's prepared for dinner—a *dal* or a curry, a dry vegetable dish, and fresh *chapatis*. Although I'm not used to eating this late, I'm resetting my body clock to Indian mealtimes. (See, I can be adjusting.) Sometimes, if Seema or Ashok is cranky from a long day, Gopal might get a scolding for a dish that's too salty or has gone cold. If they get home earlier, around eight, the three of us share a glass or two of Old Monk before dinner.

When we finish dinner, we go upstairs to stroll across the terrace and perhaps pass a cigarette between the three of us. If I'm not tired, I'll say good night to Seema and Ashok and stay for a while on the terrace, looking out over the neighbors' homes, built just last year (not unlike my parents' home in neo-California), and then at the vast field covered with scrub growth behind the development. I could live this life, with its comfortable domestic routines. Or could I? Is this the life I want? Is this the life I came to India to find? Nothing is clearer before I return downstairs and get into bed.

Recently, though, there have been welcome disruptions to my predictable evenings. I've been distracted at dinner, fielding text messages from Mustafa, my friend in Kashmir for whom I harbor feelings that are more than friendly. We got in touch soon after my arrival in Delhi and have lately been spending quite a bit of time talking to each other on the phone, instant messaging at work, and text messaging. Although we exchange the most quotidian of details at first, every utterance of his seems laden with sensuality and romance, situated as he is in Srinagar. Kashmir has always had a very distinct culture from neighboring provinces in north India, its culture and language having borrowed much more heavily from Persia and Central Asia. While Hindi-speaking people are for the most part able to make out what people are saying in Punjabi or even Bengali, Kashmiri is unintelligible.

One night during dinner, Mustafa sends a text message describing what he's just finished cooking and eating for his evening meal. "*Khatte aloo, kofte* with *palak* and apricots," the text reads. Tangy potatoes, and meatballs with spinach and apricots.

I swoon. I find nothing more alluring than a man who can cook. I send back a text under the table asking whether he cooks every night.

"The cook and servants do the cooking usually. Mom cooks great. But I find cooking very creative," he replies.

Sometimes we call each other after our evening texting sessions, and with each of us reclining in bed, our humdrum daytime banter takes a more serious turn by night. It is then that Mustafa offers up revelations—more often than not unbidden—increasingly cracking open a door to his secretive, exotic world.

Mustafa tells me of how he descends from a line of forty generations of Sufi saints, broken by his own father, who found it difficult to keep to the strict rituals and fasts demanded by the tradition and became a doctor instead. Mustafa's grandfather was the last in the family to hold the role of a *pir*, a spiritual leader of a community who offers guidance to his followers along a particular Sufi path. His grandfather prayed incessantly and paid vigilant attention to his diet and the origins of his food. For example, rice could not be grown in a field that had been sprinkled with manure or tended by women while they were menstruating.

His grandfather, however, did have one vice, as Mustafa tells me one night. He delighted in the tinkling sound of china breaking on stone and every day would spend half an hour dropping some fifteen or sixteen cups, one by one, from his upstairs bedroom window to the courtyard below.

When he was a teenager, Mustafa tried to revive the tradition his father had allowed to lapse. At seventeen years old, he began undertaking the painstaking fasts and backbreaking privations required for initiation into the role of Sufi saint. On one occasion, for forty days at a stretch, he consumed only the starchy water that remains when rice has been drained from it. He occupied himself with constant prayer, twelve times a day, with the first session of chanting beginning at sunrise and continuing until nine o'clock in the morning, and the last night vigil at three thirty A.M.

Though not a man yet, Mustafa felt strong and confident and healthy during the roughly three years that he fasted and chanted toward attaining sainthood. He loved moving up in the hierarchy to each new stage, much like I did in the U.S. when I took tae kwon do, moving from a white belt to a yellow belt and then a green. (Of course, this seems rather paltry by way of comparison, and I don't offer it up.)

Then one day, at the age of twenty or twenty-one, when his peers were all entering college, Mustafa abandoned his religious life. It wasn't because he too wanted to attend college like his friends, or even because he was exhausted from adherence to the demanding rituals. He stopped one day because he witnessed a religious uprising in the streets of Srinagar. Perhaps it was no different from the ones that regularly took place, but on this day, it looked so fervid, so frenzied, so out of control.

"I felt suffocated," he tells me. And that was that.

In these conversations I find myself at a loss for words. What interest could he have in my suburban childhood in places like Sacramento or Las Vegas or Minnesota?

Mustafa is planning a wedding for his only sister, who is a few years younger. A traditional Kashmiri banquet of thirty-six dishes, called a *wazwan*, will be laid out for the five thousand guests planning to attend, with groups of four eating from one large plate. What can I tell him of my feasts growing up? Racing to Taco Bell in my best friend's Ford Mustang after school, singing along to Wham?

Busy planning his sister's wedding, Mustafa cannot come to Delhi to see me, and although he invites me to the wedding, sending a heavy card ornate with gold lettering and border, I decide not to go. I fear I will feel out of place. The combination of traveling to Kashmir, where an insurgency is still intact; finding myself amidst thousands of strangers at a wedding, and having met Mustafa only once before years ago is a trifecta of daunting circumstances.

Plus, I've only just gotten to Delhi and am still finding my feet. My potential romance with Mustafa will have to wait a little while longer. I find his old-world charm beguiling, but I'm no less intrigued by the new crop of confident and modern Indian men I encounter in Delhi.

Vikram suggests we meet up at a place called Oz, a lounge serving Mediterranean food, on the top floor of a mall in Gurgaon. Vikram is a childhood friend of Nandini, and she thinks that while I'm still in Gurgaon, it will be nice for the two of us to get acquainted. I suspect it is more for his sake than mine—though he is married, he lives alone in Gurgaon, working overnight for an outsourcing company, and doesn't get out much. His wife lives with his parents in Kanpur.

The mall I'm looking for is situated on the same main road as the other large, shiny malls in the satellite city. They gape up from both sides, side by side, four and five stories tall, and whenever I drive down this street, I wonder how they all manage to stay in business. Our mall is the fourth on the left side of the road, quite some distance from the first three. Compared to the others, it's a tired, dingy three-story affair that doesn't fit with its glamorous neighbors. "I don't know about this whole New India thing," it seems to say, one foot firmly placed in India's past of half-hearted and slapdash construction.

I'm early for our meeting and am surprised to recognize a Chilean white wine from Maipo Valley on the menu. I order a glass and am sipping it when Vikram arrives. He has stepped out of his office, which is around the corner, for a couple of hours but will have to return later that evening. I offer Vikram a taste of my wine. He demurs. He doesn't drink. I offer him a cigarette. He doesn't smoke either. I ask him about his work. This he warms up to.

"I'm a mortgage underwriter for companies in the U.S.," he says. "I work U.S. hours."

Like millions of his peers around the country, Vikram starts work around two or three in the afternoon and stays until midnight or later. His job is to assess the credit risk of people in Arizona and New Jersey.

"That must be a bit odd if you're sitting in Gurgaon," I say.

"Well, most of these things are done by formula anyway. It's much cheaper to send the work here," he explains.

The outsourcing industry has been a boon to the Indian economy, adding hundreds of millions of dollars to the country's gross domestic product every year. It has certainly rescued untold numbers from penury, but the offshore largesse has not come as an unequivocal blessing.

While the rest of the country sleeps, young Indians toil away in Gurgaon, Bangalore, and Chennai, answering phones, developing software, analyzing stocks, and assembling legal briefs for U.S. companies. These young people, mostly in their twenties and many of them with little experience apart from English-language skills, earn far more than they would at an Indian firm.

Still living at home and with no expenses, they are suddenly flush with cash. An entire culture has sprung up around these workers, who after finishing work after midnight—some many hours after—go to nightclubs and bars with their colleagues, blow wads of money on expensive drinks, and sleep all day.

Critics of this trend blast the overnight industry for this different type of "brain drain," a bastard cousin of the one India had been experiencing for years as its finest minds left for work in the U.S. and Europe. Some argue that instead of physically leaving the country, India's youth are now finding themselves stuck in unchallenging jobs with few opportunities for advancement. They stay at these jobs for years, contributing to the productivity of the U.S. economy, not India's, because the money and the perks are too good to leave for a less well-paid but more rewarding job with an Indian company. In particular, call centers, where employees just work the phones, are becoming viewed as glorified sweatshops.

Vikram had spent most of his life in Kanpur, but unlike Nandini, he hasn't really met many people in Delhi.

"I only really have one friend in Delhi," he says. "I see him once a month, I guess."

"So you don't see any friends during the week?" I ask.

"Well, I can't really. I work so much and such odd hours." Vikram tells me he rents a tiny flat in Gurgaon for the week, and every Friday evening he leaves work early to take a midnight train back to his large childhood home on the banks of the Ganges to see his parents and wife.

I consider the twenty-nine-year-old's lonely and brutish, not to mention oddly bifurcated, existence. How many others live like him, I wonder, spurring the U.S. economy on to greater productivity with nightly conference calls to Dallas and Los Angeles even as their own lives shrink and shrivel?

That first evening that Vikram and I meet at Oz, we make a pact over our unspoken loneliness. Yes, I have made a few friends since my arrival, and there's Seema and Ashok and my long-distance interactions with Mustafa. But after moving across the world, I feel desperately alone. From Vikram's unguarded manner and lack of bluster, I sense a kindred spirit. There is something *naked* about the way we speak to each other.

I'm also drawn to Vikram's dignified bearing, which doesn't appear to have roots in an aristocratic or a nouveau riche background. I think of all the back-slapping Indians I knew back in America who throw around money and buy $200 dress shirts, thinking it gives them cachet. Vikram's confidence is innate.

He represents to me a life that I would have had if my father had stayed in Kanpur at one of his technical institutes all those years ago. My questions shift from his work to his childhood and college days. I'm hoping he can fill me in on the past I have not had in India.

Vikram senses that my curiosity about his life is real, and he opens himself up readily. I suspect it's been a long time since someone has asked him about himself. From a well-off Brahmin family, he's a diligent worker and a rising star at the office, as well as a dutiful husband and son. Back in Kanpur, on the weekends, he coaches basketball for underprivileged boys. He is used to taking care of things for everybody else. He tells me how much he'd wanted to join the army when he graduated from university, but his mother wouldn't allow it. He is the younger of two sons and his brother lives in Seattle with his family.

"She knew me too well. She thought I would take risks and get myself killed. She'd already lost one son to the U.S. and she didn't want to lose another." He pauses.

"You know, Anita, I wanted to do so many things when I was younger. I had so many interests. Well, that's why I became a mortgage underwriter," he says, throwing his hands up, a wry smile playing on his lips. I'm not expecting the quip and laugh heartily.

He asks me about my life in New York. He is the first since I've arrived in India to do so, and I feel the relief of having a past, of being a continuous human being. So often when we travel, we are only granted the present to define us. "What did you do today? What will you do tomorrow?" people will ask. And I will want to scream back at them, "Ask me what I did a year ago, or ten years ago!"

Two hours have already elapsed and Vikram has to return to work. I can tell he doesn't want to leave, and I don't want him to either. He lingers.

"*Aap Hindi bolti hain?* Do you speak Hindi?" he asks in his resonant voice.

"Yes, I speak it, but I have an accent, so I'm embarrassed a bit," I reply in my standard way to Indians who ask, afraid that they will mock my accent. Indians are unused to hearing people speak Hindi with anything other than a perfectly native accent.

"*Kuch to kahiye. Mein aap ki awaaz sunana chah raha hoon.*
Please say something. I would like to hear your voice."

I close my eyes momentarily. It is hearing Hindi, not French or
Spanish, from a man with a sonorous voice that makes me blush.
Spoken in the right way, it can be the most sensuous of languages.

"*Aap to sharma rahin hain.* You are blushing," he says, making
me blush even harder and smile even wider.

I eventually relent and we begin speaking in Hindi, switching
back to English when the conversation moves into complex
territory.

An hour later, he looks at his watch and announces he has to
go. He offers to drop me back at Seema's house since it's in
Gurgaon. As we're heading down the main road with all the
malls, we get caught behind a truck with Hindi lettering on the
back. For reasons unknown, colorful aphorisms are printed just
above the fender on most large trucks. Many, but not all of
them, read, BURI NAZAR WALE, TERA MUH KALA. Whosoever casts
an evil eye will be cursed.

I peer at the truck ahead of us, which bears a different phrase.
I slowly read the Hindi characters, but as often happens with me,
I get too caught up in making out the script to catch the full
meaning. Vikram sees me struggling and translates, "It says, 'A
car runs on the road, not in a garage. Romance courses through
affairs, not marriage.'"

"Oh, interesting," I say.

When we arrive at Seema's, we make a plan to see each other
the day after next.

We meet a few more times in those last days when I'm staying
in Gurgaon before moving to Delhi. It's usually at Oz, and it's
only for a couple of hours, since Vikram always has to return to
work. We huddle close together on the sofa, me drinking my
Chilean white and he orange juice.

It is the last evening we're together, a couple of days before I'm to move to my new flat in Nizamuddin. We leave Oz and take the escalator downstairs, and without exchanging words or a glance, we join hands. It is a physical extension of our conversation, which itself has been a dialogue, one world-tossed soul to another. We have both reached out for different reasons. Vikram is exhausted from a life of working through the night and racing into the hinterland every weekend, I from my adjustment to a new job and a new country on my own.

Sitting in his Maruti Esteem, Vikram turns to me in the passenger seat and asks if I want to see his flat. I say yes, and we drive back to his home. We enter a sprawling complex of towers, slowing at a guardhouse. The watchman recognizes him and raises the bar to admit us. We park near one of the towers and walk up two flights of stairs.

I expect his flat to be small, but it is the most threadbare of accommodations, the room furnished with just a rickety table and a cot made of rough jute. He has no food or drink in his home, only a bottle of water that looks as if it has been sitting on the table for days.

We sit down on the cot, and I tease him about his place, trying to mask my sorrow at his apparent loneliness. Soon we lie down. We are unsure what to do. He kisses me tentatively and then we return to talking. We talk, and as we talk, our clothes come off, more out of comfort than lust. Soon we are naked and Vikram is speaking about his wife.

"She's so wonderful with my mother. My mother can be difficult and my wife knows how to handle her. She's great that way. But, well, she's not very interested in sex," he says.

I've spent enough time with him by now to know that he's telling me this not because he wants sex—he's too dignified to approach it in this ham-handed way, nor even to want it really. He just wants to talk to someone who will listen.

"Right after we got married, I bought her a subscription to *Cosmo* magazine. I thought, you know, she would read some of the articles and get interested, but she hasn't really," Vikram says.

I'm not sure how to respond, but when he is finished talking, I take my turn to bare myself to him.

"You know, Vikram, I don't want to be this kind of woman forever, like this courtesan-type figure—skilled in the art of intelligent conversation and also game for a little bedroom play, but not a wife, god forbid. I also want someone to describe me as a good wife one day. I want to be that wife who knows how to cheer up my husband in just the right way or what the perfect present for his sister is, not just someone who knows how to suck down martinis and make titillating talk."

I realize then how absurd it is for me to be saying this while I'm naked in bed with a man who has a wife who's not me. And it's even more so when I'm in India to find a husband. During these evenings we've spent together talking, I've perhaps come to view Vikram as a shadow husband, someone I could have married had my father not left India all those years ago.

But this night has less to do with sex or even romance than connection and conversation. I left the bosom of good friends two months earlier in New York, and my internal monologue had grown deafening. And I don't know how long Vikram has been speaking to himself inside his own head. I don't want to know, but I'm glad in a way that I made it back to his tiny room and jute cot.

Vikram is a man caught between worlds, between working for America and living in India, between the new India of Gurgaon and the old India of his parents and wife living together back in Kanpur. And this room and this cot are the interstices of that divided life. I'm happy to have been here, to have borne witness to the only in-between place where he actually exists. Has anybody been here but him? *If a tree falls in the forest, and there's no one around to hear it . . .*

I know this will be the last intimate evening I spend with Vikram. I begin to cry softly into his shoulder, and Vikram recites an Urdu couplet from the nineteenth-century poet Ghalib into my ear to cheer me up.

> *Ranj se khoongar hua insaan*
> *toh mit jata hai ranj*
>
> *Mushquilen mujh par padin itni*
> *ke aasaan ho gayeen*
>
> When man befriends sorrow
> then sorrow itself is erased.
>
> So many misfortunes befell me
> that they became easy.

We lie there for hours, unclothed, switching from English to Hindi and back again. Do you know that lying naked with someone brings two people closer than any carnal act? That talking like this is as close as we'll ever get in this world to touching another's soul? There are times when all we want to do is talk nakedly, without artifice, to another person, and it seems the easiest way to get there is to be naked.

Later, we put our clothes on, and Vikram drives me back to Seema's house. We are silent now, and he holds my hand, though he has to contort himself to shift the gears of the car. He stops in front of Seema's house. We turn to face each other, tightening our grip on each other's hand. This time, it is my turn to do the cheering up. With a wide smile, I say, "We probably won't see much of each other after this, but we'll always have Gurgaon."

Chapter Nine

The most divisive sound in the world is the rumble of an "R."
Not the crack of a gun being fired, nor the thump-thud of a boot
kicking a body over and over on the ground, nor even the boom
of an explosion. Those are really only effects of dissent, not the
cause of it.

In the hundreds of languages spoken around the world, we
trip on the "R"s. Think about it. The "P"s and "K"s and "S"s of
the world sound more or less the same, but not the "R"s. The
American "R" is hard, the English "R" can be absent—as in
"Mahk, dahling, be a stah and bring in the lemon taht, would
you"—the Spanish roll their "R"s, and the Chinese don't have
an official "R" in their language, which is why when they re-
create it, the sound often comes out sounding like an "L." The
Indian "R"? Well, there are two of them, and that doesn't
include the two "D"s that to the nonnative speaker sound very
much like "R"s.

I mangle "R"s everywhere I go, shining a spotlight on my
difference. Raised with the decisive American "R," I am incapable of rendering the sound properly in any other language. Here
in Delhi, acquaintances make a pastime out of mimicking my
accented Hindi. And it is the "R" that separates me from them. I
look like them, many of them are of the same religion, and we
now share the same globalized culture of Angelina Jolie and psy-
trance music, but my "R"s make me an American, a foreigner,
the proverbial NRI, or nonresident Indian.

My "R"s will forever mark me as different, but I am determined in my new life in Delhi to blend in, to raise as few bushy unibrows as possible.

My first day in my new apartment, it's a Saturday morning whose gray sky does nothing to mask the uncomfortably sticky heat. I am sitting on the floor in the living room waiting for a man to come and install an air conditioner in my bedroom. Even though it's early September, Delhiites will use their air conditioners for another month, maybe two. I am not only waiting for the air-conditioning man, I am also waiting for someone to deliver my water filter—without which I cannot drink water unless I boil it on the stove—my gas cylinder to operate the stove, my washing machine, my microwave, my refrigerator, and my inverter. The inverter, too, will be indispensable for my new life in Delhi, as it's a device that allows three or four lights or appliances to continue working when the electricity blows out, as it does at least once a day. I'm also waiting for my bed to arrive, some bookshelves, and a table with chairs.

Earlier in the week, I'd gone to Sarojini Nagar market with Seema to pick up items for an Indian kitchen. Nearly all middle-class people in India employ unfathomably cheap domestic help, and I plan to hire a cook—in addition to a maid—who will need these things to prepare proper Indian meals. Seema helps me choose an Indian-style wok, called a *kadai*; different types of steel cooking utensils, or *karchis*; serving spoons for *dal*; steel glasses, plates, and *katoris*—small bowls for *dal* and curd; water bottles for storing filtered water; a roller and pin for *chapatis*; a large steel container for the wheat flour needed to make *chapatis*; a tea strainer; a steel box for daily use of the four or five main spices that flavor Indian cooking; and then countless plastic containers for longer-term storage of spices, *dals*, tea, and rice.

Later that week, I shop for the basic food staples required by any respectable north Indian housewife. I buy salt, black pepper, coriander powder, red chili powder, cumin, turmeric, cardamom, asafetida, pomegranate powder, mango powder, bay leaf, cinnamon, clove, mustard seed, and *ajwain*—a spice resembling a smaller version of the cumin seed, tasting ever so slightly of licorice and possessing salutary benefits for digestion. I ask the shopkeeper to give me every lentil available. The variety of colors, shapes, and types boggles the mind. There is *channe ki dal, arhar ki dal, masoor ki dal,* split *masoor ki dal,* whole *urad ki dal,* split *urad ki dal,* whole *moong ki dal,* split *moong ki dal,* washed *moong ki dal* (yes, washed), black garbanzos, white garbanzos, and kidney beans—to name a few.

It is now past lunchtime, and none of the deliverymen have arrived. I am starving but there is no food in the house, and I cannot leave to find any because someone transporting something I cannot live without might show up at any second. I can't even drink any water. I while away the time speaking with my new maid, Chandra, a wiry, dark-skinned woman from Tamil Nadu with a magnetic smile revealing perfectly formed teeth. I will later learn that this radiant grin will be frequently deployed as a weapon to wheedle cash and presents out of me for various emergencies and special occasions. (Gifts such as silver or artificial jewelry will be rejected outright because she only wears gold.)

Chandra, who also works for the landlord's family downstairs, tells me she has lived in Delhi for the last nineteen years and did not speak a word of Hindi when she first came to the capital, but learned it from a kind employer in the first home in which she worked. Her Hindi is rough but so is mine. She has an eighteen-year-old son and a twenty-year-old daughter. Her husband left her for another woman long ago. She says she is thirty-five years old, but her cracked hands and deeply creased face give her the appearance of someone much older. I am thirty-two.

We appraise each other. We are peers, closer in a time-space continuum than I am to most of Delhi's residents. We are nearly the same age and in a city in which we are both foreigners, drawn here by employment opportunities. We are two single women and have no one to look after us but ourselves in this bustling and combative capital. Looking at each other, a silent acknowledgment passes between us. We must take care of each other—for no one else will.

I have been waiting, pacing up and down or sitting on the floor, for the last few hours, while Chandra dusts and sweeps and wipes down empty cupboards, removing any traces of the previous residents. I haven't even brought a book, my lifelong and constant companion, since I assumed I would be busy directing the efforts of various workmen assembling my new home. I begin calling the various shops that are to deliver my items. They say the workmen have started out and should be reaching me shortly. I wait another hour and call the shops back. They feign ignorance and give me the mobile phone numbers of the deliverymen. I call the men, and they say, "Madam, tire *punkchar ho gaya tha*" ("Madam, my tire was punctured.")

I walk out onto my balcony and take in the greenery that envelops my view. There's a palm tree directly in front of me. If my arm were a few feet longer, I could touch it. Everywhere, there are India's sacred Ashoka trees, the oddly shaped, pointy, and narrow trees spotted along every roadside and in every park in the capital. Jainism's most famous prophet, Mahavira, renounced the world under an Ashoka tree. There's a banyan tree further out near the road and a neem tree to my left. A pipal tree, under which Buddha attained enlightenment, is off to the right. Jasmine fills the air, and red-orange bougainvillea, in full blossom during the summer months, still makes an appearance at this time of year.

I look down at the veranda belonging to the neighbors one floor below mine and notice the array of potted plants lining their balcony, like sentinels at attention. My balcony is a quarter of the size of theirs, but I have exclusive use of the large roof terrace upstairs. I realize I must buy potted plants to fill the empty space and look below me for inspiration. I recognize nothing. Later I will point to their patio and ask the gardener to purchase plants exactly like theirs. He will bring the so-called money plant, a large-leafed plant found in most Indian homes for its obvious properties of wealth creation, along with various other flowers and shrubs. He will place the money plant in a corner of the living room and juniper, basil, dieffenbachia, and ficus plants on the terrace. There are others for which he knows only the Hindi names, *harsinghar* and *madhumalti*.

It is now evening, past six o'clock, and two or three of the deliverymen finally arrive in quick succession. They have made it, albeit hours late and despite their punctured tires. Others don't come at all, and when I call the shops to complain, they say they will send someone out tomorrow. My bed doesn't come that first day, and so I set out for Seema's house in Gurgaon at ten P.M., fairly certain that no one will show up at this hour. As I near her home after the hour-long drive, I notice from the taxi window that the dirt and gravel roundabout that I passed every day on my way to work and back has finally been paved. It is like everything in India, from the economic boom to my deliverymen—infuriatingly late but eventually and indisputably there nonetheless.

Soon after I move in, my landlord drives me around the neighborhood in his Tata Indica. He points out the entrance to Humayun's Tomb that is used by the residents of Niza-muddin, who are allowed to walk in the grounds at dawn before the tourists show up. (Over the next year, I will never make it on time, and the one or two times I manage to drag myself out of bed to walk around the tomb, I will pass a steady stream of men and women in their fifties, sixties, and seventies leaving, having finished their brisk morning constitutional. It seems that all middle-class Indians take up walking after turning fifty-five years old.) He shows me the local market and the ATM machine I can use across the main road in Nizamuddin West. We go to the next neighborhood over, called Jangpura, where he explains I can procure larger household items at the sprawling Bhogal market that I won't find in my neighborhood, Nizamuddin East.

I realize as we drive that there are other reasons behind the long guided tour. Piyush wants to talk, and he has a lot on his mind. After nearly two decades of being a journalist, a year ago he struck out on his own to start a travel Web site and magazine. He is funding it himself and the money has started to run out. I offer to help by putting him in touch with some venture capitalist contacts I have encountered through my work. I'm pleased that I can in some way repay him for renting to me when no one else would.

The conversation takes an unexpected turn. Piyush, who's in his mid-forties, tells me he is on his second marriage. His first marriage, to a woman whom he had dated for a decade, dissolved within months. The second time around, he opted for an arranged marriage. I shift in my seat. I can't seem to get away from the subject of marriage.

Piyush continues on. Dusk has fallen, and from what I can gather we are driving around in circles. In addition to trying to launch his own enterprise, he earns a small stipend as a lecturer of journalism at a local college. There, he tells me, he has befriended a young female student who offered to help him on his Web site for free. This girl and he work long hours in the office he has built under the ground floor, where he lives with his wife, two children, sister, and mother. The girl has told my landlord that after working so closely with him, she has developed feelings for him. He finds it surprising, and flattering, because she is so much younger. His wife isn't comfortable with the relationship, but—

I cut him short. Despite usually being an avid listener of the lurid and licentious, there are simply some things about landlords we need not know.

After that initial revealing drive, I am relieved to discover Piyush is more formal in subsequent encounters, and we mainly exchange details about the flat. I begin to view him as a benevolent presence, if a slightly gloomy one.

One day, though, when I've called Piyush up to the flat to look at my faulty shower, he turns loquacious again, revealing his fascination for America and his numerous abortive attempts to settle there. This surprises me, because, as the son of Hindu immigrants from the part of Punjab now in Pakistan, he's enjoyed a life of privilege in upper-middle-class Nizamuddin. Like most long-standing residents of the neighborhood, his parents arrived in Delhi during the bloody Partition that accompanied the division of the subcontinent. These refugees quickly ranked among Delhi's most prosperous residents, using government compensation granted to those who had lost their homes to leverage business networks they formed among themselves, much like those found in the Jewish Diaspora through the ages.

For a long time, I considered the Indian idealization of America largely a function of economics. Less-fortunate Indians, like my father, looked to more affluent shores for a better life for themselves and their children. An ardent fan of jazz, blues, and rock, Piyush disabuses me of this notion. He viewed the land that had given birth to Frank Zappa, Jimi Hendrix, Janis Joplin, and Miles Davis as his own spiritual homeland.

"I wanted to be associated with the American brand," he tells me. "America had these huge roads, lovely cars, everything to do with freedom."

Piyush was blown away on his first visit to the U.S. with his first wife when he was twenty-eight years old. Upon arriving at John F. Kennedy airport in New York City, he reached down and touched the floor with his hand, which he then brought to his forehead in the Hindu gesture of *pranaam*. He was literally blessing himself with the soil of America.

They stayed with a friend of his in upstate New York, near Woodstock in fact, a detail he recollects with considerable relish. He would take the train down to New York City, and oh, the sights he would see! It was 1991, before Mayor Rudy Giuliani's crusade to clean up and beautify gritty Manhattan, and Piyush visited the peep shows that were ubiquitous in Times Square at the time.

"You would pay a dollar or two to get in, and then another two or three dollars to feel a thigh or maybe some cleavage," Piyush recalls gleefully. "Your whole life you've had this idea of white women being the best and here this nude white girl was right in front of you. Oh, it was a great thing!" Most of the patrons crowding the peep shows, he remembered, were Indians—Gujaratis, Punjabis, Tamils—all enjoying the show of a lifetime.

He nosed around for suitable work to no avail. When his tourist visa expired in two months, he was heartbroken to leave the country but decided he would return one day to live. He even had a business venture in mind, setting up kiosks of Indian rugs and fabrics and trinkets in America's strip malls, which he thought far superior to India's dirty and crowded outdoor markets.

He resumed work again in Delhi at one of the country's top newspapers, the *Hindustan Times*, but now he was a haunted man.

"I couldn't stop thinking about America. I liked everything, the furniture, the apartments, the lifestyle. I kept playing that Frank Sinatra song over and over at home in Delhi," he says. *If I can make it there, I'll make it anywhere.*

Three years later, in 1994, he got another chance to go on a tourist visa. Despite being a respected journalist in Delhi, he was hoping to find initial work at convenience stores like 7-Eleven. Before he could secure employment at such an exalted venue, he lucked out and landed a job at *India Abroad*, a New York–based newspaper for Indian immigrants.

This second time, though, Piyush was between marriages, and he felt lonely all by himself in the U.S. All the things that had enthralled him on his first visit, like the Times Square peep shows, didn't have quite the same allure—in that inimitable way men have of enjoying something prurient far more when there is a wife or girlfriend around to take umbrage. He even found himself aimlessly strolling around Jackson Heights, the area of Queens populated with immigrants from the Indian subcontinent, on weekend afternoons, inhaling the familiar odors of Indian cooking wafting out of restaurants.

He realized he would have to stay another year or two at the paper, employed illegally, before they sponsored him for a green card. So after three months, he headed back to India again. Working and earning a salary in the U.S., though, had driven home the unassailable nature of the U.S. dollar.

"I came back with four suitcases to India, one just for my dog. It was full of biscuits, dog food, those chewy bones," he says.

While his respect for America had not diminished, now he found he had a more realistic and nuanced attitude toward the country. He felt that as an Indian immigrant, he would never be completely accepted by society, and that for all his love of jazz and rock and roll, he didn't feel quite comfortable in the clubs he visited in Manhattan.

"I was more American being in Delhi than I was in America," he tells me, laughing at the irony of it. His sentiment is one I quite literally identify with, scouring New York as I did for the best *masala dosas* and Delhi as I do now for the best martinis.

He decided that if he ever returned to America, he wouldn't go alone and he wouldn't work illegally. No longer did he want to live at the fringes of society, sitting at CBGB by himself and sipping on the one beer he could afford all night.

It was now 1996, and by this time he'd remarried and reestablished himself as a journalist in the Indian capital. His career was at its peak and he was well regarded by his superiors and colleagues. Somehow, though, like the pea under the stack of mattresses, the idea of America kept him feeling restive despite his more or less ideal life in Delhi.

He sketched out an elaborate plan for this next and third attempt at becoming an American. Unlike the other times, this was a well-thought-out scheme requiring years of preparation before it would see fruition. He would apply for an immigrant visa to Canada, whose relatively lax immigration rules allow skilled professionals to settle in the country. The visa itself would take eighteen months to come through. Then, visa in hand, he and his wife, a medical researcher, would both find proper jobs suitable to their work experience in Canada, and when the time was right, two or three years down the line, he would secure a post in America—all legally, all aboveboard.

In 1998, Piyush and his wife arrived in Toronto, which to his horror was nothing like New York City. It was drab and lifeless, and people seemed downtrodden, unfriendly, huddled against the cold. All the Indians he encountered wanted to get to America as soon as possible. He couldn't bear the thought of staying a few years before getting to his ultimate destination. "If I want to go to America, what am I doing in Canada?" he thought to himself.

Nonetheless, he and his wife tried to stick to the original plan, but it didn't work out as imagined. Neither of them could find professional work, and this time Piyush didn't want to stoop to blue-collar employment despite being offered a job as a security guard—a job my father did for several years when he first arrived in the U.S. before he found work as an engineer. The couple returned to Delhi from Toronto within three months.

Now Piyush was in Delhi for good. He'd quit his prestigious position as an editor to go to Canada, and had to find a job on his return. Despite this, he felt more certain of his decision to come back to India than ever before.

"Three times, and now I'm done," he told his wife. "We've burnt our hands. Let's build our lives here. The West is no more my scene."

But you know how it is. We never really shake our demons, do we? The violence of our irrational fears, the doggedness of our outlandish dreams, the insatiable nature of our custom-made morbid curiosities. Oh, how they keep us up at night! Perhaps our bugbears, our *bêtes noires*, aren't even developed over a lifetime of missed chances or missteps. Maybe they are inbuilt, in our genes, part of us from the day we're born.

The demons tormenting my father and me proved so intractable that we both uprooted our lives and traversed continents. He left India for economic opportunity three decades ago, but, those concerns no longer relevant to the well-educated with means in this postmodern world, I leave the U.S. for other reasons—to find a spouse, for excitement, for a sense of belonging that I haven't found in the U.S.

So it makes sense to me that Piyush found himself intrigued one day in 2000—two years after he'd returned to India "for good"—by an ad in the papers for a position at *India-West*, another immigrant publication in America targeted at the Indian community. It was for a bureau chief position in Washington, D.C. It seemed too perfect to be true. Can you blame him for what happened next?

This time, Piyush's assault on Fortress America was a stealth attack. The paper, impressed by his years of experience in Delhi and the rival immigrant paper in the U.S., thought he was perfect for the job, but would only sponsor him for a work visa if he could get to D.C. on his own.

His and his wife's Canadian visas were still valid, and what could be simpler than flying into Toronto, driving across the border, and pretending to be on a weekend visit to Niagara Falls? Okay, okay, maybe he should have thought about the fact that his pregnant wife, eight months and bursting at the belly, might arouse suspicion in border officials who assumed she would try to deliver her baby on American soil, ensuring the child U.S. citizenship and paving the way for the parents to obtain legal status. And if they were going for only a "weekend visit," maybe Piyush shouldn't have piled the trunk with their four suitcases? He did have the work appointment letter in his hand—didn't he?—and he was so close, just a few hundred miles away. What could go wrong?

Piyush never made it over the U.S.-Canadian border. U.S. officials stamped a big red DENIED ENTRY TO THE U.S. on his passport.

I think about my landlord's numerous failed attempts at immigrating to America as I settle into my home in Delhi. People leave the countries into which they were born for numberless and thoroughly individual reasons. Many of us simply feel we were born in the wrong country, an expatriate at birth, and we seek to make it right. I think back to a French dot-com entrepreneur I dated once in New York, who told me, in a near-perfect American accent and while pouring ketchup over his chicken salad, how stifling he found France's business sector and how liberated he felt in the cutthroat supercapitalism of America.

These first days in my new flat, while sitting on my balcony drinking a cup of ginger-infused *chai* and looking out over the neighbors' homes, I think of other reasons Indians might leave the country. Not just for the indomitable American dollar and Frank Zappa. Also for hot showers and smooth, ribbonlike roads. The water pressure in my shower is somewhat less than thunderous; it is a trickle. And though bathing in cold water suits me during Delhi's summer heat, it is just starting to get nippy at night. When I flip on my hot water geyser and allow the water to heat up, though, the water remains warm for only a few minutes before I'm back to an icy sprinkle.

Our bodies, too, have their own dignity to them, and it is the body that knows better, that will demand we don't shower in the winter in a freezing driblet, or bump along potholed roads, or leap across trash piles when we go to the market. I will get my shower fixed, but others will migrate to a new country for stronger water pressure. I do not blame them. Sometimes the rallying cry of the flesh drowns out any other noise.

Chapter Ten

Now that I'm settled in Delhi, my thoughts turn toward escaping it. Vijay, the band manager with the long kinky hair who I'd met a few weeks earlier, has asked me to join him and some others for a long weekend in the "hills," which is the understatement Indians use to describe the imposing Himalayas. Anil, as well as Moksha's electric guitarist, Nair, who I met at Elevate, have already agreed to go, but Nandini can't make it.

Vijay has a friend who runs a small retreat more than six thousand feet up into the middle Himalayas in the Kumaon region, an area immortalized by the tales of Jim Corbett, the British adventurer who spared the lives of many villagers by killing man-eating tigers and leopards.

It sounds heavenly, just the break I need after my first couple of months in the congested city, but there are other things to consider. On the one hand, I don't know any of the three men very well, and the plan sounds a bit harebrained, not to mention outright dangerous. We'll start driving from Delhi at midnight to beat the traffic, and the trip will take at least eight hours in the car, the last few of which will be over mountain roads, with hairpin turns and ninety-degree drops of several thousand feet off to the side. If previous excursions are anything to go by, the boys are likely to be smoking hash and drinking Old Monk in the car. It may not be the most responsible thing to do.

But, on the other hand, all three of the guys are Mallus, which is short for Malayalis, the term for those who hail from Kerala.

South Indians are generally considered less aggressive than their rough-hewn and surly counterparts in the north, and many communities in Kerala belong to a matriarchal tradition. So while I may not be fending off any forceful advances, we could plunge off the shoulder of the road and my disfigured body could be found in some vertiginous valley weeks later. Soon I'm picturing the tragedy of my death—so young, so attractive, in the prime of her life, they will say. I see the aunties shaking their heads and clucking, "*Bechari ki shaadi bhi nahin hui.* The poor girl, she never even got married." Just then the phone rings.

"*Beti,* how is the marriage search going? Listen, have you found a boy yet?" my father shouts down the line from Sacramento.

Mobile phone technology in India, having leapfrogged over the decaying telephone infrastructure, is so advanced that someone calling from the U.S. or Europe sounds as if they are calling from next door. But as per my father's inability to acknowledge any change in India in the last three decades, he still yells down the line as if trying to be heard over noisy static.

I've been busy settling into a new job and country, but of course, these efforts are overlooked.

"No, I haven't, Papa. I haven't had time to meet any men," I say. "I'm just settling into my new flat and setting up house. It takes time, you know."

"You haven't met any boys at all? What have you been doing?" my father asks.

"Well, no, not really," I say. Then I think of Vijay, Anil, and Nair. They are certainly boys, and all are single.

"Hey, Papa, I'm going away this weekend to the mountains with some friends," I find myself saying. "My phone may not work up there."

"Who are you going with? Boys or girls?" he demands to know.

"Oh, both. Both. Boys and girls. A couple of boys and many, many girls," I reply.

We decide to take Anil's car, which doesn't have air-conditioning but does boast a functioning cassette player—more than could be said for Nair's car. The elements of a road trip are the same anywhere in the world, in countries both rich and poor, and they are immutable—the absence of any one element is a type of blasphemy. The elements, in no special order, are 1) a car; 2) snacks—not food but snacks, so that bags of chips or *namkeen* or wasabi peas can be passed around the car; 3) water; and 4) music. And because we are dealing with countries in all states of development, it does not matter if the music comes from a radio, cassette tapes, or an iPod. These four elements in place, as well as reasonably tolerable company, will ensure, like a mathematical equation, a successful and pleasant road trip.

Our journey begins smoothly enough. We start off at the appointed hour and make our way to Noida, which we have to cut through on our way to the hills. We sail down the same slick highway I remember from our drive out to Elevate. I've already come to love this highway, an icon of sorts of India's progress—late it may be, but under way nonetheless. Just outside of Noida, my mobile phone buzzes, indicating I've received a text message. Wondering who would send me a text message at one A.M.—particularly since I know few people in Delhi outside of those in the car with me—I click to open the message.

"Airtel welcomes you to western Uttar Pradesh. We hope you enjoy your stay," reads the jaunty greeting from my mobile provider. What technological wonders abound in this once benighted country!

I'm in the front with Anil and controlling the music, reaching into a bag of cassette tapes and pulling out whatever strikes my fancy. Many of the tapes are the same I listened to in the eighties before I overhauled my music collection and purchased compact discs. I pop in Eurythmics, overruling protest from Vijay and Anil in the back. Still, they pass me the joint.

I think back to the last time I took a road trip. I never drove anywhere when I was in New York. None of my friends had cars. And then when I was overseas, I can't recall going anywhere by car. Could it really be that I haven't been on a road trip since high school?

Though I'm not sure I see romantic potential with any of the three men in the car, I'm amazed at how comfortable I feel in their presence. I wonder if I would feel this comfortable with three American men, and I decide that I wouldn't. Later, when I am more settled in Delhi, I will notice that in urban modern circles, young men and women seem to enjoy an easier rapport with each other that I've rarely experienced in the West. I think back to how in New York, I spent little time with male friends who weren't gay, and my social life seemed to revolve around girls' nights out. In America, both growing up and in New York, I had felt males and females were locked in battle and rarely enjoyed friendship just for the sake of it. In high school, boys hung out with boys and girls with girls, and later, in our twenties and thirties, we eyed each other suspiciously, not realizing that we could be friends, not just lovers or colleagues.

Moreover, for all of India's oppression of women, it's remarkable that I can travel alone with three men in a car without being stopped by authorities. Certainly we would be questioned in Saudi Arabia or Iran, and we would have to establish that I was the sister or wife of one of the men.

I'm mulling over all this apparent modernity when all of a sudden, I hear a thud and the car jerks up and down. Anil apologizes and tells me we've just hit a pothole. Boom! Thud!

Thump! We hit three more. We bump over a pothole every few minutes and have to scurry off to the side of the road every time a smoke-belching truck comes bearing down on us from the opposite direction. India's unstoppable forward march is juddering to a halt.

Swerving to avoid potholes on Indian roads resembles what drunk driving might in other countries. But here, it's actually capable hand-eye coordination that results in the jerky side-to-side movements. Our ambling progress slows further to a walkable pace. We are now virtually stationary behind a long line of cars and trucks, inching along every few minutes. Nothing like a traffic jam to kill your road trip buzz.

I look at my watch. It reads four A.M., and Vijay and Nair have long since nodded off in the backseat, but in adherence to another unspoken rule of the road trip—that one person must stay awake with the driver at all times—I struggle to fend off exhaustion as Anil drives. I take Eurythmics out and put in some Blondie. The windows are open, and the warm, sticky air has turned noxious from all of the stalled vehicles. I feel dizzy from the pollution, not to mention dog-tired and uncomfortable in the cramped car. At the rate we're going, we've only seven more hours to go.

Other drivers have emerged from their cars and are milling around to figure out what's caused the delay. Anil sticks his head out the window and asks one of the other drivers what the problem is. There's been an accident. Every year toward the end of summer, thousands of men from all walks of life don a saffron-colored *dhoti* and make a pilgrimage to the mouth of the Ganges in the northern Indian town of Haridwar. There, these so-called *kanwarias* fill up two vessels of water, which are hung from opposite ends of a long rod and borne across their shoulders as they travel by foot from their village to Haridwar and back. The pilgrims walk barefoot on a journey that often takes days.

Anil ascertains that a car has hit and killed one of these *kanwarias*—each year, several get killed, a function of deadly driving and no roadside illumination. The *kanwarias* retaliated by starting a riot and setting fire to a dozen cars. The conflagration has died down by the time we arrive, but traffic has been at a standstill for a couple of hours now, Anil learns. Only in India would a traffic jam be caused by half-naked rioting religious pilgrims.

We lose a few hours stalled at the traffic jam and by nine o'clock in the morning, we reach the last city on the plains, Haldwani, after which our steep ascent into the mountains begins. Starving now, we decide to stop for tea. Vijay's friend Arvind, who owns and operates the retreat in the hills at which we plan to stay, grew up in this tiny town at the foot of the Himalayas. Vijay suggests we stop at Arvind's parents' house.

When we arrive at their modest home, Arvind's parents greet us warmly, though they recognize only Vijay among their unexpected guests. Arvind's mother brings tea and biscuits to us in the drawing room where we gather. Arvind's younger brother, a man in his early twenties, is also there, talking of his pending departure that very evening for Dundee, Scotland, where he is planning to find work. He'll join his twin brother, who's already there working in a hotel. I wonder how this young man with his halting English will comprehend the lilting garble of native speakers in the moors of Scotland.

My presence, which until now none of my companions have regarded as curious, finally arouses attention—in the young man. It is rare to see unattached women in small towns such as the one he lives in. He eyes me surreptitiously while I sip my tea. Soon, his gaze becomes bolder, and he follows me with his eyes as I rise to find a bathroom. By the time I return to my seat, his stare has progressed to a full-fledged shameless ogle. If he thinks I'm interesting—bedraggled and sleep-deprived as I am from my overnight journey—he'll certainly be getting an eyeful in Scotland.

India is a country where old and new, traditional and modern, the yokel and the sophisticate, meet every moment, bumping into and rubbing up against one another. They're often of the same family, a brother who has lived in Hong Kong and Paris bearing gifts upon returning to India for his elder brother who has never left Muzaffarnagar. The boy's undivided attention makes me wonder about his brother Arvind, who I will meet a few hours later. He too has grown up in Haldwani, but now runs a retreat with an extensive organic farming operation, on which visitors from all over the world descend.

We say our good-byes and start again after our brief rest. It has been a long and sleepless journey, but my mood lifts as we begin our ascent into the hills. I gulp in cool and clean oxygen. The valley falls away from us on our right, and before long we're rising above the clouds that have descended into the hollow. We career and careen our way up the perilous climb at a pace far too rapid for my taste. We climb for so long that I begin to wonder if this place, called Sonapani, meaning "Goldwater," really exists. Two or three hours go by before we stop in front of a small structure no bigger than a one-car garage. We are met by a welcoming party of young boys who relieve us of our bags, and we follow in their wake down a dirt path sprinkled with pine needles through a forest. We walk for a long time. Again I question the existence of our destination.

Some thirty minutes later, we find ourselves in a clearing. The vista opens to reveal a dozen bungalows set along the side of a mountain. We are enveloped on all sides by surrounding valleys, their slopes covered with pine trees, which I'm told were brought by the British to India.

Arvind meets us at the sturdy outdoor wood tables where guests congregate and eat their meals. He has an easy manner and seamless grace, and I notice he's quick to laugh. How different he is from his callow young brother, who is a decade younger. Arvind left Haldwani in his early twenties for Delhi, working at various sales jobs before finally raising enough money to set up this retreat in the mountains he loved. I wonder if his awkward brother will display this kind of polish too ten years hence, after being exposed to the world. Arvind mentions his wife and young daughter are currently away, and I find myself disappointed to learn he's married.

It's two in the afternoon and we are ravenous with hunger. Arvind asks the ruddy-faced boys to bring us lunch. In minutes, fluffy omelettes and toast arrive. We slather our toast with plum jam made from fruit grown on the premises. After the meal, we retire to our room to sleep off the trip. There are two large beds in the room I share with the boys. I plop onto one. The three of them crowd onto the second. I smile at the chivalrous gesture.

It's dusk when I awake, and I walk up the slope to a clearing where my friends and other guests are already gathered around a bonfire. Drinks are being served, and I ask for what is quickly becoming my default drink—Old Monk rum with plain water. Vodka or whisky may or may not be available, but you'll always find a squat, dark bottle of the inexpensive Old Monk.

As the sky darkens, guests continue to emerge from their bungalows and the momentum of the evening picks up. More drinks are poured. A dozen of us are sitting in chairs around the fire, most of us strangers to each other and most of us from Delhi. A man recites an Urdu couplet and a few guests pipe up with the expected "wah wah wah," to congratulate the profundity and felicity of the poetry.

A guitar appears and a guest sings "Free Falling" by Tom Petty. He passes the instrument to Nair, who strums Bob Dylan's "Just Like a Woman," and I listen to everyone sing along when he comes to the chorus. "*She takes just like a woman . . . she makes love just like a woman . . .*"

Our bellies are warming from the rum, loosening our tongues. I decide to join in on the next song, a Leonard Cohen number. And the next. And next. I cannot carry a tune, but then it doesn't matter up here in this dreamscape, or maybe it never does when a group sings in unison in the presence of alcohol.

As we all raise our voices to the resounding chorus of "Sweet Home Alabama," in this clearing deep in the Himalayas, I'm struck by how odd it seems that nobody is playing anything in Hindi, or any other Indian language for that matter.

When I ask Nair about it, he replies, "I don't know any Hindi songs."

"What do you mean? How can you not know any? Didn't you hear them growing up?"

"Well, I guess some stuff, but I don't know how to play Indian music. I learned how to play Western music, and my friends and I jammed to only stuff in English in college," he says. "I don't relate to Indian music."

In one sweeping statement, Nair throws over India's vast musical heritage of raga-based classical music, folk ballads, and *filmi* music for Dylan's warbling croon. What else would fall by the wayside as India pursues its irreversible advance into the future? I'm beginning to ponder this when my train of thought is cut short by the animated chords of Simon and Garfunkel's "Cecilia." I join in. "*Ce-ci-lia, you're breaking my heart . . .*"

Later, I retire to the room before the boys, tumbling gratefully onto my bed after a long day. I immediately fall into a dreamless sleep. When I awake some hours later to use the bathroom, I notice all three of the boys are snoring heavily, lying next to each other on the other bed. I make a mental note to myself to suggest to Anil, with whom I feel most comfortable, that he share my vast expanse of bed the following night.

Chapter Eleven

Have you ever heard that Eskimos have twenty-six different words for snow because it is such a constant presence in their lives? Like them, I have perhaps twenty-six different ways of expressing loneliness. There is the extremely common "having great friends, great life, but no one to snuggle up with at night" loneliness. There is the equally well-known "someone to snuggle up with at night but the charm has waned" loneliness. There is the "having great boyfriend or partner, but no friends" loneliness. There is the "all your friends are out of town for the holiday weekend and there's no one to even share a drink with" loneliness. There is the "good and edifying solitude of a trip taken alone" loneliness.

But the most wretched, the most painful, the most cauterizing loneliness is the "moving to a city and not knowing many people" loneliness. If you've never experienced it, don't. This I have experienced half a dozen times in my adulthood alone, shuttling between cities for work—Mexico City, Singapore, London, New York, Delhi.

It is always the same. The flurry of initial excitement, of being the new girl, dies down. The logistical knots are unraveled. Bank accounts are opened, always with difficulty, leaving one to wonder whether international banking has evolved much since the medieval age. (Perhaps we should return to doing what people did back then and carry around pouches of cash close to our breast?) And just when you feel somewhat settled into a city, two, three months down the line, the phone stops ringing.

The phone stops ringing, despite all your telepathic entreaties that it ring. But how could it possibly ring? You hardly know anyone here. So of course no one will call to ask you out for Friday, and Saturday afternoon, the phone will remain the strong silent type, and Saturday evening—well, who would call you? You can just forget about Sunday.

I spend those first weekends after the road trip in my new flat mostly alone, mostly revisiting the feelings I've had across several continents: Why do I always uproot myself from a city where I have decent work, a home, and good friends to hurl myself to a new city where I know few people? Perhaps it is the constant stripping down and building up again of a life that appeals to me, like a snake shedding its skin every few years. I think: When does my life go on autopilot? Maybe it never does, because I start getting restless when I'm too settled. There's something in the gypsydom that I need, that is fundamental to who I am. So instead I fight a lifelong battle with loneliness in much the same way others do with depression or chronic health problems.

This time, though, the loneliness stings more, cuts deeper. The phone has stopped ringing, and the rest of India is carrying on outside my home like it always has done—without me.

Today's Delhi feels, if not looks, strikingly different from when I lived and worked here ten years ago, when I was starting out as a journalist. Then, it was 1995, and I stayed for just under a year. Foreign investment was beginning to dribble into the country after five decades of the socialist imperative. A lone McDonald's would pop up here or there and become the subject of lively protest. Effigies would be burned in front of the restaurant. On occasion some irate farmer, angry at the foreign invader taking business away from him or dictating prices, would set himself on fire. So-called self-immolation is a popular form of protest in India. That and fasting.

I lived with my aunt and uncle, and to say the very least, I didn't get out much. There was simply nothing to do back then. At the time, Delhi had virtually no freestanding restaurants, cafés, bars, or nightclubs. There were just a few in hotels, and all other socializing took place within the four walls of a home.

Back then, after I had finished with my work as a reporter for a U.S. news agency, I would take an autorickshaw—an open-air vehicle on three wheels that if hit by a hurtling bus will crunch like a soda can—over to the Ashoka hotel, a dimly lit and cavernous hotel run by the government. There I would sit in the empty coffee shop, read a book, and drink South Indian coffee. The waiters all knew me and left me alone, no doubt bemused by my frequent presence. Then I would return home for dinner in a scooter, another word for these three-wheeled automated contraptions, even though it was just a five-minute walk. At that time, a young woman couldn't walk down the street without cars slowing down and men catcalling from their windows. And this was in Chanakyapuri, a well-manicured area that is home to many of the foreign embassies.

The Ashoka hotel is a perfect microcosm of the changes Delhi has undergone in the last decade. Then, the hotel was big, boxy, bulky, inflated, like anything publicly operated in India. There was only the coffee shop and one or two other Indian restaurants in a colosseum of space. Lots of space with no substance. I return in 2005 to discover this same government hotel has since added a Korean restaurant, a Russian restaurant, a Lebanese restaurant, a lounge bar named Soho, a happening disco called Capitol, and—get this—a Thai-themed spa and salon. Oddly enough, the coffee shop is still there and has not changed at all, continuing to serve its slapdash cheese sandwiches and its lethal South Indian brew.

I now marvel at the incongruities and ironies that abound in this country each day. I'm able to install Wi-Fi, allowing me to check e-mail from bed, but my cook, Amma—a small dumpling of a seventy-year-old woman—who prepares fresh *sabzi, dal, chapatis,* and rice each day, extracts the utterly baffling third-world rate of $18.20 a month. That same amount also buys me exactly two double vodka-sodas in a place like Soho or Capitol. Good thing Amma isn't much of a drinker.

The most ironic thing of all, though, strikes closer to home. I have set up the perfect Indian home by myself in Delhi, replete with ethnic wall hangings, cable television, and all the infinite accoutrements of the Indian kitchen. It is a feat tantamount to running a marathon or finishing one of those ten-day Vipassana silent meditation courses—in other words, something I can look back on as evidence of my general fortitude and wherewithal. But I am the only one living here. I may have re-created the consummate Indian home, yet I'm reminded every day that I'm lacking what everyone knows is the most crucial element of all: a husband.

Nair, the electric guitarist from Moksha, asks me to hold a party for him and his friends in my flat. Since I have few of my own friends, I readily agree.

Since our trip to the hills, Nair and I have been flirting on Instant Messenger when I'm at work, and on a few occasions, he's come over after his band practice to share a drink with me on my terrace. He's six or seven years younger than me and I suspect harbors a crush on me in that way that young men frequently do on women a few years older than them. They find us intriguing for our experience but aren't ultimately equipped to deal with the additional complexity (read: neuroses) that comes with age. Nair's youth puts me off, but I can also tell he's a man on the make. I doubt the sincerity or depth of his interest, so I don't encourage a romance. Plus he's a friend, and I can hardly afford to lose friends.

Romantically speaking, we may not be compatible, but I do enjoy getting to know Nair. To me, he represents the quintessential New Indian man. He works at a U.K.-based lad magazine that's just launched a local version in India, at which he will in a few months' time assume the position of editor. His band has developed a following in Delhi, where they play a couple gigs a month in some bar. He and his bandmates are regularly profiled in the city's magazines. No doctoring or engineering here.

In India, an attunement to Western culture as sophisticated as Nair's usually suggests a wealthy, or at least well-off, background. However, Nair, despite being an only child, didn't have his own room until he was twelve years old, nestling between his parents every night. The three of them lived in a one-room government flat in Nanakpura, one of the few down-at-the-heels neighborhoods in posh south Delhi. Nair grew up in virtual isolation with his parents, cut off from his extended family in Kerala. The other kids taunted him about his south Indian background, calling him "Madrasi," literally "someone from Madras"—hardly fighting words but meant to be derisive when used by kids from north India.

Despite all this, Nair derived comfort from his tight-knit family. His parents wanted to give him the best education possible and sent him to a school with kids from moneyed families. Every day, Nair would cross the main road to attend school in Anand Niketan, an affluent colony filled with foreign diplomats and rich Delhiites. Here the kids didn't seem to mind that he didn't come from money. His best friend at school not only had his own room, but his own VCR. The two would watch *Teenage Mutant Ninja Turtles* every day after school. His friend also had a piano, which Nair loved playing since he was learning the electronic synthesizer at school, where he was taught Western music. True, he was learning mostly Christian gospel music at school, but he was drawn to its upbeat melodies, so different from the maudlin ballads in Malayalam and Hindi his parents were always listening to. At home, he would repeatedly play his two cassette tapes of ABBA and Boney M—the international pop group I only ever hear about when I'm in India. When the government television station Doordarshan began broadcasting MTV for two hours every evening in the early 1990s, he made sure to be home from six to eight P.M. every single day to watch videos from Aerosmith, Bon Jovi, and Michael Jackson.

At St. Stephens, the excellent small liberal arts college to which he'd been accepted, he became exposed to an even more cosmopolitan world than the one he'd seen in Anand Niketan. There, all his classmates had traveled overseas; some had even grown up there, and nearly all planned to return for further education or work after college. His best friend, Banerjee, a diplomat's son who'd grown up in the Netherlands and Germany, introduced him to Iron Maiden and Judas Priest, and also to Bob Dylan and the Rolling Stones. Banerjee looked down his nose at most things Indian, especially Bollywood music. And he encouraged Nair to as well. With Nair on guitar and Banerjee on drums, the pair started the first incarnation of Moksha in college. But a year after graduation, Banerjee left him and the fledgling band for the University of Utah. It would take Nair years before he would get the band going again.

There was a time soon after independence when the successful Indian man was aristocratic in nature, usually hailing from landed gentry, much like the country's first prime minister, Jawaharlal Nehru. Later, in the eighties and nineties the Nehruvian ideal gave way to a slightly more egalitarian one. The archetypal Indian man no longer needed to be aristocratic, but the scion of a family well-off enough to send him abroad for education. He went off into the world, usually to the U.S. or England, and returned to start or join a company, armed with much-needed Western expertise and skills.

In many ways, Nair is a true man of the first decade of the new millennium, someone who has come from nothing and, rather than leaving India to make his way in the world, has waited for the world to come to India, which, for him, included a music upheaval that nurtured an indigenous rock and roll culture as well as a media explosion that saw the arrival of magazines like the one he edits.

A poor boy in India good at his studies, Nair had all the makings of a statistic, a stereotype, someone who would end up in New Jersey working for an IT company, like thousands of other Indian men. Instead, it is the cultured and worldly Banerjee, his best friend at college who introduced him to all the cool music, who is a software programmer living in Jersey City. And guess what? Banerjee even listens to Bollywood music these days.

The party Nair is throwing in my as yet sparsely furnished flat is for a friend who's leaving for London. One Saturday night a few weeks after I've moved in, a steady stream of young men, all around twenty-six or twenty-seven years old, begins to arrive. None of them, of course, bears any resemblance to the type of men I've met in India in the past. More than half are long haired, many have goatees, and none have paunches; some are already visibly drunk or stoned, or both. Young, pretty women in low-cut halter tops accompany the men.

I feel distinctly out of place watching them flirt and wish Nandini were here. But Nandini has been in the U.S. for the last few weeks visiting her two brothers who live there, and, more important, she's spending time with a consultant in New York she met on shaadi.com, whom she hopes to marry. With fifteen or twenty handsome men in their mid-twenties in my flat, having a good time, I feel like an auntie, or at least a *didi*—the word used by younger siblings for their elder sisters in north India. I curse my timing. I would have been ecstatic with joy at such a situation when I was their age. Now I walk around with my Old Monk and Coke, looking lost at my own party.

I look around the room to find someone to talk to. Most of the Moksha boys are chatting up the girls they came with, but I notice Nair hasn't been talking to any of the girls all night and is fiddling around with the music on my laptop. I catch his eye and sidle up to him.

"Hey, Nair, what are you doing here with the music? Why don't you go chat with some of the girls?" I say.

"Nah, I'm not that into it. I've never been good at small talk anyway," he says.

"So, you're one of those 'deep' types. Yeah, that's what has always struck me about you," I say, flirting. Nair smiles sheepishly at my dig.

It is nearing three o'clock in the morning, and guests are still arriving, which is commonplace at parties in Delhi. A petite man with a lined and preternaturally kind face steps onto the balcony, where I'm having a smoke by myself. I sense he is older than the other guests. I'm drunk by now, so I dispense with the niceties and bellow a question at him: "How old are you?"

"Thirty-eight," he says, luckily laughing at my opening line. His name is Shekhar.

What a relief! I notice one of his lower front teeth is missing, but the rum in my belly and his age have convinced me that he is the most interesting man at my party. He could even pass for the young Shashi Kapoor, the popular seventies Bollywood actor, before he got old and fat.

Shekhar tells me his family is from Bihar, but he grew up in Delhi. Bihar is India's notoriously backward and lawless state, a place where evidence of the New India is woefully lacking. When I ask what he does for a living, he says he's working on several projects, trying to start an NGO, doing some engineering work, but the details are vague. Clearly this is a circuitous way of saying he is unemployed; nonetheless, I decide that we will marry, or at least that he will be my first boyfriend in Delhi—the one every girl knows they're supposed to get in a new city to help them settle in.

Shekhar leaves around five thirty in the morning with the rest of the guests, promising to call later that week. I walk back up my staircase after having said good-bye to everyone and am surprised to find Nair sprawled out on the floor, passed out. I take him to my bedroom, lay him on one side of the bed, and try to go to sleep.

Nair is not interested in sleeping, though, and I suspect passing out on my floor is a ruse designed to push the boundaries of our friendship further. I relent to a few kisses—I've been drinking, too, after all—hoping he will let me sleep. He doesn't and continues his ministrations. I eventually manage to fend him off and move to the other side of the bed.

I wake to the sound of someone knocking. It must be Chandra, my maid, who arrives between nine and ten in the morning. I look over to see Nair sprawled next to me. I arrange the loose shift I'm wearing to fully cover myself, open the door to my bedroom, and let Chandra in.

"Chandra, can you make two cups of *chai*, please?" I ask.

Chandra raises her eyebrows just a touch and nods assent. It's the first time I've had an overnight guest. It's only been a few weeks since I moved in, and she has already warmed to me, since I'm possibly the most lenient employer in Delhi, allowing her to get away with haphazard cleaning that most *memsaab*s would balk at. Like everyone else in the world, servants too make their judgment calls: Slutty but lax employer much preferable to puritanical slave-driving maniac.

"Both without sugar?" she asks.

"No, one with sugar, one without," I say.

Chandra knocks on my bedroom door, two cups of steaming *chai* in hand. I take them and close the door. Did she just wink at me?

Nair has woken up and I can tell he's feeling a bit sheepish about last night. I hand him his tea and try to put him at ease by chattering about the party. We talk for a few minutes before he puts down his barely touched cup and says he has to leave. Today is the day he visits his parents in west Delhi. He throws on his shirt and stands up.

"OK, well, then, uh, I guess I'll see you later, maybe this week," I say.

"Yeah, see you," he says.

I go back to bed, hoping as I try to sleep that our friendship hasn't been affected by the awkward night together. I'm drifting off when my phone rings. It's my father calling from California, with my mother listening in on another line. I mumble that I had a party last night at my flat and am too tired to speak.

"Papa, can I talk to you later?"

"Who was at the party? Boys or girls?" he asks.

"Both boys and girls," I reply.

"There was alcohol too?" he demands.

"Well, of course, Papa. It wouldn't be a party otherwise," I say, trying to get off the phone.

I am not prepared for what happens next. My parents nag and wheedle and complain, but rarely do they get angry with me.

Papa blasts into the phone, "What are you doing?! You can't have parties in India! People will think you're a whore! Only whores have parties in India!"

I'm confounded, since he's never said anything about parties I've thrown in the other cities in which I've lived. Then I realize that my father is thinking of what it would be like if a single woman in Meerut threw a party for her friends in the sixties. He's quite right if he's thinking along those lines. That party would likely be thrown in a brothel.

"Papa, this isn't Meerut in the sixties! It's Delhi in 2005! Everybody throws parties. I can't have this conversation! You don't know anything about India!" I scream back.

"*You* don't know anything about India! You're just getting out of the hands," my father says, banging the phone down.

Now it's just my mother and I on the line. "*Beti*, you should really just find a nice boy. You've had enough of these party-sharties."

I try to sleep again, but the call from my parents has clearly shaken me, both for my father's rage and my mother's gentle insistence. It's true, I've had enough of party-sharties by now, probably more than most people have over a lifetime. I'm also uninterested in hookups like last night's that have no future. Now that I've found a flat, maybe it's time for me to get serious about finding a husband.

Chapter Twelve

Shekhar, the older guy I met at my party, calls a few days later. He picks me up in his Maruti Swift and I suggest a bar in Greater Kailash called Bohemia. I order a vodka-soda, and he asks for some tap water. I size him up immediately and decide he is a considerate and benign man. He is full of questions and interested in my likes and dislikes. It also becomes clear after this second meeting that indeed he is not gainfully employed, so when the bill comes, I pay for my own single drink—a whopping five hundred rupees, or around $12.

When we go outside to find his car and return home, he finds that one of his tires has been punctured (so it does actually happen!) while we were sitting in the bar. He takes me home in an autorickshaw. Despite his apparent haplessness, I feel drawn to him. He is the type of man who means it when he asks, "How are you?" and then listens to the answer. Men will never understand that this is one of the sexiest things a man can say to a woman.

I look forward to our next date. The Saturday following my party, Shekhar again picks me up—this time in a borrowed car—and he drives me to Tughlakabad Fort, a giant fortress at the southeastern tip of Delhi. It's a place unduly ignored by tourists when they make their rounds of the capital. The grounds are overgrown and the yellow sandstone structure is crumbling, but the rambling citadel boasts a forlorn charm compared with the spruced-up and well-trafficked Red Fort. No importunate tour guides here, Shekhar and I have the entire place to ourselves. We amble through the fort, one decrepit open-air section indistinguishable from the next.

We come to a parapet and decide to sit down, dangling our legs off the side of the fort and looking out over nearby villages. Shekhar draws out a ball of hash from his pocket, pinches off a piece from the chunk, shreds it between his fingers in his palm, shakes out some tobacco from a cigarette into his hand, and pours the whole mixture onto some smoking paper and rolls a joint. It would seem hash rolling, much like road trips, is the same wherever you go in the world.

Shekhar and I spend the whole day together, and later that evening we arrange to meet up with Nair and Vijay at Climax, a club that plays electronic music located off the road to Gurgaon. It will be the first time I see Nair since he sped off that morning last week. We've IM'd a few times during the week, though we didn't discuss what happened, and I'm hoping to resume our easy rapport. It's the New India, after all; people drink, fall into bed, no big deal.

Shekhar and I end up at the club before the others and decide to go in. Once inside, I ask him if he wants a drink. He shakes his head no—expectedly—so I find the bar and order myself a glass of Sula sauvignon blanc. I'm thinking about how much the wine produced by India's nascent wine industry has improved since I was last here three years ago (then what was considered decent wine is what is sent back at restaurants in the West) when I see Nair and Vijay near the door with some other friends in tow. They're arguing with the bouncer, who has barred them from entering because they are wearing open-toed sandals. Shekhar, who has been watching the fracas, disappears inside the club and brings out the DJ, who he knows from somewhere. Nair, Vijay, and their friends are allowed inside. I am suitably impressed by Shekhar's deft handling of the situation.

Shekhar: thirty-eight years old, mild-mannered, intelligent enough, educable, and likes to go out to clubs on weekends, even if he can't afford to drink. A man who laughs easily and appears to hang on my every word.

Me: new to the city, ready to explore it, and oddly charmed by aforementioned man.

Conclusion: Shekhar will be my boyfriend. I will support him.

I am relieved that the slight unease between Nair and me when we greet each other passes after a few minutes. After we've all danced for a couple of hours, Shekhar offers to drop several of us off at home. I'm the last person he drops, and he comes upstairs to my flat for one last joint. When we're finished smoking it, he gets up to leave. We've been together for more than twelve hours, but he doesn't make a move to stay. I am at once disappointed and heartened by his courtliness. The next day, I wait for Shekhar's phone call. It doesn't come. Two or three days later, I call him to see if he wants to see a movie, *Salaam Namaste*, about an Indian couple living in sin in Australia. His phone has been turned off. I never hear from Shekhar again.

Shekhar: small unemployed Bihari man with missing tooth.

Me: have lost my touch if small unemployed toothless man runs away from me.

New conclusion: Perhaps dating in Delhi is no less complicated, perplexing, and ego deflating than in New York.

Hi, I am Ravi itself. I'm a simple-living and high-thinking person with jolly nature. My thinking is very different. I think everybody living a happy and joy life because life is very cute and beautiful things is my thinking. So tell if you like my sense of humer [sic]. So please marry with me or otherwise your life is on your hand. Wish you all the best for serch [sic] for your life partner. I myself working for foreign MNC in Noida, and earning well.

Hi, I'm 35, Jain divorced male living in Delhi, India. A little attitude and very possesive [sic], that's just being a typical LEO (The very hard to find ones.) Am very particular about my work, food habits, and health work-out routine, hence look very much younger. I am from a very well-to-do business family and am a very soft-spoken, responsible, and a caring person and expect my life partner to be very caring, simple, and a very beautifull [sic] woman.

Hi, I'm divorced, reason is her extra marital affairs. And one more thing about her is I was her second husband, her first husband has also given her divorce just because of her extra affair. I was unmarried and I got married to a lady who was divorcee and had a kid (daughter). I accepted the kid and I kept her as my own child. I left my parents, my family, my society . . . for her, and she even did not give a single thought what will happen to me with her behavior, anyway more on our meeting . . .

I'm back on shaadi.com, this time perusing through the profiles of men in Delhi, a much larger and more varied pool than in the New York area. I reply to a few men who have shown interest in me, giving out my number and asking them to call. I *am* new in the city.

One Saturday evening, a man named Manumit calls. After very brief introductory remarks, he says, "Meet me at South Extension at ten thirty tomorrow morning."

I find his statement, er, rather direct and say, "Well, uh, I won't be up that early. It's my day off. Perhaps we can meet a bit later. I'll call you around one o'clock and we'll set up a time to meet."

The next day, my phone rings at 1:10 P.M. "Why didn't you call me?" Manumit implores.

"I was going to," I say.

"Meet me at South Ex at McDonald's for a brief meeting," he orders.

I'm doing nothing else that day, but I find the decision-making rather one-sided. I maneuver for room. "Hmm, well, I was planning to go to Greater Kailash to do some shopping, so maybe we can meet in that area?" I suggest.

"Well, you can meet me at Ansal's Plaza or South Ex," he says.

"Why only those two places?" I ask.

"It's convenient for me," he says. "Call me before you leave. Oh, I would like that you wear jean and T-shirt."

"Um, please don't tell me what to wear," I say, hanging up.

I walk into my bedroom and promptly remove the jeans and T-shirt I have been wearing, exchanging them for the baggiest *salwar kameez* I can find in my closet. I take a scooter to the McDonald's in South Extension, a large commercial market, buy an iced coffee, and sit down and wait for my date.

After I've been waiting twenty minutes, Manumit saunters up to the table. His hair looks odd. I try to decipher it. There is a swath of hair colored lighter than the rest swept back and hairsprayed in place. He's wearing acid-washed jeans. He's from Patna, the capital of Bihar.

I smile and he sits down. I remember his profile says he is thirty. I decide to scare him off with my age.

"How old are you?" I ask.

"Thirty," he replies.

"Oh, well, I hope it's okay with you, I'm three years older than you are," I say, rounding up my age to my thirty-third birthday, which is a few months away.

"Actually, I'm thirty-four," he says.

"Oh, why did you say you were thirty?" I ask, confused.

"I'm thirty-four."

"Yes, but you said you were thirty just a second ago," I say.

"Oh, that's because my birth date is 6/6/75," he says, a reply that makes him thirty again.

"How can you be thirty-four if your birth date is 6/6/75?"

"Birth date is 6/6/75," he says.

"Then you are thirty," I say, my voice rising a few octaves.

"No, birth date is 6/6/75, but other birth date is 6/6/71," he matter-of-factly explains.

"Why do you have two birth dates?" I ask, sighing.

I'm getting read to meet Siddharth, another man I've met on shaadi.com. He's an Internet executive at the *Times of India* with extremely fluid English. I suspect this fellow may even have only one birth date.

I try on various tops, trying to decide whether to go with an ethnic or a Western look, colorful tunic or black evening blouse. I'm scrutinizing myself in the mirror, standing sideways and sucking in my belly, when Chandra walks into my bedroom.

"Madam, *yeh mat pehnno*. Don't wear that. *Moti lagti ho.* It makes you look fat," she says, shaking her head back and forth.

"Thanks, Chandra," I say, taking off the short *kurta* and putting on the black blouse again. I'm both annoyed at her cheekiness and pleased at the free, honest advice. What use I could have made of her in New York!

"Madam, can I have two hundred rupees, please?" she asks.

"But Chandra, didn't I just give you two hundred last week? And you got paid the week before," I say.

"*Haan*, madam. But my grandson has just been born and I want to buy something for him, and the *sardar* family down the street hasn't paid me my salary yet," she says. "And you can take it out of my next month's salary," she adds, knowing I won't.

"Here, try not to make it happen again," I say, handing her the money. I guess the advice wasn't free.

I meet Siddharth at the All-American Diner in the India Habitat Centre, a catchall cultural center with several restaurants and auditoriums for staging plays and lectures that has been built since I left Delhi in 1995. An amply lit place with booths and a counter, the All-American Diner resembles, well, an American diner. We install ourselves in a booth, and I order fries and a veggie burger. It seems wrong to eat anything else in a place like this.

I learn Siddharth has an MBA from IIM Bangalore, one of the half dozen Indian Institutes of Management spread around the country; with their rigorous admissions process and even more punishing academic standards, the schools are considered to be on par with Harvard Business School or Wharton. He is well informed and erudite, and we're having a nice time talking about music and books. The problem is that I'm not at all physically attracted to him. At thirty-six years old, he has the bearing of a fussy old man, someone oddly *au fait* about India's new youth culture but yet not part of it. Nonetheless, I find myself eager to befriend him; he can be a good guide to this vastly different India to which I've returned.

We end up meeting frequently over the next few weeks, and as our friendship deepens, I discover Siddharth has also been on a marriage hunt for the last few years and he too has had a tough time of it. Like me, he is under constant pressure from his parents, with whom he lives, to find a spouse, and moreover, his younger brother was married off a few years ago, turning up the heat on him.

As successful thirtysomethings with good educations and almost too many choices, Siddharth and I find ourselves in the same bind as countless others around the world, trying to find someone we think is deserving of our attention and love without lowering our standards. But Siddharth has an added complication. He is a Dalit, the politically correct term for what was once called an untouchable, or people who fall outside India's four-tiered caste system. Siddharth belongs to the Mahar subcaste, a group that traditionally performed the function of skinning animal carcasses and later consuming the flesh inedible for members of upper castes who clung to their vegetarian diets.

The country's well-known system of categorization derives from ancient Hindu texts, which separated society into the priestly Brahmin caste, the Kshatriya warrior caste, the Vaishya merchant caste, and the Sudra laborer caste. Within these exist thousands of subcastes.

Caste is frighteningly complicated. For example, I belong to a religion, Jainism, that, like Buddhism, began as a separate religion in opposition to the hierarchical nature of Hinduism. Over the millennia, though, Jainism became subsumed within the Hindu structure, and Jainism is now largely considered a sect. Many of those who adopted Jainism thousands of years ago were merchants, and thus Jains are Banias, part of the merchant caste. Both my parents are Jains, and in their generation, marrying within the Jain community was more strictly enforced. Now even the most traditional Jain families freely intermarry their offspring with other Banias, many of whom bear the last name Agarwal or Gupta.

Caste is still a flash point in Indian culture, with many Hindus who belong to the three upper castes upset over widespread affirmative action for lower castes and Dalits. In larger cities like Delhi and Bombay, people of different castes freely intermingle and, in many families, are allowed to intermarry. Even as many caste conventions fall by the wayside, though, the stigma of being a Dalit seems to remain.

Until the age of twelve, Siddharth grew up in Nagpur, a midsized city located smack dab in the middle of the diamond-shaped nation. With its significant Dalit concentration of twenty per cent, Nagpur gave birth to the Dalit political movement. Dr. B. R. Ambedkar, the father of Dalit activism who encouraged the community to convert to Buddhism, as well as the architect of India's constitution, was born not far from Nagpur. Siddharth's family is among those that have nominally converted to Buddhism, opting out of the Hindu religion that has oppressed them for centuries. Despite this, their caste remains an indelible mark—even in this revamped and metropolitan India.

He tells me about the time he and his parents arranged to go to the home of a girl they found in a personal ad that included the line "Caste no bar," meaning there would be no caste restrictions. As is traditional in India, he was to meet the girl for the first time in the presence of both sets of parents. Siddharth and his parents went to Noida, where the girl lived with her mother and father, a navy admiral. Tea and *pakora*s were served as the two families talked. After about twenty minutes, the girl's father asked, "*Aap ki caste kyaa hai?* What is your caste?"

Siddharth's father replied, "Mahar."

"*Yeh kyaa hota hai?* What is that?" the father asked.

When Siddharth's father said, "Dalit," the girl's mother's face froze and she stopped chattering away. The girl's father began talking about the weather. Siddharth and his parents scurried out of the house five minutes later.

It was much the same on other occasions when Siddharth met girls from shaadi.com on his own, all of whom had no stated caste preference. Things might be going well, even over several dates, but as soon as the girl asked about his caste, her face would fall and conversation would come to a complete halt. After the girl recovered her composure, she'd make hurried excuses and rush out. Now Siddharth tells potential spouses his caste when they first meet. "It's just easier to not go through it," he says.

My caste may not be so exalted, but it wouldn't necessarily keep me from marrying into any of the other castes, unless a boy's family was very particular that he marry a girl from the same caste. And clearly, at this late stage, my parents aren't fussy.

Listening to Siddharth's stories, my plight seems less weighty, and I'm relieved I don't have the onus he bears. Caste no bar—except, of course, for Dalits.

Chapter Thirteen

On the morning of October 8, I am jolted awake. The bed is shaking. The movement is not violent, but almost a gentle rocking, and then it subsides after about a minute. It is a Saturday morning and I don't have to go to work. As I'm wondering what could have caused the shaking, I fall back asleep. I find out later that day that at 9:20 A.M. a massive earthquake rocked the disputed territory of Kashmir, ultimately claiming seventy-five thousand lives. What I felt hundreds of miles away in Delhi were distant tremors.

When I find out about the earthquake a couple of hours later, I immediately think of Mustafa and wonder if he's safe. It's been a while since I spoke with him and I try to call. Throughout the day, the phone lines to Kashmir are jammed, but when I get through later that evening, he tells me that he had just stepped out of the shower and was putting on some pants when the quake struck. He was thrown against the wall, one leg in his trousers, but he was not hurt and there was no damage to his home. He was lucky, because the Indian-controlled part of Kashmir in which he lives suffered negligible damage compared with the utter devastation that befell the Pakistan-occupied area surrounding the epicenter.

Alarmed by the tragedy, I think back to the time nearly three years ago when I met Mustafa in Kashmir. I'd come to Delhi for Seema and Ashok's wedding. Seema's sister, Poonam, also a journalist, was planning to travel to Kashmir to write about the war-torn region for her newspaper in upstate New York. It was an inexpensive and short jaunt from Delhi and I was between jobs in New York City. It didn't take long for me to decide to tag along. Poonam and Seema's father was formerly the head of the Border Security Force, a paramilitary group that patrols the conflict there. We would have full protection from the BSF the whole time we were in Kashmir.

Nestled amid the Himalayas, the state of Kashmir sits atop the Indian subcontinent like a crown. A vicious insurgency has raged in the region for the last fifteen years. Both India and Pakistan have staked claims to the state, which has a predominantly Muslim population, while a movement in Kashmir to declare independence from both countries has also gained momentum. Security is tight in Kashmir, and we went through several checkpoints at the airport. On the plane, Poonam pointed out the prominent leader of a Kashmiri separatist group seated a few rows behind us.

Srinagar was only a ninety-minute flight from Delhi, but when we arrived, it was as if we had entered a different world. It was the dead of winter and snowing in Kashmir, unlike in Delhi, where the weather had already taken on the temperate shades of spring. Also unlike in the capital, there were few women visible anywhere. Both of us felt slightly alarmed by the hordes of men in pajama *kurtas* crowding around the airport exit. We looked around nervously for our BSF escorts.

Two armed men in uniform stepped forward and quickly shuttled us to a waiting van. We sat in the back on a bench, men bearing long rifles seated on either side and facing us from across the aisle. I was tempted to speak with them, but I thought better of it. The daughter of an army general who had been surrounded by such rank-and-file men her entire life, Poonam would surely find it inappropriate. It was the chatty American in me flaring up, as it always seemed to do in the most untoward circumstances.

Poonam's BSF contacts arranged for her to interview a terrorist who'd been captured and was now in custody. I went along as her sidekick. Can you imagine this happening in the U.S.? A *New York Times* reporter, for example, interviewing Zacarias Moussaoui, who was convicted for his role in helping to plan the September 11 attacks, and bringing along a friend for the ride. "Hi, Mr. Moussaoui, do you mind if my friend Anita joins us while I speak to you about your role in 9/11? She won't bother us." In India, VIP status trumps protocol every time.

The scene at the barracks was a stock film-noir setup: dimly lit room, one lone lightbulb dangling over a chair, two chairs facing it. Our "terrorist" was little older than a boy. He described his wretched story of being cajoled into joining the guerrillas with promises of money, power, and an afterlife abundant with young virgins, but not seventy-two, as I'd always believed. This poor chap was promised seventy-two thousand virgins! No wonder he'd signed up. Authorities had placed him on a list with other young men active in the insurgency, and after he was nabbed, our boyish terrorist had been tortured.

The boy complained of his bleak future, perhaps viewing us as kind older sisters after being surrounded by hostile gun-toting men. He told us that if he were to leave custody, he would be under constant surveillance from not only Indian authorities, but also terrorist groups that would suspect he was a turncoat and in cahoots with India. Worst of all, he said, was that nobody would marry him given that he would be under such constant and grave danger. (For once I wasn't the only one worried about my dimming chances of getting married.)

"I wish I'd never joined," he wailed.

We, two women living in New York, nodded sympathetically, as if he were talking about taking up a new extracurricular activity that ate up too much of his time.

The next morning, we visited an orphanage for young boys who'd lost their fathers in the conflict. Hailing from a region that has seen a commingling of Central Asian races over the millennia, Kashmiris are known for their physical beauty. The man who ran the orphanage had piercing black eyes and a classical Roman set to his face. He was swathed in a dark shawl, and there was a glint in his eyes that could hardly be described as friendly. He called out to one of his underlings to bring each of us a cup of *kahwa*, a special Kashmiri green tea flavored with saffron and cardamom. Although he was overtly, even unctuously polite, it was clear to both Poonam and me that he loathed our presence. We were not only women, but Hindus. He never even so much as glanced over at me, making me feel thoroughly defiled. This time, it wasn't hard to keep my garrulous side in check. I didn't say a word. Poonam asked all the questions.

She broke the ice by describing our visit earlier that morning to another orphanage, run by a gentle Christian man from Madras in South India.

Attempting a joke, Poonam said, "Ah, we Hindus never run orphanages. We just sit on mountaintops meditating and looking for enlightenment."

The man didn't laugh, or even smile. He just nodded and said gravely, with a hint of a sneer, "That is because Muslims and Christians are people of the book, unlike Hindus."

Later Poonam asked why he only kept boys in the orphanage. He paused, boring his eyes into her, before replying with complete equanimity, "There are moral problems with females."

I flinched. When Poonam pressed him on the point, saying female orphans might also require education, the man said, "I know I am supposed to say men and women are equal, but tell me, can we really say a goat is equal to a lion?"

I was shaken by the encounter and even more rattled to discover how relieved I was to return to the back of the van with all the strapping men and their big guns.

After lunch, we made to a trip to the Srinagar bureau of a newspaper for which Poonam had previously worked from Delhi. She wanted to say hello and request the services of one of the photographers. We leaped over several puddles before entering the dilapidated building. Inside, we found the office belonging to the Srinagar correspondent. Behind the desk was the most refined man I'd ever seen. He had an elegant comportment, which I had come to expect in Kashmir, though it was very unlike that of the man who'd so disturbed me earlier that day. And he was comely, but not in the same hard way the other man was. He smiled and stuck out his hand. "Hi, I'm Mustafa. Have a seat," he said.

Again, I let Poonam do the talking, afraid I would say something idiotic. To be honest, I also feared that if I spoke too much, Mustafa would immediately discover that I was American, or worse, Californian, and write me off as an uncultivated philistine. Then, as if by instinct, knowing to leave us alone, Poonam got up and said she needed to go and find the photographer.

I was alone with Mustafa. He leaned across his desk with an outstretched palm and offered me a cigarette. Thinking this might be the only cigarette I would smoke in Kashmir without being stoned to death, I accepted. It was an odd moment. His office was a sanctuary from the conflict in Srinagar, away from the men with guns, the terrorists, and the strikingly handsome evil man who reviled the female species. Now I was being offered a cigarette as if nothing had happened. I'd like to think it was strange for him as well. I suspected not too many young women dropped by unannounced at his run-down office in Srinagar.

We puffed on our cigarettes. I was so nervous it was as if a coil were shooting electricity through me. Mustafa had a rich, mellifluous accent, one that betrayed a fine private-school education and perhaps some time overseas. I asked him about his schooling. He'd attended university in England and did some graduate work in the U.S. Desperately trying to rein in my baggy syntax, I told him that I was also a journalist and that I'd attended university in the U.S.—I thought it sounded better than saying I'd grown up there. I spoke in clipped tones in my poor approximation of Indian-accented English so as not to give away my American provenance. Ten minutes later, our cigarettes finished, Poonam returned and it was time to go. As I got up and went to the door of Mustafa's office, I looked back across my shoulder, flashed him a smile, and mouthed "Bye." He smiled back and returned the farewell.

Later, I puzzled over why a man of Mustafa's apparent capacities would be toiling away under such rough conditions in Srinagar when he could work in London or New York, let alone Delhi or Bombay. Later, when I returned to New York and struck up an e-mail correspondence with him, I learned of his saintly lineage. He would tell me over e-mail how after his father died, he quit his graduate work in Boston to return home and look after the shrine of his ancestor.

The day of the earthquake, I hear Mustafa's resonant voice after a long time. Although I'd not exactly forgotten about him, I've been caught up with my new life and thought I would hold off on the phone calls until I saw him in person in Delhi. When I was still living with Seema and Ashok in Gurgaon, our hours-long conversations into the night had filled in many of the details

I had yearned to know, but they'd also thrown up plenty of new questions. At times, the picture he'd painted of himself was a far cry from the upright, duty-bound man I'd imagined him to be. With each fresh story he told me, each new aspect revealed, I saw him as less of a dignified saint and as—no less fascinating, mind you—more of a character out of a 1920s Parisian salon, a type of bohemian dandy wastrel, if you will. The kind of man who gets linen jackets made and never wears them. The type of gentleman who likes to apply henna to women's hands. In short, the kind of man other men instinctively mistrust.

Each new disclosure at once electrified and appalled me. He described himself as a sensualist of the first order. A man whose sexual experiences started early, at thirteen, when he slept with his maid. He had experimented with sex with men in college. He enjoyed dalliances with foreign female tourists trekking through Kashmir. My image of his society as conservative and restricted was fast evaporating.

When I call him to see if he was hurt by the temblor, he tells me he will make a trip to Delhi before the new year, and I decide I'll wait until then to make up my mind about who he really is.

Chapter Fourteen

Mustafa wasn't my first encounter with a man living in India. Long before him, there was another who is perhaps ultimately responsible for my enduring relationship with the country. I haven't seen him in years, but now that I'm living in Delhi, I often find myself wondering what I would do if I ran into him on the street or in a café.

Everyone knows the stories we choose to tell about ourselves, the ones that are always at the tip of our tongue, the ones we love to regale new friends with at a dinner party, the ones our long-standing friends have heard dozens of times and at which they know the right place to laugh or groan. But what of the stories we never tell, the ones that are buried so deep under shame and denial and years of trying to forget, the ones we quickly dismiss when brought up by an old college friend with a simpering smile?

Unlike most Indians settled in America, my parents weren't particularly interested in going back to the motherland every two or three years. Growing up, I'd only been to India twice, once when I was four years old and another time at fourteen. One reason was that we never seemed to have enough money. Another was that none of my parents' relatives were especially well off either, and accommodations in their homes remained fairly modest. My parents would end up having to use a malodorous outhouse, and during the summer, the temperature in northern India rises above 120 degrees. They'd spent so much of their lives establishing themselves outside of the country, there was simply no reason to dive back into the misery.

During my first year of college, I suddenly became interested in finding out more about my heritage—hardly a novel idea for a freshman during the early 1990s, when everybody seemed to be jumping on the multicultural bandwagon. I persuaded my mother to go back to India with me during the summer.

Our main base was the home of her elder sister in Ghaziabad, a noisy, polluted city not far outside Delhi that *Newsweek* recently named one of the world's ten fastest-growing cities. From there, we made side trips to the homes of other relatives and tourist spots. At first, everything was fascinating. I loved speaking Hindi. I loved the distinct sounds and smells of India, even the ones that everyone else hates—the cow dung, the blaring horn of a bus. I even loved the dust.

But it wasn't long before the charm of my parents' India began wearing off. I found the family we were staying with petty and unrefined, focused on the most niggling of matters. There were four sons in the household and much time was spent on discussing how much dowry could be fetched for each of them. At the time, one of them was in the market for a bride, and I accompanied the family on their excursions to meet prospective matches.

When we would return home, the young lady and her family would be subject to scrutiny at the most infinitesimal level: "Did you notice when she walked there seemed to be something wrong with her leg?" "The mother didn't greet us properly, did she?" At other times, when discussion strayed from the sons' marital futures, it would become lodged in long-past arguments over money or land or inheritance or who said what to whom. Having just finished my freshman year, and fired up with all manner of collegiate inspiration, I would privately wonder why we couldn't discuss the state of India's successful democracy or the relative harmony of four or five major religions living side by side.

I wanted to have the rich and urbane relatives in Delhi or Bombay that other Indian-American friends seemed to have visited in India. No, no cool jeans-donning aunt for me. My lot was the sweaty aunties with frayed, sun-bleached saris in Ghaziabad who kept asking me how much things cost back in "Amrika." Not only did I begin to realize why my parents stayed away from the country of their birth, I understood why they had left.

During the unspeakably sultry summer nights, my mother and I and other members of the large household would sleep on jute cots strewn throughout the living room. One night I awoke with a start to discover a hand on my breast. It wasn't my own. The person to whom the hand belonged was lying on an adjacent couch, which had been empty when I'd gone to bed. I moved away, squinting into the dark to see who it was. Nearly blind without my contact lenses or glasses, I couldn't see anything but the hazy outlines of a figure that didn't have the large paunch of my uncle. I suspected it was one of the four sons, but I couldn't make out which one.

Making a fuss was simply out of the question. My mother would be distraught, and certainly everyone in her sister's household would accuse me of making up stories and being a troublemaker. And watch out if my father caught wind of this. He would fly directly to India and raise hell. No, no. I just had to be more vigilant and deal with the situation on my own.

The next night, I tried to sleep on my stomach so as to discourage the lecherous and, worst of all, anonymous culprit from attempting to molest me again. I also kept my glasses under my pillow, so that I could pull them out if need be and determine which of the four sons it was. When the figure came to me again that night, resting his hand on my hip, I bolted upright and put on my glasses. I'm ashamed to admit the blackness of night kept me from making out with any certainty which of my male cousins it was, but I did have my suspicions. After this phantom came to me a third time, I started sleeping in the same cot with my mother. Even this didn't deter him. Once, while I was lying next to my mother, the creep came and put his hand on my calf. I never did divine with certainty which of my cousins was my tormentor, and I never told my mother what happened.

Not surprisingly, I looked forward to going home. Our return was only weeks away, and I started counting the days. One evening, during the final weeks of our summer-long trip, as my relatives bickered and gossiped, my uncle's cousin Arjun arrived at the house. He claimed he was thirty-two, but his dyed black hair appeared completely white at the roots. Closer to forty, I decided.

Arjun had just finished making a film—a feature film in Haryanvi, which is the dialect used in the northern Indian state of Haryana, and from what I've gathered it is the first and only movie ever made in the idiom. It would be like making a movie in the Basque language, but even more obscure, since Haryanvi isn't a full-fledged language of its own but a dialect of Hindi. Arjun wrote, directed, produced, and acted in the film, which starred a B-list Bollywood actress named Sadhana Singh.

Me, I was a chubby eighteen-year-old (I had gained the freshman fifteen and then some) and very impressionable. A filmmaker! And in a dialect, no less. What a novel idea! After a summer of getting to know the ins and outs of dusty Ghaziabad, learning how much dowry a middle-class doctor from the Bania caste could fetch in the marriage market, and being fondled by an anonymous cousin in the dead of night, I thought, "Now this is more like it." Arjun's presence fit my image of what I expected to find that summer in India. Moreover, he would make a great story for my roommates back at school, to whom I had earlier dreaded returning with stories of sitting around watching television in Ghaziabad.

Although he'd originally planned to stay for one evening, Arjun's visit stretched out over two days, then three. I sat with rapt attention as he regaled my cousins, aunts, uncles, and mother with tales of the hurdles he overcame to make his film— how he flew back and forth between Delhi and Bombay trying to get funding for his film, how he jockeyed to get the lead actress to agree to do it, how he didn't have enough money to pay a lead actor and decided he himself would have to play the "hero," as they say in Bollywood.

Arjun, who I referred to as "uncle," and I sat next to each other at meal times, and we both broke into playful smiles when we spoke to each other. My mother quietly observed our exchanged glances. One evening, at dusk, several of us piled into the car to visit the home of another relative. And by several of us, I mean ten or twelve. And by car, I mean a Maruti 800, one of the few models plying the roads back then, in 1991. It was about five feet by four feet, and its walls were as thin as aluminum siding.

I found myself sitting on one auntie's generous lap, nestled against the perspiring armpit of another, while yet another auntie's gelatinous bicep and elbow crushed into my ribs. The smell of curry-tinged body odor hung heavily in the air. I spotted Arjun's well-formed hand, with its deep-brown, slender fingers, in front of me, holding on to the back of the driver's seat on the right side of the car. Night had fallen by now, and it was dark inside the car. I don't know what came over me: I placed my hand on his.

We began stroking each other's hands. He must have known it was mine since caressing Abha *maasi*'s doughy hand would most certainly have been the wrong move. Later, when we returned to the car to head home from our evening, we would both find each other's hands again. Arjun stayed the night, sleeping on a cot perpendicular to the one I had begun sharing with my mother to deter the night fondler. I was sleeping inches away from my filmmaker "uncle." As I nodded off to sleep, I felt a hand on my breast. This time, I knew whose hand it was, and this time it was welcome. His hand moved lower down my body, groping and tugging at my pajamas, and soon his fingers slipped inside me. My mother stirred, and like a lioness instinctively sensing danger to her cub, she flipped my body over hers so that she now separated the two of us.

I returned to spend the next two summers with Arjun. I told my parents I was doing research in Delhi. Perhaps my mother suspected I would see Arjun, but she never asked, probably too afraid to hear the answer. His world was dazzling to me, a place where people pursued the arts or journalism, not medicine, engineering, or business.

What made it even more compelling at the time was that Arjun and his friends acted, wrote, or performed in Hindi, not English, the language used by most urbane, city-dwelling people in their professions. Arjun's friends were actors in Hindi soap operas or journalists for Hindi newspapers or news producers for Hindi programs. I'd hit the real India! It was as if I'd stumbled across a mysterious key, unlocked a door, and found the vibrant world of my fantasies.

At the same time, many of his friends were Muslims. Since nearly all of my relatives belonged to Jainism, I'd never met a Muslim in India, though I knew they made up nearly one fifth of India's population. Of course, I'd heard my father, like many of his generation, rail against Muslims and Pakistan. He'd told me of the awful, bloody riots that flared up periodically when he was a child in Meerut.

India can seem the most peaceable nation on earth—it's never had a brutal dictatorship or a state-sanctioned period of terror or a civil war, the way nearly all third-world countries have—until riots break out. Then methods of murdering and killing become more inventively torturous than anywhere else. Babies are thrown up and speared. Women's wombs are slashed open. Victims are doused with petroleum and set alight.

Arjun's friendships with Muslims not only appealed to my collegiate notions of secularity and diversity but also confirmed my suspicion that somewhere India's Hindus and Muslims were interacting with each other on a genuine fraternal level, not just killing each other viciously whenever riots erupted. I had thought to myself that Muslims simply comprised too large a community in India to be swept under the rug and lead a segregated life.

The story of how Arjun and I ended was just as sordid as it began, if not more so. It was my third summer with him—if you count the one we met as the first—and I was to begin my senior year at college in the fall. Boys at school had finally started to notice me, and I'd even dated someone for the first time during the spring semester. Arjun's charms were wearing thin by this point, and his world now seemed more claustrophobic than sophisticated. His English was poor, my Hindi was constricted, and communication was forced and halted. The summer, as well as our relationship, was drawing to a close.

Arjun stayed in a one-room flat behind Connaught Place. He had no furniture, and we had slept on padding on the floor for the last two summers. There was nothing in the room besides the makeshift mattress, a few clothes, and other stray belongings.

I no longer relished this India. It was evening, and we were sitting with his closest friend, Hussain, on the "mattress." Arjun and I were nearly always with his friends, forcing me to be a silent spectator as they chattered away and ribbed each other in Hindi.

Somehow, the topic changed to one to which I could contribute: incest. Both Arjun and Hussian were making the argument that incest was largely a problem of the West and simply didn't happen in India. I thought back to the summer I met Arjun, when a spectral cousin had come to me at night to touch and fondle me. I had told Arjun what happened at the time. It may not have been as serious a molestation as that by a father or brother, but I was traumatized nonetheless, suffering nightmares and nighttime paralysis for a few years following that summer. Now I felt a strong urge to tell Hussain about it. I struggled to find the right words in Hindi to describe that summer's incidents.

Hussain turned to Arjun and said, "What is this she is saying?"

"Oh, you know, somebody just touched her on the arm or something, like this, and she went crazy," Arjun replied, placing two fingers on my forearm.

I reacted without thinking. I was enraged at Arjun's belittling of what had happened to me. Also, there was my own growing feminist consciousness. All those Take Back the Night events at college—where women got up in front of a large audience and spoke of how they had been assaulted—that I had mocked as shrill had made some impact.

I slapped Arjun across the face. Perhaps he could not take the humiliation of being struck in front of his best friend, and he slapped me back. I grabbed my bags and ran out of the flat into the evening dusk. It was sticky hot, and dust was flying everywhere. I jumped into a scooter and wracked my brains for a guesthouse. I had seen one, I recalled, in Sunder Nagar, an affluent South Delhi neighborhood where I had earlier that summer visited a friend from college. I asked the driver to take me to that neighborhood.

It strikes me now what a seedy picture our alliance made. In a cramped, sparsely, furnished room, a young girl of twenty, just becoming aware of her growing sexuality, carrying on with a man at least fifteen years older who cannot begin to understand her, nor she him. It is not clear which of the two preyed on the other. Was he the proverbial older man taking advantage of a vulnerable girl lost in an unfamiliar country, or was she the predator, sucking from him exotic experience until she had gleaned all she could and then left?

I had outgrown the relationship and thought it wise to redirect my romantic efforts toward men nearer my age.

Chapter Fifteen

The autorickshaw drivers have started wearing scarves around their necks and caps on their heads as the swelter leaves the air after Delhi's interminable summer. It is said like a truism that winter is the best season in the city, a time of year when everyone is in a jaunty mood and throwing grand outdoor parties that are impossible to plan in the heat.

Despite my long association with the city, I have never been in Delhi during the winter and look forward to experiencing this cheerful season, particularly since my summer had been less than promising in terms of romance. Perhaps since seasonal moods appear reversed in Delhi—winter and the rainy monsoon season are considered the loveliest times of the year, and no one eagerly awaits the arrival of sunshine and heat as they do elsewhere in the world—winter is the season for love here.

Already, though, I am dismayed by how cold it is. Not outside, mind you. Outside, in the open air, it is perfectly fine. A breezy, mild sixties, sometimes even low seventies. I usually don't even wear a jacket, just a sweater and jeans. Inside, it is frighteningly frigid. Arctic weather. How is this possible? I ask around and the standard response is that since Delhi's winter is only a short two months, the houses are designed for the summer. Floors and walls are made of cement, which stays cool for the scorching summers but doesn't insulate during the winters. When I'm inside, I bury myself under layers of clothing. I freeze in my own home.

I wonder whether that day back in October when the earthquake rocked me awake is the only day my bed will shake—if you catch my drift. I decide to seek advice from Nandini.

Having returned from New York a few weeks ago, Nandini meets up with me at a place called Turquoise Cottage. We repair to a table configured from a high barrel. I'm having a beer, but Nandini's not drinking. Though not much of a drinker, she usually has a drink or two. Tonight, she's drinking a Diet Coke.

Despite this, her mood is inordinately festive. I notice she's wearing a silk shawl I haven't seen before and carrying an expensive leather handbag. She looks radiant, breaking into a smile that would melt the wedding ring off the fingers of most married men. She's giddy with excitement and can't wait to disgorge all the details about her trip to the U.S. The set piece, of course, was Dilip, the consultant she'd gone to meet in New York and hopes to marry.

We are shouting to make ourselves heard over the loud music. Turquoise Cottage, or TC, as it is known, is an always-packed pub in Delhi frequented by people of Nandini's age. The girls all look impossibly young with their tank tops and jeans and heavy kohl and eyebrow piercings. The men also look too young for me, with their T-shirts and goatees and faux-hawks. TC, as I will also later learn, has a very familiar soundtrack. At least once a night, the DJ will play Guns N' Roses' "Sweet Child o' Mine" and U2's "With or Without You," and bouncy nineteen-year-old girls will pull their foot-dragging four- or five-years-older boyfriends onto the tiny dance floor to grind their hips and twirl around like dervishes because that is what the new liberated Indian female does. The night will conclude with Led Zeppelin's "Stairway to Heaven," and the girls will end up in a song-long liplock with their boyfriends. Then they will be rushed home before twelve, which is their curfew, but not before being fondled in the car by their guy. Maybe if they are well practiced, they will already have a dark spot in the city they like to go to where the police will not bother them and where they can tug off their jeans and have sex in the backseat.

"So you really like him then?" I yell over REM's "Losing My Religion."

"Yeah, a lot. He's very different from all the men I've met in the past. He's serious, career minded, older," she says, revealing that he's in his early thirties, making him nearly a decade older. "I've even agreed to stop drinking for him. He doesn't drink."

"Well, then when's the wedding?" I ask.

"That's the problem. He wants to marry me, but his parents aren't pleased. They think I'm too young and, well, he told them about my past," she says.

"Why would he do that? That's kind of odd," I say.

"I guess he wanted to be honest with them and not hide anything. He's really upstanding that way," she says.

Over late-night phone calls, coffees at Barista in Greater Kailash, and shopping trips to Sarojini Nagar's market stalls, from which Delhi girls purchase cut-rate evening blouses, Nandini will share details of her life and childhood in Kanpur with me. I listen with rapt attention to her tales, mulling over them later when I return home. I suspect if my father had stayed in India, in one of his small towns in the hinterland, my life and outlook would have been far more similar to Nandini's than it would to the upper-middle-class types who have grown up in Delhi, who I see roaming in packs of eight or ten boys and girls in Khan Market; many strike me as entitled, vulgar, churlish.

Nandini belongs to the fiercely proud Rajput caste, whose large role in fighting many of India's wars against foreign invaders is well documented. Most of Rajasthan's former prince-ly states were ruled by Rajputs. "Our caste is all about pride and honor," she says. Funny how historical caste distinctions are rooted in reality, because in my merchant caste, Bania, the focus is entirely on money.

Nandini is the baby of her family, the prized young girl following two older brothers. It is a prime position in which to find oneself in India. Indian parents will always want a son first, and, well, they wouldn't mind having another when the mother is pregnant a second time. But if she is giving birth to a third child and has already produced two sons, then of course, in that case, bring on the daughter.

In fact, her parents had cut a deal with a family close to theirs. Their friends already had two daughters—the horror!—and were hell-bent on having a son. If Nandini had been a boy instead of a girl, and the family friends gave birth to a third daughter, then the two families planned to exchange the babies and raise them as their own. The wife in the other family delivered another girl. She and her husband were devastated when Nandini turned out to be a girl.

Despite all the perks of being the precious baby daughter with two older brothers, there were some disadvantages. Her fero-ciously overprotective father rarely allowed her to go anywhere unaccompanied. She was only allowed to stay overnight at the homes of friends who didn't have brothers, which meant that the only friend with whom she could have a sleepover was the girl with whom she would have been exchanged at birth.

Nandini attended an all-girls Catholic school where lessons were given by uptight German nuns. However, while her physical comings and goings were circumscribed by her strict parents, her virtual world was left unsupervised. She grew up in the mid-1990s, after cable and satellite television had completely rewritten the entertainment landscape. (Before the arrival of cable television, India was as familiar with Western media images as the isolated neighboring kingdom of Bhutan.) After the launch of Star Television and MTV, middle-class families all over India would gather around the television every night to watch *The Bold and the Beautiful, Baywatch,* and *Beverly Hills, 90210.* Nandini told me one day over coffee, "I just thought this was how the world behaved."

Unlike her demure girlfriends, who comported themselves in line with the norms of a small town, Nandini possessed an ardent interest in the opposite sex from a young age. She was constantly developing crushes on her brothers' friends, following them around when they came to the house. And she had a lot of what are called in India "phone friends." When a girl reaches a certain age, maybe fourteen or fifteen, in a small town, she starts getting noticed by boys and even young men in their early to mid-twenties. And that's when the phone calls start. A guy might cold-call a house, and if a girl picks up, he will try to start a conversation. Most girls would hang up, discouraging such flirtatious interaction. Some would even tell their parents. Not Nandini. Once, when a twenty-four-year-old man accidentally rang the house, she spoke to him for hours. They had dozens of conversations on the phone over the next couple of years but never once met each other.

A couple of years later, the Internet came to Kanpur. Nandini's peers were spending hours in Internet cafés chatting online to strangers, and people well-off enough to afford one were getting Web connections at home. Nandini got online and stayed there from seven P.M. to ten P.M. when her father, a doctor, was at his clinic.

From her drawing room in Kanpur, nineteen-year-old Nandini entered a chat room featuring a colorful cast of characters, among them a doctor based in Delhi who worked for an NGO, a civil servant and his wife in Bihar, and an air force officer with an eleven-year-old daughter and a missing leg. There were more mainstream types as well, a boy at IIT in Bombay, some journalists from Delhi. Nandini was the youngest girl in the chat room and her new friends treated her like a princess. When she complained about her small-town life, her chat friends advised her to get out of Kanpur and do a management or communications course in Delhi. Eventually, she talked her parents into letting her go, promising to stay in a hostel and studiously avoid men.

Soon after she arrived in Delhi, she met up with her chat friends for the first time at a pub in Connaught Place called DV8. She had a gin and tonic. It was the first time she had tasted alcohol. She danced like crazy for hours that night. Her new friends nudged each other, nodding toward her and saying, "This one is going to go wild in Delhi."

"The prophecy did come true," she said to me once, with a wink.

In Delhi, she went from one man to the next, none of whom stuck around for longer than a few weeks or months. Some of them even tried to pass her on to another friend once they were done with her. She met foreigners—German, French, American—when she went clubbing and returned with them to their hotel rooms to have sex. She was desperate for attention.

Finally, she met Anil, who I met the night of my introduction to Delhi's nightlife when a group of us went to Elevate, and who subsequently drove us to the hills. He saved her from the Delhi life that would certainly have devoured her had she continued at the same pace. He was the first man to treat her like a three-dimensional person and not as a sex object or a child. She cried on his shoulder every time a boyfriend treated her badly or disappeared. She eventually moved in with Anil. Even though they began having sex and enjoyed each other's company tremendously, the two were an untraditional couple. They knew they could never marry, since Nandini's father would disown her if she married anyone but a Rajput, and one preferably from north India at that. Anil was from Kerala and from a lower caste. Knowing their relationship didn't have a future, they decided to break up after a year. Nandini continued to live with him, and it was Anil who placed her profile on shaadi.com.

I am nearly a decade older than Nandini, but we are in the same place. This girl has led a life so entirely at odds with my own but one that strikes familiar chords. I too hail ultimately from a small town in northern India, and I too have always had a wild streak, though my demons list more toward substance-fueled revelry than sexual waywardness—this perhaps because of some die-hard, quite possibly obsolete notion I have that sex should *mean* something. That said, I, too, have ended up in compromising situations with men out of desperation or loneliness that make me shudder in horror today.

And now we are both on shaadi.com, trying to find a husband.

Finally, still shouting over the music at TC, I ask, "If Dilip wants to marry you and his parents aren't into the idea, how do you expect this to happen?"

"He says that I should just wait a couple of months and then he'll speak to them again," she says. "He wants to wait for the right time to talk to them, and he wants them to agree to do it, as opposed to doing it against their will."

"Oh, okay," I say skeptically.

"Anyway, it's fine. I don't mind waiting. He's definitely the man I want to marry," she says.

"Oh, that's nice. I hope it works out," I say, though I hardly like the sound of this.

He's shared her past with his parents, which to my mind is a mighty strange thing to do. And she'd already agreed to stop drinking entirely for him when he's not even given her a commitment of any sort. Certainly, social drinking is the province of the single person the world over, and I expect my alcohol consumption would taper after marriage, but I find her sudden teetotalism a bit extreme.

I've begun to view Nandini's search for a husband as a shadow version of mine, similar as we are to each other, and I'm hoping, despite my skepticism about Dilip, that he is the one for her. It would bode well for the other if one of us could get off shaadi.com—to which we both seem to have a lifetime membership.

Chapter Sixteen

I am dancing to "Kajra Re" at Pegs and Pints, a club near the Chanakya cinema, one of the few old-style cinemas in the city that hasn't been replaced by a multiplex. It is Tuesday night, which means that Delhi's entire gay male population has descended on the club. Unlike other clubs I've been to in the city, this one is frequented by people across Delhi's social strata.

There are the men who are working professionals and dress casually, the prettier men who are from good families and probably work for Papa's business, the smaller-town boys from Agra or Jaipur looking to explore the big-city gay scene, and the working-class men from old Delhi who might be mechanics or work in shops. In the new lexicon I'm quickly picking up, this latter category is frequently referred to as "vernac," or "vernacular," since their English is more or less nonexistent. Gay men have a term for everything.

A new friend of mine, Bharat, has taken me to the club with some friends of his, including a couple, Vincent and David, who are both from the northeastern part of India that juts out from the country's shoulder like a severed limb.

I am repeating a pattern here. Bharat and Vincent will soon take me under their wings, and instead of finding a straight male with whom I can enjoy candlelit dinners and a satisfying sex life, I will be welcomed by a protective brood of gay men, who will take me to their dens of iniquity, ply me with alcohol, and drive me home safely. Again, I will be in a city where I will have *lots of fun*, but where love, like hunted prey, will dodge behind trees and elude me.

I have always found an easy camaraderie with gay men. Everyone knows about the necessity of friendship—how could we not? As well, we know about the business of friendship and how useful people with good connections are. Lately, I've been wondering about the forgotten art of friendship, for it is an art, like music, painting, or poetry. Something requiring practice and dedication—and, of course, innate talent never hurts. And nowadays, the least complicated friendship I find is with members of the opposite sex with whom having sex is out of the question. It is a friendship in which bonhomie reigns supreme over a baser kind of giving and taking. That said, when a man's sexuality is aimed in my direction, I'd rather it fall quite definitively on the heterosexual side. Not for me this post-millennium questioning of one's sexuality for the pure post-heck of it all; I would like a man's desire to be unadulterated and raw—or what's the point?

Tonight is my first night at Pegs and Pints. It is not a large, spacious club like Elevate, but a rather smallish, dark room, maybe the length of two normal-sized drawing rooms, with a bar at one end. The bartenders, though, seem heterosexual, noticing me first among the horde of men clamoring for their attention to get a drink. It is the most packed club I have been to so far in Delhi, and nobody is standing still, chatting to their friends like they do in most places. Everybody is gyrating to "Kajra Re," which soon segues into a song by the Black Eyed Peas. Now they are playing a song by Cher. Gay male icon, indeed.

After a couple hours or so, when I am soaked with sweat from dancing, I am approached by a nice-looking man. His name is Naveen and he asks me to dance with him in Hindi. I agree, and

we dance for forty-five minutes, maybe an hour. When I am
tired and want to return to my friends, he asks for my phone
number. I am taken aback, having assumed he was gay. I try to
ask him in English if he is gay, but his English is so poor he
doesn't understand the question. He is vernac. I ask him in
Hindi.

"This is a gay club. You know, men come to meet men. Er,
are you gay?" I ask in Hindi.

Naveen replies, "No, I'm not. I come here for the music. It's
the best in town."

Of course, straight men in many big cities have long known
that the very best place to pick up unsuspecting girls is in gay
clubs, so I shouldn't be surprised that Delhi men are on to it. I
take him back to my friends, who size him up and decide he
looks safe enough. I give him my phone number. Every time I
return to Pegs and Pints, vernac men like Naveen will try to pick
me up.

The next day Naveen calls and I agree to meet him at the
market near the Chanakya cinema. He has a friend with him,
which is kind of odd, but I find Naveen sweet and unthreaten-
ing. He is rather cute as well. The three of us share a plate of
vegetable *momo*s while Naveen and I carry on a disjointed
conversation in Hindi. Some details are afforded. He's a bartender at Lodi Gardens restaurant and he lives in Noida with his
mother and his brother and sister-in-law.

Later, his friend leaves and Naveen offers me to take me on a
motorcycle ride. With scarves wrapped around our necks, we
cruise aimlessly through the empty night streets of Delhi for
about an hour or so before he drops me home. It is the most
chaste of evenings and he behaves like a perfect gentleman,
waving a friendly good-bye and flashing me a dimpled grin.

*   *   *

Sometimes, when I'm sitting in Café Coffee Day at Khan Market, drinking an iced cappuccino and reading a book, I'll hear a high-pitched giggle. I'll look up and notice a table of impeccably groomed men in jeans and trainers laughing in the corner, their shirt cuffs just right and hair gelled just so. It's no San Francisco, but for all that I've heard about India's rapid social change, I'm still surprised there are so many gay men visibly out of the closet in Delhi—to their friends, to their colleagues, and many to their families.

By some lights, Indian society seems far more accepting of homosexuality than does the West, where Christianity deems homosexuality unnatural and immoral. Hinduism imposes no such strictures, and many of its gods assume both male and female forms, such as Shiva, one of the religion's three main deities, who in one of his popular avatars, Ardhanarishvara, is represented as half man, half woman.

This is not to say that homophobia doesn't exist—and indeed, homosexual acts are illegal—rather that its concerns are placed differently. A society's obsessions govern its attitude toward those who deviate from the norm. In the West, people are obsessed with sex, so they focus on what sexual acts are committed in homosexual relationships. In India, the focus is marriage, and society is more concerned with maintaining the family structure and less with what is being done in the bedroom. I've heard some gay men tell me that their parents don't care what they do or with whom as long as they end up getting married. However, nearly all my gay male friends in Delhi are out to their parents and are under no pressure to marry. Some live with long-term partners, who have been accepted as part of the family.

I may not be enjoying as many intimate dinners as I'd like with heterosexual men, but every few weeks, my new gay friend

Bharat takes me out on a "date." I'll dress up in tall boots and a skirt and sweater, he'll pick me up in his navy blue Honda Civic, and we'll drive to Stone, a cozy Italian restaurant in Defence Colony. We'll order pastas and a bottle of Sula cabernet, and when the bill comes, he'll insist on paying. Outside, Bharat will buy each of us a _paan_, and then he'll drop me home. If you're going to be a fag hag, you could do a lot worse than living in Delhi.

During one of our dinners, I ask Bharat, who now heads a public relations office after leaving a career in journalism, when he came out and whether it was difficult. It surprises me when he tells me that he came out at thirty, for he seems very comfortable in his sexuality.

"Don't tell me that only seven years ago, you were trying to pass off as straight," I say, shocked, but with an amused smile on my face. "I can't imagine you doing anything but ogling young, skinny boys."

"Well, that was kind of the problem. I wasn't," he says, wryly.

As a teenager, Bharat was a loner, which surprises me because he always knows where the best parties are on the weekends and seems to know everyone in town. He weighed two hundred and fifty pounds in high school and never went out with friends, despite constant urging by his two elder brothers and mother. His father had recently died, and perhaps this was one of the reasons he found it difficult to mingle easily with his peers.

Around this time, when he was sixteen or seventeen, he developed a crush on a Nepalese servant who lived with them in their well-appointed home in Gulmohar Park, a wealthy neighborhood in south Delhi. When Mukesh, who was in his early twenties, had finished his work at the house, Bharat would take him in his car to Nirula's, which has been serving its poor imitation of burgers and pizza since long before Domino's and

McDonald's arrived on the Indian scene. Mukesh didn't feel comfortable going inside the restaurant, so they would pick up an ice cream and go on a long drive.

Bharat would mostly ask him questions about his interests, and Mukesh would tell him about his love for Hindi film songs and his obsession with karate. When they would get home, they would box and pounce on each other.

"Oh, it was great fun. I got to touch him," Bharat says. "I could hold him down and be right on top."

It never really went farther than that, although Bharat once showed his penis to Mukesh, in which the servant did not appear to take a large amount of interest. "He didn't show me his, which was kind of disappointing," Bharat laments.

Mukesh would say to Bharat, "When you get married, I will always work for you." Bharat liked the sound of that, although he wasn't comfortable with the married part.

"I'd tell him, 'I'm never going to get married,'" Bharat says.

Mukesh eventually moved on to another family in Vasant Vihar, but a couple of years later, they got another servant who Bharat took a shine to. His name was Sufal, he was maybe twenty-six or twenty-seven, and he was from Bihar. Bharat's mother thought it would be nice for Bharat to give Sufal a little bit of education, and Bharat readily agreed to give the servant history and Hindi lessons at night.

They spent the next few months kissing and fonding during their nighttime study sessions, Bharat reaching out to place his hand on his servant's crotch while teaching him the Hindi alphabet. Bharat can still recall the exact day Sufal had to return to his family home in Bihar. It was May 19, 1989. Bharat was playing in a quarterfinal match for a local tennis championship, and he ended up losing to a boy he'd beaten several times before. He was so overwrought about Sufal's leaving that he blew the match. "I lost in straight sets. That shouldn't have happened," he says.

After Sufal, there was a decade of nothing. Bharat dated neither men nor women. He sublimated his desire for men by working well into the night and over the weekends as an investigative journalist for some of India's top newspapers, following in the footsteps of his father, who'd retired as one of the country's most admired newspaper editors.

When he was about to turn thirty, Bharat started feeling pressure to get married, but not from the usual suspects. It wasn't his family—his mother had never put pressure on any of her sons—but his friends and colleagues who had noticed that he never seemed to have female company around. Friends introduced him to a decent-looking woman, a dentist from Dehradun. Bharat thought to himself that it was best to get married and then divorce if it didn't work out. "People won't question me after that, and then I'll know what I am," he thought.

He met her with mutual friends at Delhi Gymkhana for a drink and took her to dinner alone after that. They talked about work. His friends advised him to call her every night after that.

"I did, but I didn't feel anything," Bharat says. "It was like a job interview. Something I was supposed to do."

Then his friends told him he should go see her in Dehradun. His editor, who was also one of the friends involved in the setup, ordered Bharat to take three days off, knowing Bharat never liked to take any vacation time off from work. He left by train on a Friday evening, arrived Saturday morning, and took the train back to Delhi that evening. He purposefully switched shifts with a colleague so that he could tell the young woman he had to work Sunday duty.

Bharat remembers returning home and lying in bed for a couple of days with terrible back pain, which he had never had before. Nonetheless, when the woman told him they could only continue meeting if they got engaged, he agreed to go through with it. They planned an official engagement party for a week later, but when the day arrived, the girl's uncle called forty-five minutes before the ceremony was to take place and said the date was inauspicious and they needed to postpone until a time closer to the wedding, which was a few months away. Bharat felt a flood of relief and had complete clarity of vision about what to do next. He sprang into action. One of the most mild-mannered people I've ever met, Bharat began ranting like any jilted Indian groom.

He flew into a rage. Indignant, furious, he screamed at the uncle, "How can you do this?! This is just not done! It is insulting to my family. They have all come here for the engagement. I'm calling off the wedding entirely!"

I'm not nearly as lucky as Bharat. Sometimes I wish my parents adopted the same hands-off approach to marriage.

When they next call, I find out they're coming to Delhi for my cousin Aarti's wedding next month. They plan to stay with me for six weeks, during which time they expect to marry me off as well.

I don't mind meeting a few suitors of their selection, but I fear my parents are so out of touch with the current state of affairs in India that they will choose thoroughly inappropriate men for me to meet. Otherwise-cool Indian parents can be notoriously tone-deaf when it comes to finding mates for their children.

Since arriving in Delhi I've already had to fend off half a dozen phone calls from my relatives, who've urged me to race to Ghaziabad to meet some doctor or engineer of little import. "But he is an engineer, Anita. He is graduating with M.Sc. in science from technical institute in Bareilly. He is so good. Why you don't want to meet?" an uncle will inquire, completely baffled.

At least my conversations with relatives are all over the phone, and I can make some excuse or other to avoid meeting these thoroughly hopeless cases. That won't be the case with my frightfully urgent parents. I'm not sure I will survive six weeks.

"You're coming for six weeks? Don't you think that's a bit long? Perhaps you could come for three or four?" I say.

"We need that much time. There's Aarti's wedding. Then at least a couple of weeks to find a boy, and then a few more to organize your wedding. It can't happen overnight, *beta*," my father says.

"Well, exactly, Papa. I don't think it will all happen at once. That's why I think you should come for, you know, maybe four weeks instead of six," I say.

"Mummy and I will stay in a hotel then if you can't keep us the whole time. I'm your father and this is my duty," my father says.

"Okay, whatever," I sigh in resignation.

Chapter Seventeen

I am settling into a life in Delhi, accumulating around me friends who are more or less similar to me, single and in their thirties—with the exception of Nandini. But they are usually single for different reasons—because they are gay or divorced. Up until just a few years ago, divorced women and gay men were types of circus freaks in India—they were the bearded lady, the elephant man, the Siamese twins.

Now, though, to have been married, to have been divorced, to be able to say "my ex-husband" or "my ex-wife," no longer causes jaws to drop (that low) or eyelashes to flutter (that quickly) in this cosmopolitan India. Among the younger urban set, the attitude toward divorce does seem considerably more relaxed than it was in my parents' time. I notice that on shaadi.com urban men who have never married don't specify a preference for a never-married woman.

I first meet Sonali through the Moksha gang, she being another one of the satellites that always seem to collect around music bands, whether they're from Delhi or Edinburgh. She dated Nair four or five years ago, but she doesn't see much of the band now because she lives in Ghaziabad with her husband, a prominent newspaper journalist who is more than a decade older than she is. Sonali's also a journalist, and since she writes about some of the same topics I do, I run into her at press conferences.

One day, after a Microsoft conference where the company announces the rollout of some new product in India, we decide to go for lunch at Mocha, a Middle Eastern café in Greater Kailash that a few months later, along with a host of other popular hangouts, will be shut down by the city's aggressive drive to curb illegal commerce in areas licensed for residential use. Sonali and I sit back on the low cushions and order mozzarella-pesto-and-tomato sandwiches. Soon enough, I begin to lament my dismal luck with men in Delhi.

"I don't know, Sonali, I thought it would be different from New York, but it's oddly very similar. Men here have the same short attention spans, and they are all skittish about a serious commitment," I complain.

"Indian men are only interested in sleeping around these days," she says, "especially since it's become a lot easier."

She listens to my woes attentively, nodding in sympathy and expressing rage at various suitors when required. She describes her dating life before she got married a year ago. It sounds fairly typical of what I've come to expect in this emancipated city—a few steady relationships, a few sexual encounters, a few missed opportunities.

"But that's great that you found someone eventually," I say, smiling. "I guess that's because he was older and more mature."

"The first year of marriage is so hard," she replies gravely.

I wait for her to say more. She doesn't. Sonali, earlier so chatty about various dalliances, is silent.

I change the subject. But before we leave the restaurant, she says it again, apropos of nothing: "The first year of marriage is so hard."

The evening of their first anniversary, Sonali was extremely agitated, on edge. Prakash had been so different before they got married. For two years, he'd wooed her with expensive dinners at the Imperial or the Maurya Sheraton. They'd go away on weekend trips to the hills and even longer trips to Ladakh in the Himalayas. He'd brought her gifts and listened to her patiently when she talked about problems she was having with her parents.

It was so abrupt, though, the way Prakash had stopped putting any effort into the marriage as soon as they wed. It seemed the day after the wedding, even, he was a different person. He never wanted to go out to movies anymore. In fact, he wasn't all that interested in watching movies together at home cither. He worked six or seven days of the week, and on the rare days he didn't go into work, he wanted to visit friends or sleep.

They hadn't gone out of town once together since they'd gotten married, and Sonali had hoped that for their first wedding anniversary, Prakash would agree to a long weekend away. He didn't, saying he wouldn't be able to get the time off from work. He didn't even want to go out to dinner that night, saying he had to visit a friend's wife in the hospital.

Though they'd met at a press junket and dated for two years before marrying, it still felt a lot like the kind of wedding that Sonali's mother or my own would have agreed to a generation ago. An arrangement. Two people living under the same roof, sleeping together, eating together, procreating together, but not *seeing* each other. Prakash didn't beat Sonali, he didn't drink too much alcohol, he didn't cheat on her. He was, in other words, a perfect husband by Indian standards. He did nothing wrong.

The night of their first wedding anniversary, Sonali stepped into the bathroom and took twenty of whatever pills she could find. When Prakash came home from visiting his friend's wife at eleven o'clock that night, he found her sprawled out on the bed, unconscious. He rushed her to the hospital and they pumped her stomach.

This had happened only two weeks prior to the lunch at which Sonali and I munched on mozzarella-pesto-and-tomato sandwiches. When we'd gotten to know each other better, she told me about her suicide attempt. One day, I'd hitched a ride with her back to my office after a press conference, and she began narrating the story as we drove up and down and back and forth again in her Maruti 800 down the long, wide avenues in the diplomatic enclave of Chanakyapuri, the neighborhood where my office was located.

A few weeks after the day she divulged the details of her suicide attempt to me, she filed for divorce.

Deepa is also getting a divorce. She is a friend I also met through the Moksha boys, her soon-to-be ex-husband having once played percussion with them. Deepa has just turned forty and has been married for five years. She married late by Indian standards and went through much of the same eleventh-hour panic that I'm experiencing.

Deepa met her husband on an Internet site five years ago. He grew up in Tamil Nadu but went to Chicago as a college student and had stayed on in the Midwestern city for the next twenty years, eventually finding work as a university professor. The two had much in common, as Deepa was also from south India—from Andhra Pradesh—and was also an academic. They wrote and spoke on the phone for hours each day, him running up a long-distance bill into thousands of dollars a month. After a few months, he came to Delhi to visit her. He was off-the-wall, zany, a real character. Deepa had always been the kind of woman drawn to chaotic souls, to communists, to poets, to communist poets.

They smoked some hash together and decided to marry. Within a month of meeting him, Deepa left for Chicago, the first time she had lived outside of India. It was a profoundly disorienting experience, and while her husband was certainly warm, supportive, loving, and committed, she realized after six months that the marriage would not last. Her husband wanted to stay out late in bars until six A.M. every night; he was like an overgrown child. He was a kind yet profoundly immature man. There was no chemistry.

Deepa's husband didn't beat her, he didn't drink too much alcohol, he didn't cheat on her. He was, in other words, a perfect husband by Indian standards. He did nothing wrong.

There is a shift in the metropolises of India. Women want more; they want affection, they want orgasms—clitoral *and* vaginal, even multiple—they want cunnilingus (which, by the way, notwithstanding the *Kama Sutra*, is not as integral a part of the Indian male's repertoire as I would have hoped); they want to spend time together, they want romance. In other words, they want to feel like a woman.

It wasn't always so. When I was growing up, to be a divorced woman was a type of karmic curse, retribution for faults accrued in a previous life. It was a state you would not wish on your worst enemies. I knew of this firsthand because my family was oddly tarnished by the blight of divorce.

My father may have been from one of India's luckiest families, his mother having given birth to seven sons, but it was not enough to save the one daughter she bore—the one daughter! My father's sister, my aunt, was married off to a man who beat her viciously. The beatings were so frequent and so violent that she came home to her parents after a year; had they not been so savage, she would have stayed and tolerated them. Her parents were sympathetic, but divorce was out of the question. They sent my aunt back to her husband. Some years later, after she'd given birth to a daughter, she left him for good. Many years later, she married again. This time, when the beatings started, my father's sister knew how to leave. She'd done it before, and what was the difference, really, between one and two divorces if she never wanted anything to do with men again? She was so averse to relying on another man for anything that despite repeated pleas by my father for her to emigrate to America for the sake of her daughter's future, and despite his assurances that he would support her, she stubbornly remained rooted in her job as a math teacher in a small town in north India, a place certainly not easy for a single working mother.

Then there were my mother's sisters. My mother was from a less son-blessed family than my father's. She was the second-eldest of six sisters and three brothers. The two youngest sisters of her family were still unmarried by the time my parents left for America. But my maternal grandfather, a man of good standing who worked for the Congress party government that ruled post-independence India, had already spent the family kitty on dowries for his four older daughters and had no money left to marry off the last two, or at least not enough to marry them to anyone respectable, such as, you guessed it, an engineer. No, they would have to marry schoolteachers, bank clerks, or even worse, shop assistants.

My father, who had been installed in the States for a few years, came up with what seemed at the time a particularly inspired notion, and one befitting his self-appointed role as the guardian of the rights of women. He figured he could dangle an immigration visa to the U.S. in front of a prospective groom's face in lieu of a dowry, and that would ensure that his sister-in-law would marry well. He reasoned they could even marry doctors, which possibility had earlier not even been entertained, the dowry needed for doctors being far out of my grandfather's reach. And that's exactly what happened.

It was in the eighties, and we were living in Las Vegas in one of our just-barely-middle-class neighborhoods. This was in the days when my dad was still struggling, when his moneymaking schemes were mistimed or misguided, and he had yet to hit America's jackpot, when three cherries, or three sevens, or three bars of gold would line up, and the coins would come clanging down—*chinnnnkkkkk chinnnkk chinnkk chink chink chink chinkchinkchinkchink.*

My mother's two sisters were living with their husbands together in an apartment in New Jersey. Only eight or nine years old, I could detect from the nightly impassioned phone calls to our house that all was not going well in the newlyweds' home. My parents spent a year, maybe two, on the phone with these husbands, pleading, reasoning, yelling, begging them to stop their verbal and physical abuse of my aunts, until one day, my brother, maybe eleven years old at the time, who, like me, had been listening to the fracas for far too long, suggested it, said the word—"divorce." Once the word was uttered aloud, it stayed there and hovered, hanging thickly in the air. And then my father finally addressed it: "Divorce. Well, why the hell not?! What's so bloody wrong with divorce anyway?!"

My two aunts flew out to Las Vegas, one of them with her two-year-old son, and stayed for six months. Then their husbands came from New Jersey, and my aunts went back with them. Soon after, we moved to Sacramento, where my father had found a job with the state of California as an electrical engineer.

There was some more back-and-forth, but my mother's sisters eventually moved back with us for good a year or two after their initial trip out West. It was the summer after I had finished the eighth grade, and I was poised to start high school in the fall. There were now seven of us in a family that had been only four, as my aunts and my now five-year-old cousin were living with us. This is not what my friends' families looked like. Seven of us would pile into the yellow Toyota Corolla station wagon that would become mine only two years later, when I turned sixteen. The car would eventually be replaced by a maroon Dodge Caravan in which I didn't have to sit on someone's lap.

My father felt strongly that since it was his suggestion that his wife's sisters marry doctors and come to the U.S., it was his duty to look after them for as long as was required. He was determined that my aunts empower themselves before marrying again. First, he lied about their ages, making my two twenty-something aunts into teenagers. Then he sent them to public high school. At my pleading, they were not sent to mine. Once they graduated, they were to get university degrees, then jobs, and *then* they could think about marrying again.

As for my young cousin, my father referred to him as his own son with new acquaintances, and even, strangely enough, with some old ones, as if he'd earlier forgotten to mention that he also had a five-year-old son. I tried to sympathize with my aunts' plight, but I couldn't help but feel resentful—at my mother's attention being drawn away, at going from a nuclear family to an extended one, at having to explain their presence to friends who came over. It would take me years to understand that my father was trying to make up for all of the flaws he saw in Indian society, as if he alone could turn back years of oppression of women, as if he could reverse the practice of dowry, of harassment or violence or death over dowry, of women being treated like servants or chattel by their parents-in-law.

I left home for college four years after my aunts moved in. It would take them much longer to leave my parents' house, which they did, after both getting university degrees in biochemistry, some ten years later when I was working in some far-flung city as a journalist. My parents helped them both to remarry, the older one finding a man from India and my younger aunt marrying an Indian man who was already settled in the States. The younger one, who did not have a child from her first marriage, gave birth to a baby girl after a year of marriage. Both are working in the Bay Area and are far happier in their second marriages than they were in their first. My young cousin graduated from Berkeley and is now working as a management consultant in San Francisco. And I still call him my little brother.

Chapter Eighteen

So you could say divorce haunted me while I was growing up. No, not in the way that it haunts children of divorce, who become determined never to repeat their parents' mistakes. Divorce possessed me differently. I couldn't let my father go through it all again.

I watched nearly all of my close female friends from college marry a few years after they graduated, and I watched many of them—some Indian and some not—divorce a few years after they married, many of them remarrying. Perhaps by design, I steered clear of marriage in my twenties.

I wouldn't blame you if you've come to the conclusion by now that I'm unmarriageable. I, too, on many a night, have had the same thought. But I should tell you—as well as remind myself—that there have been opportunities, one in particular that haunts me to this day.

I met Rahul, my first proper boyfriend, my penultimate year at Harvard. We had much in common. He was Indian-American (Bengali, in fact), from California, and, like me, assiduously avoided the pre-med or sciences route that most Indians are apparently born to pursue. Moreover, he was a graduate student in the English department, and for a graduate student to take notice of a lowly undergraduate was a *big deal.*

A friend of mine—it was Nadia again!—had taken me to a party thrown by graduate students one evening. When I walked in, I noticed Rahul standing across the room. I'd seen him on campus before. He always wore a tweed blazer and round spectacles for effect, which combined with his full red lips to make an exceedingly attractive package—in that English-graduate-student sort of way. He looked like he was the kind of person perpetually on the verge of quoting Auden. (And later, after I got to know him, he often was.) In other words, Rahul was the type of guy I never thought would take a second look at me, let alone ask me out. But he did both. At the party, he walked across the room toward me and introduced himself.

"Are you in a graduate program?" he asked.

"No, I'm an undergraduate," I said, shifting my weight from foot to foot nervously.

Rahul called a couple of days after the party. When I told some friends that I was going on a date with the Indian graduate student in English, the one with the glasses and tweed blazer, they knew who I was talking about, since they were taking a graduate seminar he was in.

"He asked *you* out?" one said suspiciously.

"I thought he was gay," another said, taken aback. I wasn't in any graduate seminars. I was no budding scholar; in my circle, I was considered the dumb one.

On our first date, Rahul and I went to a bar on Cambridge Street between Harvard and Central squares and awkwardly spoke about post-colonial literature. He did most of the talking. I just nodded, afraid I would say something stupid. I felt like I was in class and he was the discussion leader.

I didn't think Rahul would call to go out again, assuming he had plenty of pretty English graduate students with mermaid hair, a much larger vocabulary, and a photographic memory for Keats to choose from. He called a few days after our first date and asked me out to dinner at Tandoori House. It was much the same as the first date, with me eagerly listening for the brilliant bons mots I expected to fall from his lips. This time, after the date, we went back to his apartment, a filthy little place with books stacked up on the floor a half-hour walk from my dorm. I assumed cleaning, or more practically hiring someone to clean, was just out of range of his "life of the mind."

I saw him a few more times before the summer break arrived a month later. I cavorted in India as usual that summer—it was the one where my ongoing liaison with my "uncle" came to an end—thinking I wouldn't hear from Rahul again. Rahul had left Harvard that semester with a master's degree in English and was planning to attend Oxford in the fall for a second graduate degree in philosophy. To my surprise, though, Rahul sent letters to me in Delhi all through the summer, and in the fall, he wanted to pick up where we left off. My senior year and his year at Oxford, Rahul sustained our relationship through more letters in his calligraphic handwriting and books by his favorite Indian author, Upamanyu Chatterjee—who would soon become my favorite author—that he sent by post. During his visits to Harvard, he took me out to our old haunts, like Casablanca on Brattle Street, the restaurant with the Humphrey Bogart wall murals and the strange wicker cabana seats.

Then I graduated and Rahul and I maintained an on-again, off-again relationship, crisscrossing continents. At one point, he was trying his hand working at an investment bank in Hong Kong, where his father lived; I had wandered to Mexico City on a lark and found a job as a journalist. Then a couple of years later, I began working in Singapore. By this time, he'd left investment banking (work not suited for the academic) and became a journalist as well. Then he bagged a swanky job with a finance magazine and moved to Singapore, and all our continent-hopping came to an end; we were in the same city for the first time in more than three years since the graduate student party in Cambridge.

By this time, my illusions about him had long since dispersed and our relationship was marred by a certain rockiness. No longer was he the imperious English graduate student and I the diffident undergrad. We knew each other much too well to assume those roles. Though we had fought bitterly on many an occasion and over many expensive phone calls—this was in the era of prohibitive long distance rates—I'd always credited the difficulty in some part to the distance between us. Perhaps now that we were in the same city for the first time ever we could possibly start all over and begin our new life together?

The first night he was in Singapore, I met him in the lobby of the Ritz-Carlton, the new "six-star" hotel his company had put him up at. He strode toward me, smiling, and kissed me warmly, his hands in my hair. Then he grabbed my hands and brought them to his face. "Oh, the same little girl's hands. I love these hands," he murmured.

We immediately went up to his room and made love, and then took a bath together in the capacious bathtub with water jets. As I sat in the tub looking out the large hexagonal window dozens of stories above the city, Singapore remade itself in my eyes. No longer was it the lonely, sterile city I'd despised for the last few months I'd lived there. No, now it was sunny and inviting and green.

Rahul and I got out of the tub, dressed, and went for dinner. Afterward we repaired to his room, and soon enough, we began fighting as we were wont to do. After a colossal and soul-piercing few hours of arguing, he threw me out of his room, saying that I was definitely Not His Girlfriend.

It was after midnight, and I found myself, hair matted, weeping uncontrollably, outside the grand glass doors of the hotel as security guards looked on at me worryingly. That is to say, they were not worried *for* me. In spankingly safe Singapore, I *was* the threat. Reeling from confusion, grief, and desperation, I began walking the three miles home—I quite literally had no one to fear but myself, as the hotel guards had made abundantly clear—to the depressing flat I shared with two messy, hard-partying, babe-loving stockbrokers. At twenty-three years old, I had never felt so gutted.

As I put one foot in front of the other, I thought back to the night we'd spent together less than two years earlier in Berkeley, which we figured was a somewhat halfway point between Sacramento and Pasadena, where Rahul's mother lived. We'd found a room at a Motel 6 on the seedy part of the main drag and made love several times that night, taking particular glee in the sleaziness of our backdrop. At dawn, after a couple of hours of sleep, Rahul nudged me awake to look at the sheets. I'd been menstruating, but we hadn't taken notice of how bloodied the sheets had become.

"Anita, Mr. Patel and family are going to be looking for a dead body soon. I think we should get out of here," Rahul said. We jumped into the shower together, rinsing each other off as we giggled about our "murder."

"Rahul, I'll get off with a lighter sentence because I was only the accomplice, and I'll turn state's evidence, whatever that means," I said. We left our sullied room as day was breaking.

How much it smarted now that he was throwing me out of his hotel room after all we'd been through. And how much I wished it were a Motel 6 and not the Ritz!

Even though Rahul told me repeatedly over the next year in Singapore that I was definitely Not His Girlfriend, we still spent a great deal of time together, though now he turfed me out of his home whenever he saw fit. It was an increasingly untenable situation, even for a drama-seeking woman in her early twenties who had adopted with especial gusto the motto "It's better to feel bad than nothing at all." When Rahul broke up with me a final time, I moved on to someone new.

But we remained friends of a sort, and he wanted to meet for lunch a couple of months after our break. It was New Year's Day.

"So, Anita, it sounds like you really like this guy then?" he said.

"I do, yeah. It's weird, because he actually seems to want to make me happy," I said, adding with a smirk, "I guess that just wasn't a priority for you. You know, that's okay though, Rahul, people do have different priorities."

"Point taken," Rahul said, chuckling.

During lunch, Rahul seemed unusually attentive to my needs.

"How do you take your coffee, Anita?" he asked, pouring me a cup.

Clearing my throat, I said, "Like I always take it, Rahul. Milk and no sugar."

"Right," he said. "And do you want some dessert?"

"Rahul, you know I don't have a sweet tooth. Why are you acting like you're seeing me for the first time?" I said, though I was actually touched that he was finally asking. Later I realized he *was* seeing me for the first time.

We walked out onto the street after our long lunch, and Rahul lingered. He wanted to say something. He suggested we go for a drink. It was a Sunday afternoon and I had nothing better to do, so I agreed. It was around four o'clock when we stepped into a nearby bar. There was no one in the bar. It was dark inside in that way bars are when in stark contrast to the brightness outside. Only drunks seem to feel safe in them at that hour. There was a soccer match on the television. We sat down at a table and Rahul gazed across at me from the other side. We hadn't ordered drinks yet.

"Will you marry me?" he asked.

Nobody had ever spoken the words aloud to me before, made a formal proposal. What does a woman feel like when a man says those four words, when women have, in a way, been wanting to hear those four simple words their entire lives? I'll tell you. The words feel like they pull you into a long string of humanity flowing through the annals of history. Someone is choosing you, making you unique, but at the same time joining a chorus of other men who have asked the same exact question of someone else. It connects you. How can you be a freak if someone wants to marry you?

I gulped. It was an odd way to propose—in a dark bar during daytime and with the detritus of a long and painful relationship lying at our feet.

"But, Rahul, we don't even like each other. Isn't that kind of a prerequisite for marriage?" I said, smiling awkwardly. I didn't know what else to say.

Rahul explained himself. The usual stuff—how he had done a lot of thinking and how he had been wrong and immature, and how he loved me.

And from the vantage point of a new relationship, I tried to explain my side: "It's like this, Rahul. You have always thought that your manhood was constituted by, or rested on, your intellectualism, or your education, or your family pedigree, or your job, or even your prep-school-boy good looks, but I guess what you're realizing, now that someone else is making me happy by simply being nice to me, is that your manhood was actually never defined by those things. You are less of a man because you didn't want to be nice to your girlfriend."

Looking stricken, Rahul said, "You're right, Anita. That's exactly what I've been thinking, or at least something along those lines."

We left the bar and spent hours walking down the streets of the sunny and antiseptic city, Rahul trying to convince me he was serious about the proposal. When we finally ended up propping ourselves up at another bar, after dinner, at ten P.M., I swiveled on my bar stool to face him.

"Rahul, if I were to marry you, you would have to be a completely different person," I said, echoing the last words Nora speaks to Torvald in Henrik Ibsen's play *A Doll's House*, one of the first feminist dramas ever written.

"I want to be a completely different person," he replied.

"Rahul, to use just a tiny example, one of many, mind you, you'd have to be the kind of person who did the dishes," I said.

"Anita, I would do the dishes, not because you wanted me to do the dishes but because *I* wanted to do the dishes," he said.

I was stung by his words. They are among the bravest words, to this day, I've ever heard a man utter, but after years of trying and failing, I wasn't certain it was enough.

"I know, Rahul, I know you would do the dishes," I said, a few tears now slipping from my eyes. "But, it's just that, well, I don't know if I can ever forgive you, or at least forget so many of the things you've done to me. I think I would be too angry. I'm still angry."

"Anita, I don't have words to express how sorry I am," he said, forlorn. "I behaved so badly."

"You know, I would never do that to anybody," I said, thinking of him throwing me out of his hotel room the first night he was in town. "Not even somebody I disliked."

"I know you wouldn't," Rahul said. "I'm so sorry."

*   *   *

A few weeks later, I received a letter in the post—perhaps the last actual letter, as opposed to e-mail, I've ever received of a personal nature.

I opened the envelope to find a letter in the chiseled handwriting I knew so well by now. It read:

Dear Anita,

We've hurt each other to such a breathtaking extent that it can hardly be put into words. Why have we, recently and over the years, done into each other so much damage? Why have we been to each other like some hate-filled ledger, divided down the middle, where we've both tabulated our furies, column by column? I think it needs consideration. What is at play here?

My hours and minutes are awash, shot through, with pictures of your face. I wish to god that the world could spin backwards and I could do all the things you say I never did: hold you tight over a phone line, in bed, on the street. You've walked briskly away from my folded arms and into something that I have neither the right nor the knowledge to describe. It seems to be giving you happiness. You're getting even, Anita. Do know that.

Your flaws are dazzling, Anita. So are your gifts. You're the most brilliant girl I've ever met. Your capacity for growth is limitless. You talk, think, enquire, like someone who knows the world can be drunk down like a cold glass of water on a hot day. It can. And you *will.* Always believe that I've believed this. Always.

And your flaws? Only one comes to mind with a piercing clarity that you will surely know the origins of: A need for adoration that can, among those you love, sometimes twist into viciousness.

I won't hear your voice for god knows how long. I'm so intensely sorry and I love you.

—Rahul

He was right, of course. We both were always right about each other. As journalists, and he a would-be novelist (aren't all former English literature Ph.D. students?), we both searched for the perfectly turned phrase to highlight each other's shortcomings. We wracked our Harvard-honed vocabularies to make certain our barbs were as accurate as possible. We were heat-seeking missiles in the damage department. And I was crueler than he was. Women always are—with their words.

And why was I so cruel? I was young, of course, and perhaps better schooled in reading text than I was in reading human emotion. But also, I think it was because Rahul was so close to everything I'd always imagined I'd find in a man, as well as eminently acceptable to my parents, being Indian and well educated—and yet he fell so infuriatingly short of the mark. He was not perfect.

So I never married, not Rahul nor anyone else. It's now a decade since I received that letter, and if I had turned back then, I could have been just like all the other women whose lives I envy so much. The ones who married in their mid- to late twenties, and have two or even three children, and have careers and are married to successful and intelligent men who can afford to whisk them away for the weekend to Paris. I could have had all those things—none of which I have now. I didn't know then that what I was choosing instead was a ceaseless merry-go-round of mostly empty dates, barring a couple of exceptions, for the next ten years. And perhaps with 20/20 hindsight, I would have chosen differently.

But then I think, would I really be with Rahul right now, ten years later? We'd tried for nearly five. Could we even have survived for another year—another month, another day—let alone the four decades that my parents have?

I don't know the answers to those questions, but I could not allow my father, whose only sister had divorced twice and who felt personally responsible for the twin divorces of his wife's sisters, to see his only daughter get divorced. I had to be sure it was right before I married—for my father's sake.

Chapter Nineteen

My parents are arriving in a couple of weeks, and once they do, it will be a flurry of meeting potential husbands as well as shopping for my cousin's wedding. I will be under pressure-cooker heat to get married; I need to blow off some steam before they descend on my life here in Delhi.

We are careering down that sleek highway to Noida, heading for Elevate, the club that had initiated me into Delhi nightlife all those months ago. I'm with the Moksha band members Nair and Amarjeet, and their sagelike manager Vijay. Vijay is driving Nair's new rust-orange Maruti Swift too fast. We are passing around a joint and pouring Old Monk rum into our plastic cups and taking shots.

I am quickly becoming a Delhiite, for I see nothing reckless about this behavior. I'm also noticing phrases slip off my tongue that are part of the youth argot here, like "Let's take his trip" or "We screwed his happiness," both sentiments that imply messing with someone.

Vijay is probably drunk or stoned or both, but has insisted on driving. Nobody protests, even though Amarjeet is perfectly sober and should be the one driving. Amarjeet is always sober. Amarjeet is an Amritdhari Sikh, which means that he took an oath at the Golden Temple in Amritsar—the one Indira Gandhi stormed in 1984 preceding her assassination by her Sikh body-guards—vowing to never smoke, drink, eat meat, or engage in physical relations with women before marriage.

Guess which of these has been the hardest for him to abide by? How'd you guess? Apparently, Amarjeet would really like a girlfriend. The others have told me that it's been nothing short of torturous for this twenty-eight-year-old man who's never been kissed to watch his bandmates go to bed with a steady stream of female groupies. Certainly being with a woman would contravene one of the strictures of his oath, but then we all tinker with our personal codes, making exceptions here and adjustments there, don't we? Like the vegetarian who has a hamburger once a year or the teetotaler who drinks champagne on New Year's Eve and at other celebrations.

We take the glass elevator up to the club. Tonight is Friday night, so the city's aficionados of electronic music have turned up for the British DJ. None of the guys I'm with are interested in dancing, so we buy drinks and stand around watching as strobe flights flicker across the bodies on the dance floor.

I turn to Amarjeet, who's drinking a Coke, and ask him about being an Amritdhari Sikh. He tells me that his mother wanted him to take the oath when he was fifteen years old because she didn't want him to turn out like his alcoholic father. He agreed to it and had not flouted any of the injunctions—so far.

"Is it difficult?" I ask, a vodka–lime soda in one hand and cigarette in the other.

"No, not really. I've never really been that tempted to smoke or drink, so it doesn't seem like I'm missing out on much," he says.

"But you're not really allowed to go out with girls either, right?" I dig deeper. A mischievous idea is forming in my head.

"I'm not supposed to," he says, but I notice a sheepish tone.

"So you've probably never kissed a girl then," I probe.

Amarjeet laughs but doesn't answer.

"You know, Amarjeet, I wouldn't, you know, mind helping you out in that direction," I say. "I would, in fact, really want to help you, love to, really."

Registering something like shock, Amarjeet gulps and his eyebrows shoot up. But his smile is now as wide as can be. "Anita, that's so kind of you. Thank you," he says.

We join the others, Amarjeet's mood having considerably improved in the last few minutes.

Later, when we are in the car again, I sit close to Amarjeet in the backseat. He puts his arm around me. It is a collegial feeling we are sharing, being in on a joke that no one else is part of. He offers to drive me home, asking Vijay to drop him off where his car is parked outside of Vijay's flat. The suggestion arouses little suspicion since Amarjeet is *never* on the make with a girl.

I see no harm in kissing Amarjeet and helping him to overcome that initial hurdle of being a newbie, before the removal of which we conjure the bogeyman of an imagined lifetime of celibacy. I recall feeling desperate for my first kiss—albeit at a much younger age—and wondering when my exile in never-been-kissed land would come to an end. However, as Amarjeet drives me back to my flat, I find myself feeling nervous and wonder why. I'm supposed to be the femme fatale, not the one with butterflies.

When we arrive back at my place, we go through the motions of pretending we don't know what's going to happen.

"So would you like to come up for a few minutes for, um, you don't drink, that's right, okay, so to listen to some music then?" I ask.

"Yeah, maybe I'll just come up for a few minutes," Amarjeet says.

When we get inside I ask Amarjeet what he'd like to listen to. He doesn't care. I play some bossa nova.

I want Amarjeet to feel comfortable, and I suggest we dance a bit to loosen up. He says he doesn't dance, but agrees to sway with me. We do a version of the dance I remember doing with boys in the seventh grade at after-school dances, the one where you both stand with your arms around each other and move back and forth arhythmically to the music. After a few minutes of this nonsense, I suggest we sit down on my low divan.

Although we both know what's supposed to happen, we are finding this more uncomfortable than we had imagined. I'm especially surprised at how nervous I feel about this. Am I really confident enough in my own kissing prowess to be inaugurating someone else into the ritual?

We're both looking at each other and then away, neither of us sure who should start. I put my hand on the side of his head, on his maroon turban. Kissing a man with a turban is awkward, it turns out. Instead of human hair or skin under my hand, I feel cloth. I smile and lean in. He does the same. Our lips meet, and his are soft, surprisingly soft. Unlike the two other members of Moksha I've kissed (I've also kissed TJ in a drunken fumble), Amarjeet doesn't thrust and jab with his tongue. He lolls his tongue around mine gently, invitingly. Amarjeet is a really good kisser, a natural.

"Your hair smells so nice, it's so soft," he says, learning at a startlingly rapid pace.

Amarjeet begins kissing my neck, simultaneously stroking my hair. I caress his turban. He wants to move lower with his mouth and his hands are traveling in wider circles over my body. I'm uncomfortable with going too far. I want to leave it at a kiss, to stay in this realm of innocence that I feel I've created. Kissing *is* innocent in a way, isn't it?

I move his hands back up to my face, to my hair, and murmur, "Let's just stick to kissing. You're a great kisser, you know. You're perfect."

"Thank you," he says, pleased.

Later, when I stand up to stretch and tell Amarjeet it's late, he gets the hint and leaves—with a spring in his step. As I watch him leave, I wonder if I've done the right thing by trespassing on his innocence. I hope that now that the door has opened to this new world, he will be able to harness the crescendo of its passions and emotions much better than I have over the years.

The next day, I receive a text message from him: "I'm still floating. Yesterday was nice and sweet. Thanks, *masterji*."

Maybe Amarjeet will be just fine.

Mustafa, the Sufi saint in Kashmir, and I were in sporadic touch in the fall, but communication has fallen off lately. I'm aware he will be coming to Delhi in mid-December. I'm still curious about how much my fantasy of him matches reality. Given my failure to find love of any duration since I've moved to the city, I revive my hopes of a romance with him as his visit nears. I haven't seen him since that day in his office in Srinagar, now nearly three years ago.

The week I recall he's supposed to arrive in Delhi I'm in my office, feeling shiftless and perusing the Indian newspapers for some story ideas. I have a separate room, which is basically one of the bedrooms of a flat on the top floor of a residential home. It's not the most kinetic of newsrooms; there are only two of us, me and the bureau chief, who is often away traveling in the region. We have some support staff in the form of Mr. Singh, our office manager; a driver; and the tea lady, Kamlesh, who seeks weekly updates on my marital prospects and who, like my maid, Chandra, gives unbidden sartorial advice—"Madam, that dress doesn't suit you. You looked better yesterday."

For his part, Mr. Singh could have been plucked from central casting. Having worked in several news bureaus in Asian cities, I recognize his prototype—a dithering old fellow who's been with the company for eons and appears to spend all day drinking tea and sifting through papers on his desk until you realize after two weeks he's a wizard of dark and mysterious resources and you'd be utterly lost without him.

On days like today, the ones in which I'm sorely lacking in motivation, I often wander out to the main area and make small talk with Mr. Singh and Kamlesh. But today I'm feeling a bit low and reclusive, perhaps Mustafa's failure to get in touch playing in the back of my mind. I've just turned from the newspapers to my e-mail when Mr. Singh pops his head into my office to tell me there is someone here to meet me. I walk out of my room into the foyer and am greeted by a young bespectacled man. He introduces himself as Mustafa. He's much smaller than I had expected—he'd been seated during our first encounter. Not quite the stately presence of my imagination, he is reed thin. It's amazing what whorls of fantasy our minds can weave given half a chance and a whiff of mystery.

He doesn't have much time, so we drive back to my flat for a cup of tea. Since I had spent so much time during the summer describing how I would furnish my flat, Mustafa is eager to see it. When we arrive, I make him tea, into which I crush ginger, clove, and cardamom, and we climb up to my roof terrace so that I can show off my view of the Mughal-era tombs. We stand there for forty-five minutes, maybe an hour, resting our teacups on the ledge and making small talk. We are formal, our conversation bearing no resemblance to our late-night rambles over the summer. He soon has to go, but we make plans to see each other later that evening. When I get back to the office, I'm too distracted to work, though a story has come in. I'm trying to make my deeply ingrained image of him jibe with the real person I've met.

I still have no sense of who he really is and am hoping a drink this evening will loosen us up and allow us to recover the intimacy of our previous talks. After all, I have harbored a years-long infatuation for him. I return home from work and wait for his phone call. It doesn't come until around ten o'clock, when I am tired and in no mood to step out. Also, I'm a bit baffled as to why he didn't call earlier. Mustafa apologizes profusely, saying he has been delayed in a meeting. He says tonight looks difficult but we should go out the following evening. I'm dismayed at his nonchalance, but then wave away the annoyance and begin to look forward to tomorrow.

At work, I'm unable to concentrate again, but this time out of anticipation for the evening rather than the general malaise afflicting me the day before. Perhaps I no longer expect us to embark on a romantic relationship, given that it hasn't happened already and I've been in the country for six months, but curiosity, not to mention hope, dies hard.

That evening, he calls and cancels and says we'll do it later in the week. The call never comes. It's clear that, as they say, he's just not that into me. I'm devastated. I take a sleeping pill and go to bed early that night.

I distract myself as much as I can from the abortive encounter with Mustafa with the pending arrival of my parents, who are still determined to marry me off in a wedding before they leave Delhi.

I have not heard from Mustafa for a couple of weeks, so on the morning of New Year's Eve, I call him to wish him a happy new year. It turns out he is still in town, working at his newspaper's Delhi bureau. I'm surprised and, of course, miffed that he has not bothered to get in touch. He is friendly enough, though, so I ask him if he'd like to accompany me to my friend Deepa's New Year's Eve party later that evening. He says he has to work—he's unfortunately been assigned to duty that night.

He says he is returning to Srinagar in the next couple of days, and I fear I will never get closer to him than that stilted moment on my terrace. I suggest dropping by his office to say hello—as well as good-bye—on my way to my party. He agrees and I feel my old hopes rekindle.

My parents have arrived in full bustle and my mother and I are to spend the day shopping for Aarti's wedding, which is the following week. She is my first cousin and eight years younger than me, but of course, like everyone else in my extended family, she is getting married before me. She is marrying a friend of her brother's who she's dated for a few years, but the official line is that it is an arranged marriage and they met through a newspaper advertisement, as per Indian society's perverse insistence on the façade of parents' involvement in their children's marriage.

If you are going to a wedding in India in which a family member is getting married, then shopping is not just an excursion, but a journey spread over days. There are at least two or three saris to select—one for the *sangeet* (music night), one for the wedding, and one for the cocktail reception. Or if any of the aforementioned are combined, then surely there will be a separate *mehndi* ceremony or *vidaai*, the official tearful farewell the bride's family gives her when they send her to her new home with her in-laws. I only ever wear saris at weddings, but when I do, I relish garbing my body with the six-foot ornate fabric. I'm in full agreement with the oft-made statement that the sari is the most exquisitely feminine, not to mention sensual, of apparel. In addition to saris, to be worn in the evening, there might be one or two *salwar kameezes* to buy for daytime wear when we're sitting around aimlessly drinking *chai*. Then jewelry to match each sari. Also bangles. Shoes. The list is endless.

My mother and I, neither of us much of a shopper, race through the process, collecting three saris at one go in South

Extension. We move on to a jeweler in the same area, and within ten minutes, without too much deliberation, select a gold necklace with rubies and matching earrings. We plop down a credit card for the one lakh rupees, or about $2,000—a paltry sum compared with what others blow on wedding jewelry—and quickly move on. My mother and I are demolishing world records for shopping for Indian weddings.

We move on to Khan Market for shoes, *bindis*, other odds and ends. It is our last stop before we will return home and I will get ready for my evening. I'm exhausted by the shopping. I'm also looking forward to going home, dressing up for the New Year's Eve party, and meeting Mustafa in his office.

My mother is haggling over some item or other in some store at Khan Market, while I step out to get some fresh air—which in Delhi is a bit difficult given the heavy pollution. It is dusk now, and the air is thick with particles. My eyes alight on a young woman. Her head is thrown back and she is laughing. My gaze lingers for a moment and then shifts to the man with whom she is walking. Mustafa enters my vision just as they pass me on the sidewalk. He walks past me a few steps, and then we both turn around in a classic double-take.

He introduces his companion to me. Her name is Nafisa. I don't know what to say.

"I thought you were working," I blurt out.

"Oh, I was. I managed to get out," he says.

"Oh, that's great. Well, happy new year," I say, and turn away. They are the last words we ever exchange. I choke on the dust in the air as they walk away.

I return home, feeling socked in the stomach. I am dejected and confused. It's true that Mustafa's presence in my life was more or less an apparition, a product of my overactive imagination. Of course, it's one of the most unbearable feelings in the

world to be betrayed. But it's also painful to not have the right to
feel betrayed, but to feel it acutely nonetheless. What I feel is a
phantom sensation, not quite the real emotion, but the black
shadow of it that follows us on the ground.

I put on my carefully selected New Year's Eve party outfit, no
longer quite as enthused as I was when I thought I would be
seeing Mustafa. I am wearing black fishnet stockings, a black
low-cut top, and knee-high black boots. Nobody wears "ethnic"
clothing to parties in the New India.

I arrive early at Deepa's house, despondent. My mood is
bleak, glum, far from festive. I plan to get drunk to numb the
phantom pain. I am one of the first to arrive, and I pour myself
an Old Monk with soda and sit down on the couch, where I'm
planning to remain planted the entire evening. I gulp down my
first and get up to make another. I'm not talking to anybody. By
my third drink, I'm managing to greet arriving party guests.

Amarjeet notices me sitting reclusively on the couch. Seeing
that I'm not my usual buoyant self, he sits beside me and asks me
what's wrong. I tell him the story, feeling the falsity of the note it
strikes even as I describe it. How can one feel betrayed by
someone one hardly even knew? Amarjeet puts his arm around
my shoulders to comfort me. What is there to say, ultimately, to
a phantom emotion? We sit huddled like this, close, our kiss
having initiated us into a familiar intimacy.

"Ten, nine, eight . . ." the countdown to the new year has
begun. I, for one, have no intention of moving joyfully into the
new year. What could it possibly hold? What could possibly
change my downcast mood?

"Three, two, one . . . Happy new year!" People are shaking
hands, hugging, kissing each other. They are now mingling and
wishing as many people as they can a happy new year. I remain

rooted to the couch, observing the holiday cheer around me. Amarjeet is no longer sitting next to me. I look up to see him with his bandmates, laughing and punching each other in the arm.

Deepa walks up to me and pulls me off the couch. "Happy new year, Deepa," I say.

She orders me to circulate. I begin walking around.

"Happy new year, Vijay."

"Happy new year, Nair."

"Happy new year, Vaibhav."

"Happy new year, Rohit."

"Happy new year, Chetan," I say to a young man who I've seen at parties before. Flamboyantly gay, Chetan is always seen meticulously attired in some colorful ensemble. Tonight, Chetan is wearing kohl around his eyes, which admittedly he does most of the time, and a red *churidar kurta*. Okay, maybe *some* people wear ethnic clothing to parties in the New India.

I'd seen Chetan enter the party earlier with a handsome young man wearing eyeliner. I take him to be one of Chetan's lovers, or at least a homosexual friend. Chetan's friend stops me as I'm doing my rounds.

"Are you Anita?" he asks.

"Yes," I reply.

"Anita Jain?" he asks.

"Yes."

"You have a Pankaj *chacha* and a Gautam *chacha*?"

"Yes," I say, thoroughly shocked that this young boy somehow knows my uncles.

"I know you. I'm Aristu. We've met. We went out to dinner and a movie with your cousin Aarti and your aunt Mira when you were visiting from New York a few years ago."

I peer at this young man and wrack my brain to remember him. And then I recall my visit to India three years ago—the one on which I had met Mustafa—and how on the last night before I was to fly back to New York from Delhi, I'd gone out to dinner with my cousin and aunt. Yes, I remember, Aarti had brought along a friend that evening, a young boy.

"Yes, yes. I totally remember now. We went to TGIF's in Vasant Vihar. And then we saw that dumb movie *The Hot Chick*," I say, the details of the evening drifting back to me.

"Do you remember how I was hitting on you?" Aristu asks.

"Oh, were you?" I say.

"I told you I was learning Spanish and said, '*Eres muy bonita*,'" he says.

"Oh, that's right! You were hitting on me, but you were, like, twelve years old, right?" I say, smiling.

"Well, I was twenty-two. I'm twenty-five now," he says.

I study him. He's a classically good-looking young man, his hair worn longish to his chin, similar to the style sported by Bollywood actor John Abraham. Then, I had been thirty, a journalist in New York, and he had seemed a mere kid. I'd also just returned the day before from Srinagar and was probably swept up in my new infatuation with Mustafa. Now, with that behind me, and after a few drinks, and it being a new year, well . . .

"Are you single?" Aristu asks.

"As a matter of fact, yes I am," I respond. "Are you?"

"Yes," he says.

And we embrace. I am no longer forlorn. I am now elated. My mood has U-turned, and I now look forward to a bright new year of new opportunities, new people, and new relationships.

Aristu and I parade through the party linked arm in arm, and I introduce him to everybody as an old friend. I think to myself, "Ah yes, maybe the man I was supposed to meet on that momentous and near accidental visit three years earlier was not Mustafa at all but this young man. Yes, yes. It's all making sense." Hope springs eternal.

The party concludes when it is nearly dawn, and Aristu offers to take me home. As he drives me home in the wee hours of the morning in his gold Honda City, he explains his connection to my extended family. Aristu's father had been a pilot in the Indian Air Force, as was the youngest of my father's six brothers, Pankaj. The two had been close friends before Aristu's father died in a plane crash in Kashmir when Aristu was seven years old.

His proximity to my extended family at once unsettles me and draws me closer to him. He's a known quantity. Also, I notice a feeling I've never had before—that of being part of a clan. I've spent little time over the years with these uncles and aunts and cousins, but an extended family is a tribe after all. Somewhere, our tribe's blood runs together.

We are now parked outside my house. My parents are in town, so there is no chance of him coming upstairs to my flat. We kiss each other in the car. I try to pull away, thinking I should go upstairs to sleep, but I can't seem to cut it short. I can see the next door neighbor's night *chowkidar*, or watchman, glaring at us through the dark, which is already beginning to soften around the edges.

In India, the car becomes a crucial site for physical intimacy, since few young people live on their own and society forbids public displays of affection apart from hand-holding—which is still frowned upon in smaller towns. Almost everybody I've met in India has made out or had sex in a car at one time or another.

Unfortunately, the car thus becomes not only a place for consensual physical relations, but also rapes. The newspapers report rapes in Delhi daily—Delhi is considered the rape capital of India—and a surprising number of them occur in moving vehicles. Two or three men might ask a woman they know if she wants a ride home, and she will be raped in the backseat, while the car keeps moving.

With parents in town, I now encounter the dilemma faced by most young people in Delhi. Where to fool around? I've never done this before in a car in the West, apart from some initial fondling in taxis on my way home with someone I'm dating and after a boozy evening. It's embarrassing and silly to be making out like a teenager in a car parked outside my own apartment, but Aristu and I can't stop. Are the windows really fogging up? I didn't know that literally happened; I'd always thought it was one of those metaphors.

Aristu's hands have reached under my top, and mine are on his groin. He wants to take it further, but since I don't want to risk the wrath of my parents or the opprobrium of the neighborhood, I tell him we need to stop. He promises to call the next day, and I creep into my home silently, hoping not to wake my parents. I go to sleep, marveling at the evening's sudden turn-on-a-dime series of events.

Chapter Twenty

I have exactly ninety minutes and need to have a dozen different treatments done at the beauty parlor before we're to go to Aarti's wedding, which is being held over three days at a farmhouse in Gurgaon. I have to get my underarms and legs waxed and my eyebrows and upper lip threaded—threading is the practice, pioneered in Indian beauty salons, of using twisted thread to entrap tiny hairs and yank them out. I have to get a pedicure and a manicure, and a facial as well. My hair needs to be oiled, washed, and straightened.

Perhaps more than in any other country, the beauty salon is a veritable institution in India, as crucial to the functioning of society as the legal system or the free press. The importance of feminine charm and beauty has been entrenched since ancient times, with most Hindu epics devoting at least a few stanzas to a woman's doelike eyes, her golden skin, or her silk-like hair. I would be willing to wager that the beauty salon was invented in India, the concept later branching out to the rest of the world, much in the same way as the game of chess and the number zero did millennia ago.

It is unheard of for an Indian woman of any means to have never stepped inside a salon. The first time I ever visited a beauty parlor was in fact on a visit to India when I was fourteen. Then, I got my beetled eyebrows and downy upper lip threaded for the first time. It was akin to a deforestation.

I decide to go to the Ambassador Hotel, where they have a no-nonsense parlor. I know if I go to one of the other ones, like the

Spa Zieta near my office, the attendants will be decorous about everything and it'll take much longer. I tell the manager at the Ambassador salon what I need to get done.

"And I only have an hour and a half," I say.

"*Ek ghante mai ho jayega.* We'll do it in an hour. Abhishek, Bhavna, Shilpa, Puneet, Shanti, *idhar ao!* Come here!"

Abhishek, Bhavna, Shilpa, Puneet, and Shanti leap on me. Abhishek starts oiling my hair. Bhavna sits on a low stool and begins waxing my legs. Shilpa threads my eyebrows. Puneet lifts my arms to wax my armpits. Shanti is starting a manicure on my free hand. Pulled in all directions, I feel like a basted turkey. No danger of decorousness here. I emerge from the beauty parlor waxed, threaded, moisturized, blow-dried—radiant!—in exactly one hour.

A man is bent over my hand, squeezing curlicues and spirals onto my palm from a tube of *mehndi*. After he is finished I will have to sit idly for at least an hour, maybe two, giving the henna sufficient time to stain my palms. Various aunties will come by with cotton swabs and dab my palms with a lime-and-sugar concoction, deepening the color. Female guests only get their palms done, but a bride's hands and feet are decorated nearly to her elbows and shins, heightening her feminine appeal on her wedding night.

Anticipating hours of boredom, I turn to Gita, a young cousin of Aarti's from her mother's side, who is also getting henna applied, and strike up a conversation. I have known her since she was a young child and now she is sixteen, the silky-haired, doe-eyed, golden-skinned daughter of a wealthy businessman.

"I hear you'd like your parents to send you to NYU for your undergraduate studies," I say.

"Yes, I'm trying to convince Mummy and Papa to let me go," she says in her singsongy Delhi accent.

"What would you like to study there?" I ask, feeling like an auntie.

"Hmm, well, I don't know. I just think it would be fun to go to New York City," she says brightly.

"Would you plan to stay in the U.S. then after your studies?"

"Oh no, not at all. If I stayed in the U.S., I'd have to work. Everyone in the U.S. has to work," Gita says, less brightly.

"So then what would you do after you get your degree?" I ask, slightly confused.

"Well, I would come back to India and get married and sit at home all day and spend my husband's money!" she announces.

I try to digest this. This young girl believes that after being in a place as exciting, cosmopolitan, and ferociously independent as New York City, she will come back and be happily married off to some businessman's chubby son. Maybe it's possible. Look at me; I left dazzling New York City to get married.

More likely, I think, is that Gita will go to NYU, and some white skinny emo guy who plays in a rock band and gets stoned a lot will find her terribly exotic and woo her. They will date for one, two, maybe all four years of college, and then she will find it hard to leave him, and she will finally tell her parents about Jake and ask them if she can marry him. They will say no, and she will be unhappily married off to some businessman's chubby son.

There's a lot of sitting around at this wedding. It reminds me of something, and I'm trying to recall what it is. The tea, coffee, and snacks available around the clock. The way everything revolves around meals. Bumping into the same familiar faces over the days. Ah yes, it's like a business convention, like those mutual-fund conventions I attended in various cities like Geneva or Barcelona when I was working as a reporter in London.

Here, at the wedding-cum-convention, my identity has been neatly elided with my father's. No longer am I Anita, but Naresh *ki beti*, Naresh's daughter. I am also Naresh *ki beti jiski shaadi abhi nahin hui*—Naresh's daughter who is still unmarried.

Whenever I pass a familiar-looking auntie and uncle, in accordance with what is expected by elders when I see them, I smile and chirp, "*Namaste*, Auntie. *Namaste*, Uncle."

They stop and say, "*Tum Naresh ki beti ho, na?* You are Naresh's daughter, right?"

"Yes, Auntie. How are you and Uncle?"

"Good, good. You are still looking?"

"Yes, I'm still looking. *Abhi tak koi nahin mila.* I haven't found anyone yet."

"We will come to your *shaadi* next! Ha ha!"

"Yes, Auntie. Yes, Uncle."

During the *uptan puja*, when the bride's female relatives gather to apply a paste of turmeric, mustard oil, and gram flour all over the bride's body, the older female relative conducting the ceremony singles me out. She calls me to come to the center of the circle and she begins to smear my palms with various unguents—the turmeric paste, yogurt, sandalwood paste. She places marigolds in my palms, folds my fingers over them and utters various incantations. When she's finished, I return to my seat. I am the only one who receives this special treatment, being the only female of marriageable age who is as yet unattached.

Despite trying to deflect attention from myself, I have for inexplicable reasons agreed to perform a dance tonight onstage at the *sangeet*, to "Sajna Ve Sajna" from the movie *Chameli*, the one in which Rahul Bose falls in love with the prostitute played by Kareena Kapoor. The reason I'm doing it solo is that everyone else has already formed groups and has been practicing their number for weeks. I have "learned" my dance in a mere few hours from the dance trainers on-site hired by my uncle.

At my brother's wedding in Sacramento ten years ago, I did a solo dance to "Mere Khwabon Mein" from the film *Dilwane Dulhaniya Le Jayenge*. It had been a hit, and many of the guests had come and twirled cash around my head, as is the custom, before dropping it at my feet. I'd made out like a bandit that night, scooping up my few hundred dollars from the floor. Then, too, I'd only had a day or two to practice, or maybe it was three. In any case, I'm sure I'll be just fine here at Aarti's wedding.

Certainly weddings have always been grand occasions in India, but lately they have morphed into spectacles of the first order, as witnessed in the 2006 extravaganza thrown by New York hotelier Vikram Chatwal and his bride—guests included Naomi Campbell and Bill Clinton. Weddings being proportionate to the bride's family's wherewithal, my uncle, perhaps the only wealthy one in my immediate family, has arranged to serve a hundred separate dishes tonight at the wedding reception. Every time I run into him, Aarti's father butonholes me to ask what I think of the wedding. I tell him each time that it's wonderful, "*Haan chachaji, shaadi bahut acchi hai.*"

These days, the *sangeet* often immediately precedes the wedding dinner or reception, an instance of immigrant practice boomeranging back to the mainland. According to tradition in India, the bride and groom hold separate *sangeet* ceremonies for their own largely female relatives and friends. The women from each side gather to play the harmonium and sing, and perhaps the younger girls dance. This practice of largely female and separate *sangeet* ceremonies fell by the wayside in Indian weddings staged in the West, where time to organize and attend events was limited. Weddings that would normally extend over four or five days have to be crammed into one or two. So, in the global Indian culture, the *sangeet* is no longer a private ceremony, but one held for guests from both sides and in which male and female relatives both participate.

My dance instructor is a dark young man with acid-washed jeans and greasy hair. He's twenty-one or twenty-two years old, and he sure can move. When I try to mimic the way his hips sway and his legs shake, my moves are all wrong and I can never remember the next sequence. I don't have much time and I'm trying to learn in a sari, which I've hitched up between my legs. Big mistake. Everyone else is still wearing jeans and T-shirts, planning to change later tonight. Why did I agree to this again?

That evening, when my song comes on, I scurry onto the stage and find myself in a blinding spotlight. I perform the first eight beats of the song as taught, and then stop for a few long seconds on stage, doing nothing, blinking dumbly at the audience, a deer in headlights. I have blanked out in front of hundreds of guests. Then I make a dash offstage. My song continues for the longest ten seconds of my life before being mercifully turned off. Aarti's mother doesn't compliment me on my dance as I brush past her, the way she has with all her other nieces. Needless to say, no one showers me with money. But my ever loving and doting parents, sitting in the front row, are awestruck by my performance.

"You were the star of the evening," my father says, beaming.

"Anita, you looked so beautiful, more than any other girl," my mother says, oblivious to my humiliation. I shake my head and walk away.

I'm beginning to wonder if my parents' constant fawning has something to do with why I'm not married. I'm sure all the other guests are nudging each other and saying, "*Woh Naresh ki beti thi. Haan, jiski shaadi abhi nahin hui. Bechari ko naachana bhi nahin ata hai.* That was Naresh's daughter. The unmarried one. The poor girl, she can't even dance."

My sari is now falling off. Great. The entire wedding party thinks I'm some unmarriageable spinster who also can't dance, and I'm stepping all over my sari as it slides off my body. Although I know I shouldn't care what all these mostly anonymous aunties and uncles think of me, I do. Head bowed, I walk out of the outdoor tent to the hall where the *mandap* for the solemn wedding ceremony has been set up. It's empty, and the marble tiles and high ceiling make it especially chilly. It's also one of the coldest nights of the year. I'm freezing, but I don't care. I want to be alone. I take one of the long strands of marigolds that adorn the hall's pillars and bring it up to my cheek. It is unexpectedly cool to the touch and surprisingly heavy to lift. It feels oddly reassuring. There's nothing like a wedding to make one feel like getting married.

Chapter Twenty-one

One of the things my father loves to say is *"India hamesha hi India rahega. Kabhi change nahin ho sakta hai*. India will always be India forever. It can never change."

Perhaps on this trip he will be impressed by the wireless broadband I have installed at home or notice all the Hondas, Toyotas, Hyundais, and Fords on the road. I am pleased when he registers some change from the country he left, such as when he comments on how young women now wear jeans and Western-style tops and not *salwar kameezes*. "They are wearing Amrikan clothes," he comments approvingly.

He also notices how these young women are holding the hands of their male companions as they walk down the street, another thing he never saw back in his days. "Once when I held your mother's hand on the street, everybody started shouting and catcalling," he tells me, the memory of his roguish behavior causing him to chuckle.

And of course, he is horrified—dumbstruck!—by the rise in prices. Despite possessing an academic grasp of the concept of inflation, my father never expected prices in India to change—ever. He still tries to get my regular taxi driver to drive us around Delhi all day long for fifty rupees, or just slightly over a dollar.

When I hand over the twenty dollars the taxi driver has asked for, my father glares at me. "The problem with you, Anita, is that you have no conception of the money. *Mein garib baap ka beta hoon, tum aamir baap ki beti ho.* I am the son of a poor man, but you are the daughter of a rich man. Tell me, do you even know where the money comes from?" he asks, disgustedly.

"Of course, Papa, it grows on the money plant that I have upstairs," I say gleefully, eyeing him for a reaction. I can tell my father is struggling to suppress laughter—it's one of his trademark gestures when someone in our family teases him—but on principle, he can't bring himself to laugh outright about money, to make a joke of something so sacrosanct.

"Anyway, prices have gone up, but besides that, I see no difference in this country," he says, shaking his head back and forth dismissively, completely unmoved. I live in India now and have seen firsthand the massive changes wrought by the booming economy. My father has not lived in the country for more than three decades. What could he know?

My parents are in India, as they have emphasized, for one reason and one reason only—to find me a husband. They do not want to waste too much time visiting my relatives, so we decide to dispense with both of their hometowns in exactly one day each. My mother's hometown, Ghaziabad, is a mere thirty or forty minutes from Delhi, and my father hails from Meerut, ninety minutes away.

Two days before we leave for Meerut, a rough-hewn town in western Uttar Pradesh where men keep a tight rein on their women and honor killings are not unheard of, my father's hometown is catapulted into the national news. In an incident reported on the front page of the newspapers all over the country, police in a planned operation pounced upon several couples, some of whom were married, sitting together in a park. Outraged at their flagrant immodesty, police officers used sticks to beat the couples, who were apparently doing nothing more salacious than resting their hands in the laps of their companions. The case sparked outrage over police brutality and the role of the state in regulating society's mores.

Reading the papers, watching the television news bulletins, my father is triumphant: "*India kabhi change nahin ho sakta hai. India can never change.*" I steam at his "I told you so" attitude, but quietly concede the point, even as I think about the young couples groping each other in all the city's nightclubs.

One of my mother's sisters lives in Meerut. This aunt has three daughters. The first one they named Asha, which means "hope." Perhaps they would be blessed with a son next. The second one they called Nisha, or "night," in a reference to what had befallen them. When the third daughter arrived, they'd had enough. They named her Kshama, which translates into "forgiveness." They asked god to pardon them, and he did. Two sons followed.

Nisha and Kshama are Irish twins, only ten months apart, and Nisha is my age. I am not close to any of my three dozen first cousins living in India and the U.S., but I suspect if I had grown up in India, these two, being of the same age and sex, would have been like sisters to me. I can only recall meeting Nisha and Kshama once before, when I was eighteen, that fateful summer after my first year of college. We had stayed up all night during my visit, comparing notes and taking the measure of the vast chasm between our lives. My mother tells me both girls married when they were twenty-one or twenty-two and have two children each. Both live with their in-laws, Nisha in Meerut and Kshama in the nearby and equally unprogressive town of Muzaffarnagar.

Now I am preparing to see them again after all these years. Nisha and Kshama have convinced their mothers-in-law to let them leave their houses to meet me at their mother's home. My mother, father, and I arrive at my aunt's modest home in Meerut bearing gifts. Next to my aunt's home is the kiosk her husband and sons run from which they sell cigarettes, cold drinks, and mobile phone cards.

My mother enters the dimly lit home first and embraces her younger sister. Despite being two years younger, my mother's sister has aged far more dramatically. Though the resemblance is striking, my aunt looks the better part of a decade older than my mother. My aunt's face is lined, haggard, and her body is shrunken from osteoporosis. My mother is fresh-faced and robust, America-large and estrogen-injected. Tears well up in both their eyes as they clasp each other. I rarely see my mother affected, moved like this; grand sweeps of emotion I have always left to my father.

My father and I feel slightly out of place, and we look around the room uncertainly. This is not about us. It is about a part of my mother's life neither of us can claim or even know much about, my mother being far more reticent about her past than my father. My uncle is also milling about, folding his hands in *namaste* and man-hugging my father. He offers his extended hand to me. Greeting him gives my father and I something to do. We sit down on the couch tentatively, waiting for my mother to finish. Finally, when she is done conferring with her sister, she joins us, and my aunt grabs me from the couch and embraces me. I stand only five feet one inch tall, but I tower over my aunt. I have never held such a tiny adult before.

I look around the home, at the discolored cement walls, the tacky trinkets placed here and there, the small dining table with the clear plastic tablecloth. My aunt disappears to the kitchen, where my cousins Nisha and Kshama are preparing dinner. Soon, my two cousins emerge with trays of *namkeen* and steaming chai.

I am not prepared for their appearance. These two forest nymphs, this duo of light-footed sylphs, these wasp-waisted houris, swish into the room soundlessly, gliding across the floor. Both are wearing blue saris, with a cardigan on top to protect against the chill. Their thick hair is plaited, and they are bedecked with gold everywhere—around their necks, on their forearms, on their fingers, dangling from their ears. Everything is perfectly in place. Their elegance and grace astounds and chastens me. They bestow radiant smiles on me. Then I notice the children nipping at their knees. It is the reverse of my mother and my aunt. I, in my jeans and turtleneck sweater, am the one who is small, shrunken.

My father too is visibly impressed with his nieces. He intones respectfully to my uncle, "You have beautiful daughters." My uncle has heard this before. He knows he is a lucky man. It was not difficult to marry off his comely daughters.

Nisha and Kshama return to the kitchen to finish cooking dinner. And I am left on the couch with my parents. I join my cousins in the kitchen but feel awkward as they expertly roll out and deep-fry *pooris*, turning them over as they inflate in the *khadai*. They are busy and it's difficult to break into an easy rhythm of conversation, our lives so inscrutable to one another.

I ask to use the toilet, and Nisha guides me to the small room used for bathing. Here, there is a bucket and mug, a sink, and a drain in the ground. I'm confused. I tell her in Hindi, "I have to pee." She has not misunderstood. I am meant to urinate on the ground, into the drain.

Later, after dinner, I join Nisha and Kshama in the bedroom in the back of the home. Here, away from our parents and the kitchen, we recover some of the camaraderie we shared all those years ago. While their small children caper about the room, with frequent nuzzling breaks from their mothers, we shoot questions at each other. My cousins are nothing like I expected. They are not shy, demure, squeaking half-answers about their lives with a downcast gaze. They look me in the eyes, give me direct and revealing replies, and break into laughter whenever I express horror at their hidebound lives. They are the most high-spirited and charming women I've met since I've come to India.

They tell me what it is like being a *bahu*, a daughter-in-law, in a traditional Jain home in a place like Meerut or Muzaffarnagar. They must seek permission for everything they do from their mother-in-law. When Nisha wanted to take the bangles off of her right arm, so that she could wear a watch, she asked her mother-in-law for consent. They rarely leave the home. They spend all day cooking, cleaning, looking after their children or their husbands. They tell me how difficult the *bahu*'s first year of marriage is, how everyone in her new home—from her husband to her husband's brother to her husband's brother's wife—will eye her every move, scanning for signs of insolence, hesitation, or resistance.

Our conversation eventually even unlocks the mystery of the missing toilet. Why was I taken to the drain to pee? You see, Kshama explains, they are so accustomed to using the drain to pee that they forget others might want to use the toilet. In their in-laws' home, my cousins can only use the drain because if they head for the toilet during the day, their mothers-in-law assume they are defecating, which they are supposed to do along with their morning ablutions before they bathe and dress for the day. If for some reason there is midday defecation, then, well, they will have to bathe again and put on an entire fresh change of clothing. I ask if this was expected of them in their parents' home growing up. They laugh and say, "God, no!"

I shudder and think of my free-for-all anything-goes American-ness, emptying my bowels at whatever time of day I see fit, sometimes even several times a day. Would I be able to survive their lives? I doubt it, but if their demeanors are any indication, they don't seem dismayed by their fate.

I venture, "Are you happy with your lives? Would you want something to be different?"

Nisha pipes up, "Well, I did want to go for more studies, but Papa wanted me to get married. It's okay, though, I don't mind."

"And your mothers-in-law and husbands?" I say vaguely, throwing out a bait for them to complain, to see if they bite.

"My mother-in-law loves me! I'm her favorite," Kshama giggles.

"I wish I saw more of my husband, but he works so much. He's very nice to me," Nisha says.

They are equally perplexed by my life. I ham it up, telling them I live alone—all alone!—in a three-bedroom flat in Delhi, where I stay out all hours most nights, drinking and smoking in bars with men. They shriek with laughter. They don't look down on me. They are my cousins. I tell them when they come to Delhi to see me, I will dress them in jeans and sexy tops with plunging necklines and take them to a bar and get them drunk. We all know full well they will never make it.

Then there is Ghaziabad, the town neighboring Delhi in which my mother grew up, a place I had always thought of as the armpit of the universe—congested and provincial, but not even deep enough into the hinterland to justify it being so. Now, I am told that *Newsweek* magazine has ranked it among the world's ten most dynamic cities, alongside Las Vegas, London, Moscow, and Munich.

One of the most heavily industrialized towns in India, Ghaziabad is also laying claim to being the country's fastest-growing city. With land prices in Noida and Gurgaon reaching unaffordable levels, property developers have recently set their sights on poky Ghaziabad to erect luxury high-rise buildings and strip malls.

Ghaziabad? Among the many less-than-exalted memories I have of the place is a visit when I was fourteen years old. Next to my aunt's home was a vast dustbowl of an empty lot, which we would cross—a short five-minute walk—to get to my mother's childhood home, now occupied by her youngest brother. A nomadic community of migrant workers had set up tents in this vacant expanse where their dusty children, with shirts but no bottoms and uncombed bronze-colored hair, wandered around, dazed. Seeing those people marked the beginning of my ethnic or racial consciousness, in a way, because I recall thinking to myself at the time, "These people here are closer to me in blood and spirit than my best friends Jennifer and Rachel and Stacy."

Back then, none of my relatives had an indoor bathroom that I found usable, only smelly outhouses. That summer, I stopped defecating nearly entirely. I would wait for a week or ten days, until it was absolutely necessary, and then my father would take me out to the neighboring field when night had fallen and wait fifty yards away while I answered nature's call in the great outdoors.

I'm eager to see this new rapidly developing Ghaziabad I have only heard about from the newspapers. Although it is only a short drive from Delhi, I have waited for my parents to make the visit. We arrive in Ghaziabad in a taxi from Delhi in less than an hour, pulling up outside the house in which my mother was raised.

My cousin Gaurav is expecting us, waiting in the shop he runs right outside the house. It is the same government-licensed sugar wholesale business my grandfather, my mother's father, operated more than half a century ago. Gaurav emerges with a wide grin, revealing teeth thoroughly stained brown by years of *paan* chewing. He is wearing a tattered and faded synthetic button-down shirt and trousers, the uniform of the small Indian town.

I look around for evidence of *Newsweek*'s dynamic Ghaziabad. My mother's home is a fossil, and there is no discernible change in its immediate environs. The adjacent empty lot is still there, although it is no longer home to migrants.

My mother's brother and his wife greet us warmly, and we are introduced to the young woman Gaurav married a couple of years ago, the *bahu*. There are no couches to sit on in their tiny living room, only the jute cots topped with bedding used for sleeping at night. Gaurav's wife, only twenty-one or twenty-two, has recently given birth and has filled out like the timeless women of Indian townships. She hardly looks like the young lithe slips her age I see in Delhi. She tells me she saw Gaurav once for five minutes a few months before they married. She did not exchange any words with him.

I look around for a morsel, a scrap, of modernity here, forty-five minutes from my flat in Delhi. Then Gaurav takes me to his computer room. There, in this tiny room, is the biggest computer I have ever seen. He lovingly removes the plastic cover from the terminal and boots up the computer. It whirrs and clunks, and three or four minutes go by before light flickers on the screen. He is so proud of his dinosaur machine that I am afraid to say anything. I tell him it is a lovely computer. "Very nice," I say. "*Bahut accha hai.*" He grins his *paan*-stained smile at me.

As much as I resist the notion, my father isn't wrong in his dead certainty that India hasn't changed a jot since he left more than three decades ago. His world was Meerut and Ghaziabad, and it's true, that those cities, at least the parts I've seen, haven't registered India's leap toward modernity the way Delhi has. And to Papa, India is Meerut and Ghaziabad, not Delhi.

Later, during the short drive back from Ghaziabad, I notice the touted modern flats and shopping complexes here and there, which become more concentrated as we near Delhi. Clearly, *Newsweek*'s journalists didn't get as far as my mother's childhood home.

Chapter Twenty-two

My father is on a mission, and the first thing he does when he arrives in Delhi is take out an ad for me in the *Times of India* matrimonial pages, which appear on Sunday. Not the ads in microscopic print that line the section's columns, though. No, he takes out one of the large ones that dominate a corner of a page, the one that has a border separating it from the other listings. Despite large-scale migration to the Internet, newspaper matrimonials are still the mainstay of Indian arranged marriages.

The "*bordervala*" ad reads, "U.S.-educated Jain girl, thirty-three years old, Harvard graduate and working for international newspaper looking for broad-minded groom."

Clearly, my dad thinks that stating my particulars will bring only the finest candidates and that he doesn't need to specify what we're looking for in a groom. I'm just hoping the print matrimonials will bring a more suitable match than I've found on the Internet.

Papa sits back and waits for the deluge of replies that will certainly flood in, demanding to wed his precious, beautiful, brilliant daughter, no matter that she is a decade beyond prime marriageable age. He's provided his e-mail address in the ad and eagerly checks it every morning following the Sunday that it first runs. There are no replies in his inbox on Monday. Nor Tuesday. On Wednesday, he gets one or two. Thursday, another two or three trickle in.

My father is thoroughly confused. Perhaps his e-mail account isn't working correctly? Something must be wrong. And he's none too satisfied with the quality of the responses either. No high-powered U.S.-returned business executives. No doctors either—his fascination with doctors persists despite years of trying to convince him I have no interest in them. The fathers of a couple of middling IT engineers and bank workers have written to him on behalf of their sons.

Desperate to get the show on the road, to whittle down the huge pool of candidates to one upstanding, fine individual, he invites a fellow who's answered the ad over to my flat. His name is Lalit, and he works as a clerk at a shipping company. Lalit earns 8,000 rupees, less than $200, a month. He's never been to my neighborhood before. When he arrives, he greets my parents first, "*Namaste*, Auntie. *Namaste*, Uncle." He asks them how they are as he's sitting down at my dining table, and once he's seated, he surveys the place, clearly thrown by the style in which I live alone. Finally, he turns to me and says, "Hello"—I'm the last thing he notices.

My father busies himself in the kitchen, preparing tea. He comes out with four cups, one each for my mother, me, Lalit, and himself. It is not an entirely unstudied gesture. My father is showing this young man what he expects of him if he is to be my husband. My father, the unlearned feminist, knows what even the most seemingly liberated Western men do not. It is this: If masculinity is synonymous with a type of self-sufficiency or not asking for help, it is the most unmanly, the most weak-willed, the most *feminine* act of all to be served, to expect a woman to wait on you. And conversely, to spring from a table to clear away or wash dishes, this is what the honorable, brave, secure man does.

For added effect, later in the conversation, I ask my father to get me a glass of water. Papa rises from his seat dutifully and scurries to the kitchen, returning with the water. (My father and I will later giggle at our ingenious dramatics.)

Lalit continues his conversation with my father and mother, stealing glances over at me only occasionally. He tells us he lives with his parents, and the "girl"—meaning his future wife—would be expected to live with them. My father, who is now quite enjoying shocking the poor fellow, butts in, "Well, all that is fine, but my daughter has lived alone for ten years. She has lived in Mexico City, London, Singapore, New York. She may find it difficult to adjust to living with your parents. And she doesn't do housework."

Searching for the appropriate reply, Lalit says, "*Theek hai.* Others in the house are there. My brother's wife is there. A servant is there."

The suitor asks my father about his work in the U.S., but he has yet to pose a question to me. He has not even made direct eye contact with me. My father says, "Why don't you talk to the girl?"

Lalit turns to me and says, "How are you?"

"I'm good," I say, embarrassed myself by the entirely novel situation of meeting a suitor with my parents. Even though I don't view Lalit as a serious prospect, the situation has undone me. I begin to understand why Indian maidens usually cast their eyes downward and don't say a word at these marital introductions. Of course, prospective wives don't speak in these introductions because they might be considered lippy by the boy's parents, but also I feel infantilized in my parents' presence. Now I identify with the mind-set of a young woman in this situation: Mummy and Papa are taking care of it, like they would buying a home, a car, or a piece of furniture. What need is there for me to be here?

After Lalit and I converse politely, if awkwardly, for a few minutes, my father interjects once more: "Well, thanks for coming. Think it over. If you like my daughter, give her a call. She's the boss."

We all heave a sigh of relief after Lalit leaves, all knowing of course that he was far from suitable. "He didn't know what hit him," my father says, shaking his head and laughing.

Later that evening, we have another assignation, this one with a far more promising candidate. He is a corporate lawyer at one of India's top law firms, Luthra & Luthra, and we are to meet him at the coffee shop at the Oberoi hotel.

Vinod is already there when we arrive. He greets my parents respectfully and takes a long look at me, sizing me up, as we sit down. Unlike Lalit, he addresses me first: "You know, there's no reason for you to be in India. You can earn thirty to forty times more in the U.S."

I'm taken aback. This is the most unexpected opening line I've heard in my life. I am quite speechless. Finally, I say, "There are other reasons that I've chosen to be here. It's not just financial."

I'm wondering if this man thinks I'm so dim-witted or out-of-touch that I don't realize the U.S. is a first-world country and India a third-world one. Anyway, I suspect the wage differential between the U.S. and India is hardly that large.

Getting angry, I say, "You don't earn thirty to forty times more in the U.S., unless you are comparing a corporate lawyer there to a taxi driver here. I would suspect the differential from a corporate lawyer there to one here is three to four."

Vinod listens but is unmoved. "Well, in the U.S., you can make a lot of money. I wish I'd gone earlier, but now it's too late. I would have to start out at the bottom if I went there. I'm stuck in India, but I make good money for here."

Sensing a recurring theme in his conversation, I try to suggest that there are other guiding motives in life apart from money. "I really like it here in India. It's so exciting and interesting. It's in a state of flux."

He nods but doesn't say anything.

My father is also money obsessed, and in classic "it takes one to know one" fashion, Dad immediately recognizes a kindred spirit. Yet the trait is hardly desirable in a son-in-law. My father's fixation on lucre is different, derived from years of privation in his childhood and, later, trying to make ends meet for his family in an unfamiliar country. Money-mindedness in a young, wealthy man, a potential husband to his daughter, is despicable in my father's eyes. It reveals the man to be chintzy, utterly lacking in a generous spirit.

My father wants to see if there is more to the fellow. He believes only one question is required to take the measure of a man. Leaning in, my father carefully chooses his words in Hindi: "If my daughter Anita is sick and cannot cook, who would cook dinner?"

Waving his hand as if shooing away a fly, Vinod answers, "I have a maid."

Knowing how decisive the question is, Papa gives the fellow another chance. "The maid is sick. Who cooks?"

"I have two maids," he says, notching up his attitude of arrogant dismissiveness.

"Your other maid is sick too. Who cooks?" my father says, relentlessly.

"I'd hire a third," Vinod says, unblinkingly.

Neither is backing down. It is a face-off. "Forget the bloody maids! What do you do?" Papa bellows at Vinod.

With little deference to his prospective father-in-law, Vinod grunts, "What, these hotels and restaurants are going to shut down all at once?"

My father has gotten his answer, and the corporate lawyer drives us home in his white Mercedes. I'm beginning to feel sorry for Papa. It is dawning on him that finding a "broad-minded" groom in a few weeks may be harder than he'd assumed.

To cheer him up, I offer to meet more suitors—as many as we can. In the same way that dating many men makes one feel that one is getting out there, *doing something* about being single, meeting multiple suitors makes Dad feel he is *doing something* about getting his daughter married.

A few days later, my mother, father, and I meet a round-faced, seriously chubby guy with ringlets and his father at the Ashoka hotel, my former haunt of ten years earlier.

My father speaks with his father. And I thought it was infantilizing to meet a suitor with my parents. Now the boy and I are both here with parents. We are doubly infantilized. We are mute, like toddlers at a playdate.

Looking at me, the boy's father says kindly and with a smile, "We would treat her like our own daughter. *Bilkul beti ki tarah.*"

I shift uncomfortably in my seat. Who says I want to marry his fat Little Lord Fauntleroy son? The boy's father suggests to his son and me that we sit apart and get to know each other. It is more like giving us permission, as if we are doing something racy, modern.

We walk to a nearby table and sit across from each other. I have nothing to say to this guy. I wish Papa were here.

Papa tries to cram in one more suitor the night he and my mother leave Delhi, mere hours before their flight is scheduled to depart. We have arranged for a Gurgaon-based software engineer to come over to the house after I return from work.

At the appointed time, two young men arrive. We are confused, but one of the two quickly jumps in and explains, "This here is my cousin, Ashish. He's the boy. I am only here to provide company and any assistance. My name is Ranvir," he says with a smile and a flourish.

Ranvir and Ashish sit down in chairs facing the couch where I am seated. My father joins me, but he is distracted by his coming flight, and as well—dare I say it?—he has become disheartened by the process. Papa's finally lost his steam.

It doesn't really matter, because Ranvir, a handsome, quick-talking man, carries the conversation for all of us. Turns out Ranvir is a civil lawyer, frequently preparing cases for the Supreme Court. Apparently, he's from Bihar and has been in Delhi since law school. Ranvir asks about my job as a journalist and enthusiastically discusses the latest political developments. Looking at my book-shelf, he notices *Shantaram*, the opus about the Australian prison escapee who flees to Bombay, where he joins the underworld mafia, and we begin a lively conversation about it.

I sense Ranvir would happily cook dinner and make *chai*, but he is only the chaperone. Unfortunately, Ashish, my intended, has not said a word since he walked in the door. Looks like my parents will be flying out of Delhi tonight groomless.

After another twenty minutes, I usher the men out, since on this final night, I'm taking my parents out to dinner. After the men leave, I help my parents finish packing and call a taxi for dinner. Papa doesn't say anything about this last introduction and is silent on the way to the restaurant, a new place called Veda in Connaught Place opened by a New York–based chef.

At dinner, as we push our nouvelle cuisine around on our plates, my parents speak about details pertaining to their im-minent departure and we avoid the topic of marriage. I feel I have disappointed them and think I should say something.

"Papa, Mummy, I want to get married too, you know, just as much as you want me to. It's just that I haven't found the right person," I say.

"I know, *beta*. There is a time for everything. *Jab tumhara time ayega, ladka bhi mil jayega*. A boy will come when it's your time to find him," my mother says, putting her faith in god like she always does.

"Don't worry, *beti*. We love you anyway, whatever you've become," Papa says.

"Er, thanks, Papa."

Chapter Twenty-three

It's been a few days since my parents left and I've been feeling glum, largely because things with Aristu, the handsome young boy I met on New Year's Eve, or was reintroduced to, are cracking up, or rather they never really got started.

Lately I've been finding it hard to get started in the morning and have been arriving at the office later and later each day. I spend the morning lingering over my breakfast, which Chandra delivers to me in bed, and aimlessly surfing the Internet, both the computer and my eggs resting on a raised wooden tray I have purchased for precisely this use.

Chandra hands me breakfast and *chai*, but I notice she's standing by the door, watching me. I assume she's about to ask for cash and I prepare for my answer. One has to draw a fine line in these matters; I can't live without her, but I also don't want to be taken advantage of. She already views me as the softest touch of all the families she works for, coming to me first when she wants extra money. I decide if she asks for more than five-hundred rupees, I will deduct it from her salary next month.

I'm readying my firm employer tone when Chandra says, "Madam, can I ask you a question?"

"Yes, of course, Chandra."

"Madam, *aap ko shaadi karne chahiye*. You should get married. *Mein to hoon tumhare sath, lekin ek aadmi bhi hona chahiye ghar mein.* I'm here for you, of course, but there should be a man in the house as well," she says.

"Yes, I know, Chandra. I . . . I'm looking," I tell her, feeling ashamed that even my maid is highlighting my singledom.

She doesn't leave. "Madam, *ek aur cheez bolun?* Can I say something else?"

"*Haan, bolo,*" I say, preparing again for the cash request.

"Your mother, well, your mother is very concerned that you get married," she says.

Tell me something I don't know. "Yes, I know that," I say.

Chandra goes on, "She loves you very much. More than your papa even."

I find this hard to believe, but continue to listen.

"*Jab tumhari mummy mere sath baat kar rahi thi, rone lag gayi.* When your mother was talking to me, she started to cry. She said, 'When I die, who will look after my daughter?' *Bahut dukhi thi.* Your mother was very upset. I didn't know whether to tell you or not."

"No, it's fine, Chandra. Thank you for telling me," I say.

My father's gung-ho insistence on marriage is one thing, but my mother crying on my maid's shoulder is quite another. My mood becomes even bleaker and I set aside my breakfast tray and go back to sleep.

My "relationship" with Aristu, which started with so much fanfare on New Year's Eve, is over by Valentine's Day. He is golden limbed, with a smooth, sturdy body and athletic build. I'm pockmarked with desire, physically drawn to him in a way I haven't been to a man in a long time. I do not usually date very good-looking men, because I suspect they are out of my reach, but also on general principle. Good-looking men are rarely deft conversationalists or in possession of plumbable depths. I suppose I impart too much significance to Aristu's connection to my family, and this, combined with his preternatural attractiveness, make me giddy with infatuation. It will take me a few months and 20/20 hindsight to recognize Aristu is an Adonis-like cipher, a gorgeous zero.

At the time he tells me he is confused about entering a relationship, and I use his explanation to justify his cruel behavior, which includes constantly hanging up the phone on me and rejecting outright my desperate entreaties to meet and discuss our "issues." I will later realize that it is the other way around, not his confusion that causes him to be cruel but his innate cruelty that undergirds his confusion.

The aftermath of our fledgling romance lasts two or three months, marked by phone conversations that proceed like this: "Hi, Aristu, listen, don't hang up, I just wanted to talk, please don't hang . . . shit, you hung up." There's perhaps nothing more woefully pathetic than an older worldly-wise woman groveling at the feet of a surly and inarticulate boy nearly a decade her junior. I have dated far more sophisticated, intelligent, and powerful men, but I am stuck on this hot-tempered kid, like an older gay man infatuated with a young, mean hustler.

It has become clear to me that I suffer from a deep-rooted high-mindedness when it comes to romantic love. I can be practical, yes, and when it comes to financial matters, I have never been late when paying my bills and have managed to hold down jobs in several leading international cities that have afforded me a comfortable urban lifestyle of nice dinners and designer jeans. But when the blandishment of love is held out invitingly, I do not understand the impulse to recoil or even to think twice.

Is there any worthier pursuit than that of finding love, nourishing it, and then luxuriating in a closeness that is at once physically gratifying and emotionally rewarding? I've gathered, of course, that while this may make perfect sense in theory, romance is far more complicated in practice. It rarely goes according to plan, years of disappointments causing a marked skittishness among the world's singles. Yet still, still—I don't understand.

This so-called "fear of intimacy" or "fear of falling in love," what is this? It seems rather unfathomable to me, like a "fear of success" or a "fear of being happy." I have always been a fool in love, rushing in headfirst with a backward wink and nod to my long-suffering, cringing friends.

It is a strange moment in this New India: I meet few available men in their mid-thirties, most men in this age range being proverbially gay or married. But there is an abundance of youthful men—bars and clubs are filled with these cash-rich, brashly confident youngsters. Statistics bear out my observation. Owing to improved infant mortality rates, nearly three quarters of the population of India is under the age of thirty-five, and over half is under twenty-five. The country is a juvenocracy of the first order, where bravado and flash trounce experience and age. The reverence with which Indians traditionally regard somebody older than them, even by a few years, is rapidly falling by the wayside.

Over my year in India, for lack of choice, I will date several of these young cads and discover a marked emotional tone-deafness among all of them. I date Karan, a well-educated twenty-five-year-old Hindustani classical musician—albeit struggling and negligibly talented—for several weeks, before he tells me he does not find women he meets in the ordinary course of his life, including me, pretty, but Bollywood actress and former beauty queen Aishwarya Rai is stunning. He tells me that despite having an active social and professional life, he considers only one person in the world a friend, someone he has known for twenty years.

When I'm sick in bed for four days with the seasonal flu, I phone Karan and suggest, in a fit of vulnerability when I'm feeling jittery and weak from the antibiotics coursing through my body, that he call me later that day to check on my health. He refuses, saying if I want to talk I should call him. Appalled, I say, "Why should I call you? I'm the one who's sick. It's just a nice gesture."

Coldly, he responds, "I don't believe in gestures."

When he calls a few days later, and I have recovered my health, I dump him. By way of explanation, I parse through his worldview, parroting his words back to him. "For a woman to be pretty, she must be Aishwarya Rai. To consider someone a friend, you have to know him or her for twenty years. Calling someone you're dating and intimate with while they are ill is an empty gesture.

"This is a very emotionally ungenerous way of looking at the world, and I suspect it will hurt you in the long run," I lecture him. "As you get older, you may want to rein it in."

"I don't see it the same way. I think it is a matter of having high standards," Karan says.

Karan comes months after my run-in with Aristu, as well as a few other of these twentysomething boys, but it is he who causes my epiphany regarding the city's Generation Y youth. In the same way that India has leapfrogged all the intermediary technology of the seventies, eighties, and early nineties, moving directly from antiquated telephone circuitry to cutting-edge mobile phone platforms and wireless Internet, the country's urban twentysomethings plugged directly into the rampant casual sex, or hookup, culture of the West without bothering to travel through the intermittent stages of dating and romance.

Delhi's youth are in lockstep with their counterparts in cities like London or New York. In the West, however, once people tire of freewheeling sex, they can fall back on a well-established culture of romance and dating, a path paved by previous generations. In India, the previous generation for the most part had arranged marriages. Here, urban youth might move from one sexual partner to the next without ever developing a taste for real emotion. I, of course, had come to India expecting just the opposite—that because of the heavy focus on family and marriage in previous generations, men in India would be more commitment-oriented than those in the West.

Honesty has become a dishonest buzzword tripping off the tongues of these pierced and tattooed, callow young men. They, as well as their peers in the West, think that if they tell a girl to have "no expectations," they are doing the young lady a valuable service. I find this the most scurrilous phrase a man can utter. Most women are not looking to marry every man they date, but to tell her to have "no expectations" is, of course, to say to a woman she is good for one thing and one thing only—sex. If a man must be honest, then he should just tell a woman it is purely sexual and nothing more. If there is any room for ambiguity, if perhaps this man would also like to occasionally enjoy the woman's company over dinner or a drink, then, in my opinion, he should just keep his trap shut. I hear the first few notes of a death knell every time a man kicks off a relationship with the pure narcissism of "I don't want you to have any expectations."

In line with young men's attitudes, Indian women—like I fear they do all over the world—adopt the same breezy attitude toward sex and pretend not to care when a man disappears.

It's hardly surprising that this coarseness is absent in Indian men who are a bit older or men who have grown up in small towns. Both retain an old-world charm.

Predictably, it is Ranvir, the voluble civil lawyer from Bihar who had accompanied his tongue-tied cousin on his "introduction" with me when my parents were in town, who calls me to take me out on a date.

"Hello, this is Ranvir. You may recall that I visited you and your lovely family for the purpose of furthering a matrimonial alliance between you and my cousin Ashish. I have proposed to him that perhaps I might make your acquaintance instead, as it seems that you and I are sharing many more common interests. I would also like to tender my deepest apology if you are not in agreement with my perception," he says to me in a phone call a week after we meet.

"Ah, sure, I'm in agreement that we seemed to get along better than your cousin and I did. He seemed rather quiet. Not my type really," I say.

"Perhaps then we can strategize a time suitable to both of us to meet. Usually I'm free on Wednesdays and Fridays, except for this week, there are some minor aberrations. Would it be acceptable if I were to make an impromptu phone call?" he says.

"Sure, that could work," I say.

"In the circumstance that you do have a particular commitment, we may defer it for another evening. Are you in agreement?" he says.

"Yes, I'm in full agreement," I respond, amused by his syntax. His English is a sandwich—Bihari-learned English is the bread, stuffed with a filling of odd, archaic phrases from his legal textbooks and dressed with a condiment of formality used when speaking with a woman.

Ranvir plans a date for us, dinner and a movie, and I realize it is the first proper date I've been on in Delhi in the eight or nine months I've been here. He has already purchased tickets to *Mixed Doubles*, one of the recent crop of Bollywood movies tackling "modern" themes. This one takes a look at spouse swapping. I shift in my seat uncomfortably during the movie. Perhaps this was not the best choice for a film on a first date.

We discuss the movie over dinner and I am perhaps unduly combative. Being well-versed in the art of argument, the lawyer launches into a cheerful defense of the practice of open relationships. After a good twenty minutes of this, my eyes narrow to a slit, and I query, "Have you ever had a girlfriend?"

"No," he replies.

"If you've never had one girlfriend, why would you already want two?"

Maybe I shouldn't have been so hard on the poor chap, because after all, he had taken me on a Date, this elusive concept that appears so far beyond the ken of the average Delhi male that you might think I was suggesting he smear his body with blue paint and serenade me with a flute in the manner of the god Krishna.

A Date is a movie and dinner. A Date is a drink or two at a bar. A Date is even a relaxed coffee with the intention of getting to know someone. A Date is not being called at eleven thirty P.M. by a man and asked if he can come over and spend time on my terrace. A Date is not sitting squashed between a man and three of his best college mates in the backseat of a Maruti Swift while another friend drunkenly careers through Delhi's wide moonlit avenues at ninety miles an hour. These things might be fun, but they are not Dates.

In the great "form vs. content" argument, I favor structure—in books, poems, films, and yes, evenings. A Date with a not-so-interesting person can be rescued by the trappings of the evening—that nice bottle of wine, the low lighting and appealing décor—whereas a bumbling, disorganized mishmash of a night with someone sexy and promising leaves one vulnerable to all manner of crossed wires and mixed signals.

Soon after my date with Ranvir, I meet a director of television commercials from Delhi on shaadi.com who takes me out for an exquisitely planned evening. He is in his late thirties, clearly an explanation for his gentlemanly behavior.

Gurpreet, a mild-mannered Sikh with a sky-blue turban, picks me up in his Toyota Corolla and ferries me to an unprepossessing-looking house in Lajpat Nagar. From the top floor of the residence, a sect of Tamil Brahmins provides a uniquely Indian service. These men, naked but for their brahminical thread running across their chest and a *lungi* covering their legs, read people's futures, not to mention pasts and presents, through *naadi* leaves. Unbelievably, every one of us on earth has a separate one of these ancient parchments, which look like six-inch-long pieces of aged, thin tree bark and correspond only to our individual being. So if these remarkable seers are to find my leaf—not everyone's is found—it will bear my parents' names, their professions, my own propensity for stomach upsets, and so forth.

A great and not to mention logic-defying start, and our Date has only just begun. Gurpreet has arranged for us to see *Brokeback Mountain* at the PVR Priya shopping complex in Vasant Vihar. (It used to be that only Hollywood blockbusters like *Spider-Man* showed in India, but now somewhat less than half of all movies screened at cineplexes in Delhi come from the U.S. However, far fewer Hollywood films make it into the hinterland.) As we wait for our showing, my companion and I nibble on some chocolate mousse at the Chokola café. After the film, we step into the Hookah bar and talk about the movie over some hummus and pita and a couple of glasses of Sula white.

While both Ranvir and Gurpreet prove themselves to be the most courtly of escorts, I am ashamed to find that I am still hung up on Aristu. I even find myself doing that horribly annoying and gauche thing of talking about him on my dates with them. Despite this, I stay friends with both.

Gurpreet and I meet sporadically that spring, but he has work in Bombay for a few months and I return to California for a long visit with my parents. When we meet again for the first time in many months, he will surprise me with a clean-shaven face and head. I'm shocked to see him shorn of the beard and the turban that had left only a portion of his face visible. The Sikh tradition mandates that its followers not cut hair anywhere on their body, and the turban identified with Sikh men is worn to protect the unshorn and long hair. Lately, young Sikh men have been defying tradition by wearing their hair short and trimming, as well as shaving, facial hair, especially those who are not particularly religious, like Gurpreet.

Now that I can actually *see* him, I realize he's kind of cute. Without prompting, the first thing he says is, "My love life has skyrocketed."

I let out a loud laugh. "That's fantastic! Well, you know, a girl does want to see what she's dealing with. How does it feel, though, not having a turban and all?"

"Well, when I first did it and got out of the shower, I was like, 'That's it? I can just leave the house?'"

"So then it would take a long time to tie your turban in the morning, I guess?" I ask.

"Not only that. On good days, it would only take fifteen minutes. But you know how people have bad hair days? Well, I would have bad turban days. Sometimes, I'd tie it and it would look lopsided or just all wrong. At least twice a week I had a bad turban day, and it took me thirty or forty minutes to put it on," he says.

Gurpreet is now a cut *sard*, the commonly used term for Sikh men who don't wear a turban and have cut their hair. It's said

often enough that cut *sards* are the best-looking men in India,
given their strapping physiques, angular bone structure, fair skin,
and refined bearing. I do not disagree. It's not the turban, the
most dignified of headdresses, that I find off-putting, but the
sheer hirsuteness of Sikh men who are not allowed to trim their
beards or cut their hair—in some severe cases, only inches of a
man's face are left visible. Many of my girlfriends here in Delhi
have said the same—that they would find it difficult to go out
with an uncut Sikh.

Earlier in the year, on a business trip to Punjab, the state
where Sikhism was born, I decided to make a detour to the
Golden Temple in Amritsar, which I'd never seen. It is not often
in Delhi that one is blessed with an attractive taxi driver, but
there in the state of Punjab, I was delighted to spend four hours
in a car driven by a strikingly handsome gentleman. His hair was
cut short, but when we reached the Golden Temple, he escorted
me inside. Before he did so, he elegantly wrapped a navy-blue
turban around his head. He was a cut *sard*. I thought, "Now,
wow, here you get two great looks for the price of one."

Sikh elders are up in arms about the number of young men of
the faith shearing their hair and grooming their beards, but with
the country modernizing at breakneck pace, there's likely to be
many more razors purchased and quite a lot more hair on the
barbershop floor.

I spend the spring moping over my thwarted romance with
Aristu and wish I could discuss it with Nandini, but she's been
incommunicado lately. It's not just that she more or less stopped
going out because she isn't drinking anymore, but also that a
tragedy has taken her out of Delhi in the last few weeks.

One of her close friends has been the victim of an acid attack,
a particularly vicious form of assaulting women favored by men

in the subcontinent, that left her face completely disfigured. When I finally reach Nandini, she's in Agra, spending her days and evenings sitting by her friend's bedside in a hospital.

Nandini's friend had recently married. When a male relative, who was also married but had always held a torch for her, found out about the marriage, he followed her onto a train to Delhi from Kanpur. En route, he threw acid in her face. It was Nandini who was among the first to arrive at the hospital after the attack and she who removed the bandages from the face of her friend. The victim's mother and sisters were still in shock.

"I'm so sorry," I say, when I hear about the incident. "Take care of yourself."

"I will. I should be back in Delhi in a week or two," she tells me.

I hang up the phone, shaken. Those of us who live in Delhi, but for the most posh and cloistered, live in this liminal space between an old and new India. Nandini may be a woman who can date several men at a time and dance until dawn at a club, but she is also the very same woman who might be called upon to remove bandages from the face of a friend at whom acid has been flung, or worse, she might one day find herself in the place of her friend. India may be moving into the twenty-first century, but, like many countries, it's keen on retaining its most cherished traditions, including acid throwing.

Chapter Twenty-four

Every Delhiite, from my maid Chandra to my friends to shopkeepers, is a weather pandit, and there are a few things everyone agrees upon. One of the most incontrovertible tenets of Delhi weather trends is that the brief winter ends on Holi, the spring festival that falls in early March when revelers throw water and crimson red, bright pink, deep purple, cerulean blue, and sunny yellow powder on family members and friends, leaving blots on clothing and stains on skin that take a few days and much scrubbing to fade. Traditionally, the tossing of colors—once made from natural herbs and spices, such as turmeric and *neem*—had a medicinal purpose, which was to ward off illnesses caused by the changing season.

I arrive around three o'clock in the afternoon to a Holi party thrown by the Moksha boys, not realizing that festivities for the holiday start in the late morning, around ten or eleven o'clock. The band and the fifteen- or twenty-odd people who always collect around them are already unrecognizable. Nair has green hair, TJ's face is smeared red, and Amarjeet's clothing and turban are marred by a blurry mélange of colors. I see several people sprawled out on various couches and beds around the house, passed out from *bhaang*, the potent cannabis concoction traditionally drunk on Holi.

I have missed the peak of the fun, but a few merrymakers stumble toward me and halfheartedly dump fluorescent pink and green powder over my head.

I am surprised at how accurate conventional weather wisdom in Delhi is, and like clockwork, the days following Holi are springlike. Apparently these days are even more short-lived than the winter, and the season will in a month's time give way to the uncomfortably sticky, mind-meltingly hot summer. The month-long "spring" in Delhi is the only season that bears any passing resemblance to its counterparts in other places I've lived, in terms of temperature and general corresponding mood.

"Ah, what lovely weather we're having," Delhiites will say, and for the first time—for they have said the same during the winter and during the monsoon—I will nod my head in agreement.

Certainly, others around me are squiring around new love interests like they do in other cities when the flowers and trees begin blooming again. Nair has started dating an Australian girl named Genevieve, who followed her best friend Lisa to Delhi to work for a call center. Both have since quit, and Genevieve is pursuing a singing career, while Lisa has found a job in market-ing. Soon after Nair and Genevieve embark on a relationship, Lisa and TJ also start dating.

Even Amarjeet, my kissing novitiate, has a girlfriend, an Indian woman in her early twenties who he met on the Internet. Before he met her and soon after our kiss, Amarjeet lost his virginity to a German woman. I am delighted, perhaps taking undue credit for removing that initial, seemingly insurmoun-table hurdle of being a newcomer to the world of physical intimacy. Having kept all but the celibacy part of his oath, Amarjeet is following the spirit, if not the letter, of being an Amritdhari Sikh.

One day that spring, when I am sitting in the passenger seat of Nair's car and we are on our way to a party, I complain to him of my abortive relationship with Aristu. Even as I recount the story,

I feel ashamed of my attachment to someone so flimsy, so lacking in gravitas.

"And look at you," I say, "you make it seem so easy to find someone. You just met Genevieve a few weeks ago, and now you're going strong."

A shy smile plays on Nair's lips, and he offers unusual words of sympathy. "Anita, you just picked the wrong person," he says.

I have never sought comfort from the glib, arm-punching Nair, and yet he rises to the occasion. Or maybe it is that when we are lovelorn, anything proffered is reassuring.

"Maybe I just picked the wrong person," I repeat to myself. "Yes, I suppose I did."

India has attracted foreigners through the ages, but in the late twentieth century, they were usually one of three types in Delhi: foreign journalists—many of them old Asia hands bouncing from China to the Philippines and on to India—diplomats, or senior business executives with wife and children in tow. They lived in Jor Bagh, Golf Links, Friends Colony, and Nizamuddin.

A new group of fresh-faced and pale-skinned foreigners has arrived in Delhi recently, and they are coming in hordes. For many of them, it is the first time they have lived outside their home country. Every time I'm in Khan Market, perusing the bookshops or eating penne arrabiata at Big Chill, or buying hundred-pill sheets of prescription-free generic Xanax, I notice the place is crawling with *goras*. No longer are they diplomatic wives lunching together and discussing which schools are best for their children—the American School or the British School? They are young, in their early to late twenties, and they are often tucking into a heavy meal to recover from their hangovers. Their conversation might proceed something like this:

"So what did you do last night?"

"Oh, I went to this party in Defence Colony last night. Do you know this French girl, Delphine? She's in fashion." (All French people in Delhi are in fashion.)

"Oh, yeah, I heard about that party. Was it any good?"

"Yeah, they had a DJ playing on the roof. Loads of people were there. Where were you?"

"We went to this farmhouse party. It was way out past Gurgaon. I didn't know anyone there, but I met some cool people. Have you met that Swedish guy Carl? He does these multimedia collage paintings with Indian themes."

"Yeah? Cool."

A fresh boatload of young people like Genevieve and Lisa seems to land in Delhi every week, as a result of two separate but complementary trends. First, India is becoming more integrated into the global economy, and foreign companies are finding the need to be in India or risk losing out on a huge market; second, India is becoming the place to *be*, as a center from which a new type of fusion music or the latest mode in fashion is gravitating out to the world. When I'm out at a bar or at Defence Colony market and I see a number of white faces stream past me, it strikes me that Delhi has become the expat destination that Hong Kong or Bangkok was in the go-go nineties.

India's longstanding love affair with white skin means that many of these young foreigners find unexpected success in India they wouldn't find back home. Genevieve and Lisa, friends from back home and college dropouts, both initially came to India to work at call centers. And they both eventually left, Lisa finding a senior position at a marketing company that would have taken her years to get to back in Australia, and Genevieve turning her singing into a skyrocketing career.

The two twenty-five-year-olds met in boarding school in Sydney. Both are from the Australian countryside and neither completed her university degree in public relations. They both spent time in London working in pubs and at other odd jobs on the two-year work visa for which all Aussies are eligible and which all of them seem to have taken advantage of at one time or another.

The more outgoing and adventurous of the two, Lisa was the first to come to India, in early 2005. When her work visa in London ran out, she returned to Australia, but was bored after the excitement of London. She didn't do anything but surf for the first few months. She would idly glance at the employment section in the newspaper every once in a while, and one day, on her way back from the beach, she came across an advertisement looking for someone to work in Delhi in a call center selling Indian vacations to Australians, Brits, and New Zealanders, the idea being that customers would respond more readily to an accent they could identify with.

Genevieve followed Lisa to India six months later, after her stint in London ended. Genevieve secured the same call center job from her perch in London and trained at the headquarters there. When she arrived at the call center in Okhla, a gritty industrial district in southeast Delhi, she was appalled at the conditions. The only upside was that she worked from noon to seven in the evening with Lisa, which allowed her to get to know Delhi nightlife.

Like me, the duo was intimately familiar with the handful of bars, lounges, and clubs in the city—Shalom, Elevate, Urban Pind. When the company tried to change her shift to one starting at midnight and ending at five in the morning, Genevieve balked. She'd had enough and left the call center after being there only a few months. Lisa had worked there for nearly a year and found the work mindless and rote, and she quit as well in solidarity. All the other expat staffers viewed their stays as short-term ones, doing it for the experience of living in India or working just long enough to save to travel around the country for a year. Genevieve and Lisa decided to stay in Delhi while they figured out what they would do next and whether they would stay in the country.

Around this time, Genevieve started getting singing gigs. Her first had come as a lark after she attended an open-mike night at Tonic, a bar in the Siri Fort auditorium complex. The manager was impressed and asked if she would do regular gigs. On Friday evenings for the next two months, Genevieve sang covers of Sting, Sheryl Crow, and Lisa Loeb. Soon, Genevieve had penetrated the Indian underground music scene, much of it focused on electronica. She also came to be friends with various well-known DJs around the city. Genevieve and Lisa were asked to DJ on a few occasions, once for $1,500 for just an evening, even though neither of them had any experience. "It was the novelty factor. We were two white women in the DJ booth. We didn't know what we were doing. We just played some house and some Bollywood," Lisa told me when I ran into the two one night.

Even more shocking, the girls tell me they were hired to dress up and attend polo matches, their attendance as white women raising the cachet of the event. They were paid two thousand rupees each to drink wine and mingle—to be guests at a cocktail party.

Within a few months, Genevieve met Talvin Singh, the U.K.-based artist whose fusion of Hindustani classical tabla and electronica has sold millions of albums around the world. The musician, who has worked with Madonna, Björk, and Massive Attack, invited Genevieve to sing with him at an exclusive party at the Ashoka hotel. "Here I was doing covers of Karen Carpenter and all of a sudden I'm sitting onstage with

Talvin Singh, with Indian classical instruments and kneeling on cushions. I was thinking, 'How did I get here?' " Genevieve said.

I wonder how much of her success was attributable to her skin color. The city's doors had certainly not opened as readily for me. In India, I'm conveniently treated like an Indian where privileged access is concerned—that is, no red-carpet treatment for me—and treated like an outsider, an *American*, the worst possible kind, when I don't behave like everybody else—speaking my mind, laughing loudly, drinking too much, or in any way calling unnecessary attention to myself, which I tend to do often enough.

Nandini wants a white boyfriend. No surprise there.

"I'm so done with Indian men," she tells me over vodka-sodas at Urban Pind. She's back in Delhi and has started drinking again. After waiting months for Dilip to talk to his parents about marrying her, she's fed up. And she's fed up with not having a life in Delhi while he carries on with his in New York.

"Now that I've been here awhile, I don't blame you," I say, adding, "Maybe you'll meet someone tonight."

It's Thursday at Urban Pind, and it will get crowded later because it's "Expat Night." For seven hundred rupees, patrons are given a bracelet with which they can drink all they want. The "pay one fixed price for all you want" concept doesn't work very well in India, because here only one person among a group of friends will pay the seven hundred rupees and fetch drinks for everyone else. This is why the bracelets, which have to be shown to the bartender before each drink, are designed such that once affixed to the wrist, they can't be removed without tearing them off. But even so, the one time I go to Urban Pind on a Thursday with some Indian friends, only one of them buys a bracelet and returns repeatedly to the bar after an acceptable ten to fifteen minutes, eventually procuring drinks for the entire group.

Tonight, I'm planning to introduce Nandini to two young expatriate men I recently met. One is a twenty-three-year-old named Robert from Copenhagen, who is setting up an IT office in India for his Danish company, and the other is a twenty-five-year-old venture capitalist from San Francisco called Greg. Sadly, they are too young for me.

As the night progresses, the bar becomes packed with Europeans and North Americans. It is standing-room only. I am reminded of my own first forays abroad, in Singapore in the mid-nineties. There, most bars were filled with expatriates and only a smattering of locals. The foreign men would, of course, try to pick up local women, while we expatriate women were shunted to the sidelines. In India, it appears to be the reverse. Local, or Indian, women are less responsive to white men, largely due to social restrictions, while it's the white women who usually have Indian boyfriends.

The owner of Urban Pind greets Robert and Greg warmly. He sends them free drinks and food. I've met him countless times at his bar and other parties with *goras*, but he always seems to forget who I am, though he's clearly on back-slapping terms with all the foreigners. Typical.

Robert and Greg both chat up the charming Nandini, but she has a taste for older men. Nandini has flitted off somewhere, leaving me to spend the evening talking to them. She returns an hour or so later, in her wake an attractive and polite thirty-two-year-old management consultant from the Netherlands named Patrick.

After the debacle with Dilip, Nandini returns to her man-juggling days. She's been seeing Patrick for a few weeks, but he's planning to leave the country in a month—also in contrast to the past, many of the recent crop of foreigners in India are on short-term contracts.

Knowing that it won't go anywhere with Patrick, Nandini is also seeing Nigel, a photojournalist friend of mine she met at one of my parties when he was going out with Rekha, another friend of mine. After a messy breakup with Rekha, Nigel called up Nandini and asked her out. Although Nandini shares intense physical chemistry with Nigel—they're both Scorpios, she tells me by way of explanation—he's not ready for another serious relationship.

Nandini and I are back in the same boat again. Sure, we're keen to step off the endless churn of dating and meaningless sex, but one does have to keep oneself occupied in the meantime.

Chapter Twenty-five

A city's measure can be taken by the people who find a haven in it. While young Silicon Valley venture capitalists may be clinking champagne glasses in dimly lit lounges in Gurgaon, another migration to the capital and its suburbs has also accelerated. On previous trips to Delhi, I'd paid scant attention to the large population from India's northeastern region, people who Indians refer to as "chinky." While political correctness has wrought some changes to the country's lexicon—such as the usage of "Dalit" for the caste formerly called "untouchable"—it still has some distance to go. Now it seems every third or fourth person in Delhi hails from this disenfranchised region, whose fractious Christian and tribal population bridles under Indian control.

When I go out with Bharat and Vincent to Pegs and Pints or the Concord on Saturday nights, we are joined by a gaggle of diminutive boys from the northeast. Bharat is a self-confessed "rice queen," finding men with East Asian features more attractive. For years, he was obsessed with Bangkok and would fly there every other month. Recently, though, he's realized that many of the young men there find his wallet far more attractive than they do him, and he's started dating a twenty-two-year-old fashion designer from Assam, one of India's seven northeastern states. None of us much cared for his last boyfriend, a Thai who was living with him and his mother for a couple of months, so we applaud his new interest.

Bharat tells me that years ago when he was introduced to Vincent, he had a massive crush on him. Apparently a lot of Bharat's friends were taken with the shy, articulate Vincent, who had dreams of becoming a playwright. I can see why. Although I find all my friends in Delhi well versed in Western music, films, and literature, it's Vincent with whom I can share my more esoteric interests. We talk about the tragic demise of Maria Callas—Vincent sings opera—and the memoirs of Edmund White. We argue over which David Mamet plays are worthy and which aren't. (He likes *Oleanna*. I prefer *Speed-the-Plow*.)

Vincent frequently comes over to watch some of the foreign films I've bought from the copyright-defying merchants at Palika Bazaar. For these occasions, I prepare ahead of time by going to the Khan Market liquor store and buying two bottles of Sula red, usually the Satori but sometimes the cabernet. Going to the *theka* is always an experience. Male patrons, with few exceptions the only kind, are barred from entering the shop and call out their purchases to the shop assistants, who fetch the bottles for them. I wonder how many of these men, wearing tattered clothing and some of them already soused and wild eyed, are spending their day's wages on booze, denying their family dinner. As a woman, I'm allowed to enter the empty store and choose my wine at leisure, but first I have to make my way through the crowd, which I do, elbows up and ready to jab. Actually, the *theka* in India is the one place I do get the red-carpet treatment.

"You know, Maria Callas just wasn't a life-ist. She couldn't carry on anymore," Vincent says, during one of our marathon conversations.

"Vincent, what's a life-ist?" I say, wondering if he's coined the word.

"You know, people who even when life isn't great and has set them back, they feel the need to have fun and enjoy themselves, rather than the instinct to recoil from the world. She just wasn't like that, our Maria," he says, shaking his head mournfully.

Vincent bears the least outward resemblance to me of all my friends in Delhi. The others are all varying hues of brown. Some of us who are from the north have sharper, more European features as a result of the Aryan invasion many millennia ago. My south Indian friends might have softer and rounder noses and lips. But Vincent—well, Vincent looks Japanese, or maybe Korean. He could walk down the streets of Tokyo or Seoul without anyone batting an eyelash.

But when Vincent tells me of his childhood, its lack of high culture, and his autodidacticism, it resonates deep within me. I am reminded of my own determination to rise above my past, which, if not an impoverished one, was too rooted in an immigrant struggle, too philistine, or just too pedestrian for my lofty imagination. I had always wished my parents were artists, dancers, or musicians, or at least showed an interest in the arts other than *Love Connection* with Chuck Woolery and *Three's Company*.

There are other similarities as well. In a place as concerned with being from an "established" family as Delhi, Vincent and I like to thumb our noses at the establishment and chuckle over being of unknown provenance. And when it comes to romantic love, let's just say Vincent and I have been known to devote many an obsessive or delusional thought to the wrong man.

If most of my friends who have made Delhi their home arrived from somewhere else, Vincent's journey is by far the most harrowing. The youngest of seven children, Vincent spent the first fifteen years of his life in a small town in Nagaland called Mokokchung. He belongs to one of the prominent tribes in that region called the Khasi, which he informs me follows a practice diametrically opposite to that of primogeniture, the English law that stipulated that property be inherited by the eldest son in a family. In a Khasi family, the youngest daughter is eligible to receive all the spoils. (My father clearly has a few drops of blood from this tribe.)

His mother was a schoolteacher, while his father ostensibly managed a movie theater that played Hindi films, but his main occupation was drinking. A comparison can be drawn between India's northeast and the Native American population in the U.S. and aborigines in Australia, where the imposition of a civil society, technology, and modernity on what was a tribal way of life may have caused such serious damage to the fabric of those communities that many of its people have turned to drinking. One of Vincent's brothers died from alcoholism, while others have battled severe drinking problems.

Growing up, his five older brothers were layabouts, while his sister was the town harlot. They all lived in one room and shared a bathroom with six or seven other families. Their cramped home was made of concrete, and a mixture of mud and cow dung was used to plaster the kitchen walls. "I never felt I belonged in the poverty I grew up in," he says one day, sipping wine on my terrace.

I find it hard to digest that Vincent, whose friends in Delhi are top socialites, fashion designers, and writers, could have come from such privation. He is quirky, and he has flair and an offbeat sense of humor, all things I associate with growing up in a type of luxury that allows one to develop idiosyncrasies. He should at least be middle class, shouldn't he?

At fifteen, his family finally moved to the big city—Shillong, the capital of Meghalaya, another state in the northeast. He had no real consciousness of India as a nation at the time. He knew that he lived in a state that was part of a country called India, but he certainly didn't know any "Indians."

"I couldn't even string a sentence in English together when we moved to Shillong. Nobody did, and I grew up watching a lot of Hindi, not English, movies," he says, explaining that at the time he spoke a mishmash of tribal languages. "In Shillong, people were speaking English, and I was determined to speak it properly."

Everyone in Vincent's family recognized him as the "bright" one, and he was encouraged in his studies, not that he needed to be, as he himself was looking for a way out. Not surprisingly, he was pushed in the direction of the sciences. He studied economics at university in Shillong and showed little overt interest in the arts. When he graduated, family relatives suggested he apply to the Indian Institute of Management, India's premier business school. He applied to all six campuses and was accepted at the one in Calcutta. "I didn't know what management or marketing was, but I wanted a well-done-up flat, with sofas and nice furniture," he says.

IIM was nothing like university. All the other students, mostly male, were bespectacled, serious, and studious. Vincent was lost in his classes in statistics and finance. "I couldn't for the life of me fathom what they were about," he says. He was miserable, and when a research project took him to Delhi four months into his first semester, he decided to stay in the vast, dirty metropolis, where he could vanish into the anonymous swarm. He didn't tell his family that he'd left the business school, and he made no contact with home for two years. Later he heard that his family back in Shillong had asked a police officer to discover his whereabouts. Vincent squatted in a residential building under construction in Mayur Vihar in East Delhi, bedding down in a flat with only three walls on the seventh floor. The summers were impossible. "There were tons of mosquitos and pigeons," he says.

He'd jump off buses before the conductor approached him. He ate one meal a day in a nearby slum for a couple of rupees. "When you're in it, living in penury doesn't bother you too much," he says.

During the day he would scour the city for work. Somebody told him he could get part-time work from All-India Radio and Doordarshan doing voice-overs for small dramas. Back in the mid-1990s, Delhi wasn't the kind of city where you could wait tables or work at a Barista or Café Coffee Day. He found he was good at the voice-overs, and it sparked his interest in theater work. In the evenings, he'd read plays by Oscar Wilde or Tom Stoppard that he borrowed from friends or the library. A couple of years later, he would begin writing full-length plays and would even get them produced at the India Habitat Centre and the Kamani Auditorium, Delhi's premier theaters.

Few writers from India's northeast have found widespread success, and Vincent's plays so far have focused on "Indian" India, not the region from which he hails, both because he doesn't think India is ready for northeastern themes and because he, like me, is intrigued by the wave of modernization sweeping through urban India, which provides the backdrop for his works.

I've always been ensnared by questions of identity, in large part because mine is so precarious—Indian, American, citizen of the world?—and I often pepper Vincent with questions about his.

"So, okay, imagine this scenario," I say. "You're in London, and you're this big famous film director being fêted."

"I like the sound of that; go on," he says.

"Now you're seated at a table with two people that you've never met before. One is Indian, and let's say his name is Rakesh Agarwal. The other fellow is from Japan, and his name is Ken Watanabe. One is your countryman but you don't look like him, the other one you resemble, but his culture is alien to you. Who do you identify more with, feel more kinship with, so to speak?"

"Hmm, interesting, Anita. Let me think. You know, I think I'd have to say Ken Watanabe, because he looks more like me than Rakesh Agarwal," Vincent says, bemused by his own reflexive answer.

This disconnect is another thing Vincent and I share. We are two sides of the same coin. I look Indian but am not, while he *is* Indian but doesn't remotely look it.

Bharat and Vincent are doing their best to introduce me to "interesting" straight men they know in the city, but mixed messages, crossed signals, unequal desire, and lip-locks with no follow-up phone call seem to prevail here just as much as they do back in New York. I'm still pecking away at shaadi.com. If the pool on the Web site is a little less interesting, at least we're all looking for the same thing—*shaadi*.

One day I'm contacted by an Indian fellow who lives in Luxembourg. I check out his profile. He seems perfectly fine, and if he was in Delhi, I would meet up with him straightaway. I forget to write him back. I get a brief message a week or so later,

Hmm, you appear to be rather laconic. But if we're meant to take this forward in any way, you do need to say something. I'd even take a "boo" at this point. Manoj

I'm utterly charmed. The level of communication on shaadi .com rarely rises to involve SAT-appropriate words and correct spelling, let alone dry wit. I write back, a simple reply acknowledging the wry humor in his message. Sensing that his audience appreciates wordplay, Manoj, a management consultant, sends back a parody of a matrimonial query "addressed" to my father.

Dear Shri Jain, this has reference to your most auspicious matrimonial posting for your dear Anita. It is a pleasure to be able to speak with you directly-thanks be to

Shiva-Parvati, Krishna-Radha. Also, Vikram, Juan Carlos and the gym girl in *Pyaar*, by
Brin and Page, who provide a modern setting for the magic of romance, yet allow,
in these non-doctor, non-engineer boys, the useless types lurking outside shaadi.com,
some naughtiness to flourish.

Useless types.

I have triple degrees from IIT-D, AIIMS, and IIA-ETIDKWTFITA. My patent-
the one about double cantilever arms on titanium prostheses-saves lives. Undeniab-
ly false, even absurd claims paint me a (mild) rogue, but the honest truth is that I
am merely a 34-year-old boy, seeking a Harvard-educated non-smoking virgin, and
wish simply to make a connection with the woman of my dreams; if she is non-
wheatish and comes with a dowry, so much the better. I earn $200,000, am
vegetarian, independent, annoyingly confident and would enjoy a night at the
Sacramento Bharata Natyam Company, watching Madhuri Dixit. Finally caste no
bar, but only around the auspicious midnight hour please, that would be perfect.

Sir, in today's world where children are bullheaded, I stand as a shining exception.
I would like nothing more than for you, in your wisdom, to pull the rabbit out of the
hat, as it were, and make your daughter's life full. Doing less would mean the fertility
freezer, and deny, let us be honest, wanton desires that lie secretly beneath every breast.

That would be the father I would want to be to my little girl.

In conclusion, let us just say Arpita and I are fated. Like the tree with a name
entwined by the creeper of different name. Fated. Even if the creeper does too much
and the branch falls. I hope to hear back from you, and can be reached at this e-mail or
through Mr. Ramesh Gupta of Mississippi, or thereabouts. A reminder—I have posted
on shaadi.com—my profile is "manoj_1971."

Yours, but not in Kentucky only,
Manoj

The message makes winsomely silly references to an article I wrote for *New York* magazine on arranged marriages a few years ago, indicating Manoj has clearly Googled me. It's a bit disjointed, yes, but I'm terribly amused. I write back, saying I'm delighted by his letter and would like to meet him the next time he's in Delhi. Manoj is busy traveling and I only hear from him two or three weeks later. He asks if I noticed the message within a message, directing me to "read every other line starting with the second line."

I'm confused by his response but scroll back in my e-mails to find the one with the letter. I follow his instructions and begin to read every other line. Another message forms.

Dear Anita. It is a pleasure to be able to speak with you directly—thanks be to
Brin and Page, who provide a modern setting for the magic of romance, yet allow,
some naughtiness to flourish.

I have triple degrees from IIT-D, AIIMS, and IIA-ETIDKWTFITA. My patent-
ly false, even absurd claims paint me a (mild) rogue, but the honest truth is that I
wish simply to make a connection with the woman of my dreams; if she is non-
vegetarian, independent, annoyingly confident and would enjoy a night at the
bar, but only around the auspicious midnight hour please, that would be perfect.

I would like nothing more than for you, in your wisdom, to pull the rabbit out of the
freezer, and deny, let us be honest, desires that lie secretly beneath every breast.

In conclusion, let us just say that Arpita and I are fated. Like the tree with a name
and the branch falls. I hope to hear back from you, and can be reached at this e-mail or
on shaadi.com—my profile is "manoj_1971."

Manoj

Wow, I'm astounded, confounded even. Clearly this is a far cry from what I've come to expect on shaadi.com, which is more along the lines of "I am myself Manoj looking for girl of sweetest natur [*sic*], family orientation, and blend of East and West." Our Manoj is a wordsmith of the first order.

I discover the embedded message while on a trip to Dharamsala, the Dalai Lama's haven in the Himalayas, with my friend Sonali, who's accompanied me to distract herself from her crumbling marriage. After reading the letter in an Internet café, she turns to me and says, "Marry him, Anita. Don't let this one get away. Men like this don't come by very often."

We're now jostling our way down the filthy central thoroughfare of Dharamsala amid the ranks of the dreadlocked hippies who make the town a long-term destination. "Yes, you're right. A man who can craft a message like that is likely to keep me happier on a lifetime basis than a pretty face. His picture was decent anyway, didn't you think, Sonali?"

"Yes, yes, of course, he was fine. Snag him now or someone else will," she orders me.

"Okay, okay. I'll write him as soon as I get back to Delhi," I say.

When I return home a few days later, I'm in a phenomenally buoyant mood. The fresh, cool mountain air and breathtaking views have done me some good, a perfect break from relentlessly urban Delhi, where the ovenlike summer is in full swing. Also, it's hard to ignore the fact that I will be getting married soon to my betrothed, Manoj, of the dazzling Nabokovian message-within-a-message.

Chandra notices something different about me one morning soon after I've returned as she comes in to deliver breakfast and *chai*. And it's not that I'm not wearing any clothes. She's used to that by now. At first when the heat started getting uncomfortable, I would sleep in as little clothing as possible, in a shift or T-shirt, but the scorching 120-degree temperature has lately made that impossible and I have to strip down completely. But I would still try to hastily throw on the shift before I opened the door for Chandra in the morning, or even hold it in front of me to cover myself, which looked pretty silly.

Chandra dispensed with that charade a couple of weeks ago when she said, "Madam, *mein bhi ladeez hoon, tum bhi ladeez ho. Kyaa* problem *hai?* I'm a ladies, you are also a ladies. What's the problem?"

She's right, as always, in her inimitably direct way.

Today, referring to my high spirits, she says, "Madam, *aaj to tum bahut kush ho. Kyaa ladka mila?* You seem very happy today. Have you found a boy?"

Bright-eyed, naked, and typing a reply to Manoj, I tell her, "*Haan*, Chandra, *ladka mila*. I've found a boy."

To Manoj, I express my divine pleasure at uncovering the hidden message. "When will you be coming to Delhi?" I implore in my e-mail.

I hear back from Manoj a few days later.

So Delhi men haven't quite swept you off your feet, eh? Can't say I'm surprised, since on average they're a bit boorish. But clearly average isn't your thing, so fingers crossed?

Anita, I've met someone since I wrote last, and it's moving really well. It's all happened quite quickly, and while I'm not yet sure if it's leading to a relationship, I think it is only right that I tell you this. I'm going to drop off the shaadi.com scene till I know one way or another.

However, again either way, I would love to meet for a coffee and a chat when our paths do cross, perhaps in Delhi. I shall also call you sometime later this week to say hello.

Till then,

Manoj

And he's anomalously honest too. Did I mention I'm unlucky in love?

Chapter Twenty-six

I mope for a few days after receiving Manoj's deflating reply, bracing myself for a return to shaadi.com's rampant garbled syntax and malapropisms. Rather fortunately, though, I don't have to wait long before shaadi.com serves up another aberrant (read: literate) sort. On his profile, Sanjeev cites Norman Mailer, Henry Miller, and P. G. Wodehouse as his favorite authors and describes himself as a wizard at crossword puzzles and Scrabble. He plays racquetball and cricket and has traveled extensively through Bhutan, Nepal, and India.

Unlike with Manoj, there is no long drawn-out banter and repartee. Sanjeev simply calls one day, we have a brief conversation, and he asks me out for the coming Saturday. While preamble can be titillating, forthrightness is a never-fail virtue. Over the phone, I learn he works in IT and lives in Gurgaon, and he's from Gorakhpur. I pull out my map of India and locate the city in eastern Uttar Pradesh, the state of my own provenance, and some sixty miles from the Nepalese border. Gorakhpur is a big city by comparison with those around it, and it's an hour from Kushinagar, the town where Buddha breathed his last.

I've been in Delhi eleven months and have come to the conclusion that men bred in the city, growing up in Friends Colony or Vasant Vihar or my own neighborhood, Nizamuddin, are more often than not boorish and possess an unearned sense of privilege, while men from the hinterland, like Vikram, the mortgage underwriter from Kanpur, are far more charming and complex, if a little less exposed to the world. So I'm intrigued to meet Sanjeev, this well-read man from—where was it again? Oh yes, Gorakhpur.

On the appointed evening, Sanjeev arrives at my door and bounces into my living room. He has an animated spring in his gait, causing him to bob up and down. His hair is cut close to his head, revealing it to be a perfectly symmetrical sphere. He has eyes that always seem on the verge of shutting, and he's rail thin. He's a little goofy, putting me in the mind of a gnome, a word I will later use as a term of affection for him. And he seems a bit cocky, though not in a churlish, entitled Delhi way. I later learn that Sanjeev from Gorakhpur has had to develop an attitude to survive in this aggressive city, one that says he's equal to anyone here.

I'm still getting ready when Sanjeev arrives, so I let him in the door and give him a glass of water before returning to the bedroom. When I come out to the drawing room five minutes later, he's looking around my flat, taking it in. We walk downstairs to his car, a beaten-up Maruti 800 of indeterminate color. I can't tell if it was originally white and has now taken on a greenish tint, or if it was initially mint green and has faded. There's no radio and no air-conditioning, or rather, as Sanjeev tells me, the air-conditioning works by rolling down the windows. I might have expected such a car from a Gurgaon-based IT guy who grew up in Gorakhpur, but that's the only apropos thing about him.

In the car, he tells me his roommate is an Austrian woman. I learn he studied architecture at the University of Roorkee, a few years before its campus was brought under the aegis of the Indian Institute of Technology. My father, if you recall, also attended the University of Roorkee, similarly entering the college as a greenhorn from the Uttar Pradesh interior. I realize later that the parallels end here, since it turns out that at age twelve, Sanjeev plowed through Henry Miller's entire trilogy of *The Rosy Crucifixion*—*Sexus, Plexus,* and *Nexus.* The last book I remember my father reading cover to cover was *How to Buy a House with No Money Down,* which he read about twenty-five years ago. I bought him Bill Clinton's autobiography when it came out, certain he would absorb every last detail about his hero. My mother told me later he just flipped through the tome looking for the dirty parts.

Sanjeev suggests we go to Turquoise Cottage—the loud pub where all the kids dance around to Guns N' Roses and Nirvana. I sway him in the direction of Aura, a quieter lounge in the Claridge's hotel. When we enter the sleek bar from the lobby, he looks around suspiciously at the décor, perhaps calculating how much lighter his wallet will be by the time we leave. But Sanjeev is too gracious to mention it, and remember, he's equal to anyone in Delhi, right?

I order a double vodka-lime-soda, the first of three at *that* bar, a fact that will not only be imprinted on the bill Sanjeev pays, but on his mind. Despite himself, he will be dismayed. He thinks his reading and extensive solo travels have given him a cosmopolitan outlook, but I will put him to the test.

We lean forward from our large leather chairs situated too far apart. We talk about Woody Allen's new movie, *Match Point,* set in London, and how it's the director's first decent movie in years. I bring up the Truman Capote biopic that's just been released, and Sanjeev tells me he read *In Cold Blood* when he was seventeen years old.

"I picked it up from a sidewalk sale in Gorakhpur. It didn't have a cover on it, but it looked interesting, so I read it. Great book," he says.

I am relieved to be conversing with someone so articulate and well informed, and so *normal* in some fundamental sense. As in any big city, New York or Paris or London or Delhi, it's a colossal misconception that people are having intelligent conversations. I've always considered myself to possess the most conventional, the least arcane, of interests. Simply put, I like to read, watch decent films—mind you, they need not be nonlinear and subtitled—and drink. But you'd be surprised at how many people don't perform these three very elemental activities.

As my insides turn warm from the vodka, the gnomic Sanjeev is exceeding all expectations. I can't decide whether it's a good or bad sign when he tells me he's a Bania, the same merchant caste that we Jains marry into. His mother is even a Jain. Think of two Jews who aren't fussy about whether their partner is Jewish or not meeting up for a date. Obviously, being of the same caste eliminates virtually all family-related issues, but then the soundtrack in the back of my mind is saying it would seem too goody-two-shoes if I were to marry another Bania. After the life I've led, I'd probably rather want to break the rules a little, no?

But I do like that when I tell him that my father is very into wealth creation, Sanjeev doesn't miss a beat when he replies, "Well, he's genetically programmed to be."

Sanjeev is a year younger than I am. He's perfect. We will marry and my parents will be thrilled. "So, I think we should go dancing," I slur happily. Perhaps counterintuitively and to my detriment, I tend to overdrink when I'm having a good time with a man, even if it's on the first date. Isn't the point to see if you have fun with someone? It's with someone boring that I order one beer and sip it veeerrry slowly until the encounter is over.

He's game, and I take his arm to avoid stumbling as we walk out to his shoebox of a car. I take off my heels and put my feet up on the minimalist dashboard as we zoom through the fairly empty avenues to Turquoise Cottage. I wiggle my freshly painted pink toes and chirp along merrily about this and that, mentioning at one point that dating has been hard in Delhi. It's also a good sign if I'm chattering. I smile politely and let loose a barrage of questions when I'm *not* interested in a person.

"Is this a date?" Sanjeev asks.

"Yes! Of course it is! Whee!" I yodel and grin stupidly.

Oh, I know I should be a bit more proper. I can tell he's a little unnerved by my blithe and giddy behavior. He's from Gorakhpur, after all, but I'm having too much fun. We arrive at TC, but it's shut down early because of the fracas surrounding the Rahul Mahajan case. Rahul Mahajan, a famous politician's son, and his father's closest associate overdosed on heroin. The adviser was found dead, but Mahajan survived. I don't see how shutting down bars in Delhi early for a week will solve any issues relating to heroin use in the city, but then logic rarely prevails in India.

Sanjeev and I try to get into a couple of other clubs in south Delhi, but they have all closed early. He turns to me and says, "Well, you know what this means?"

"No, what?" I say.

"Well, there's only one place to go now. It's called Last Chance, fittingly enough, and it's in Gurgaon. You up for it?" my sweet little gnome asks.

"Of course! Yay! Whee!" I trill.

Later, after we have danced to Bollywood music for two hours, we emerge from the club into the parking lot, drenched with sweat. We are now holding hands and giggling like teenagers, though we have yet to kiss. As we're ambling toward Sanjeev's Maruti, we're accosted by two blond potato-faced men.

"We are from Finland, and we cannot to get a taxi. Do you mind to drop us just down the road?" one of the men says.

"Sure," Sanjeev says gamely. "No problem."

The Finns pile into the back as Sanjeev starts the car. We are too wrapped up in each other to make conversation with the men, so we ignore them entirely.

"Listen, Anita, I'm happy to drive you back to Delhi. Of course, I would anyway, but then I'll have to drive all the way back to Gurgaon, so . . .," Sanjeev says.

"Oh, no worries, you can stay over," I say. "I mean, you could stay as long as you want."

"As long as I want? How long is that?" he says, looking over at me playfully.

"You could stay . . . oh, I don't know . . . forever, maybe?" I say sweetly.

"Forever?" Sanjeev says, grinning.

"Yeah, would you like that?"

"Yeah, I would like that a lot."

And with that, Sanjeev leans over and we share our first kiss, as we're racing down Mehrauli Gurgaon Road with two drunk Finns in the backseat. Sometimes it is just like the Bollywood movies.

The next morning, Amma makes *paranthas* for us and we eat them in bed and watch two films I have lying around. When I walk into the kitchen to bring the dirty plates, Amma and Chandra are particularly solicitous.

"Would *bhaiya* like something else? I can make more chai," both say in unison.

While both have seen evidence of male guests before, this is the first time a man has stayed throughout the afternoon. Sanjeev *looks* like a nice fellow, and they like him.

In the evening, Sanjeev and I go out for dinner and some wine at the upmarket restaurant in Lodi Gardens. Again, the restaurant is my suggestion, but Sanjeev dauntlessly pulls out his wallet when the bill comes. Later, when people at his office will ask him about his forty-eight-hour date, the first thing he will say about it is that it was expensive.

Over dinner, I talk more freely than I did the previous night about my past and my life in various cities. I'm finding Sanjeev's company perfectly delightful and have decided to like him—it's usually a decision after all, isn't it? But I can tell he's hesitant, not as unequivocally into this as I am.

I, of course, am rather unreserved about my delight. It is a full moon. I bray at it.

Chapter Twenty-seven

I do not consider myself a good lover. Just ask any of my previous lovers. In fact, although I hardly wish to overstate the case, I may even be a poor lover. I am neither extremely generous, nor inventively acrobatic, nor indefatigable. I'm not terribly experienced or irresistibly sexy, and worst of all, I'm far too interested in postcoital affection and conversation. But, oddly enough, for these reasons I consider myself a connoisseur of love—a tabula rasa on which can a man can paint his desire.

Once when I was twenty-three years old, an Irish lover told me that for a woman to be a good lover, all she had to do was allow herself, to present herself, to be loved. I was impressionable, and somehow the words dovetailed with my nascent ideas of lovemaking. So while I may not be the most kinetic of lovers, my body is like a very sensitive Richter scale, responding to the briefest tremors of a man's desire. I follow his lead. If his desire does not register, my performance is, in concert, lackluster.

It's been a few weeks, and the needle on my Richter scale is barely moving with Sanjeev. He has previously dated mostly women from the northeast and even admits to having a marked preference for them. Ah, a fetish for the East Asian woman. I know it well. I lived in Singapore, remember, where white men would sing the glories of the East Asian female's taut body, her flawless skin, her silky hair, her uncommon grace. After being with a succession of East Asian women, these men could no longer date other women. European or Indian women seemed large-ish, bulky, ungainly. I am surprised to encounter the fetish here in India, but then my year in Delhi has thrown me so many curveballs, I should hardly be shocked.

Sanjeev and I trudge on with our *pas de deux*, despite constantly stepping on each other's feet. After a month together, he suggests we go away on a long weekend to Rishikesh, a religious town on the Ganges, located at the foothills of the Himalayas. I agree, hoping passion will ignite outside of the city.

On the eve of my first-year anniversary of living in India, Sanjeev and I set out in his car, and the pitiful Maruti shudders for the entire eight-hour journey. I have purchased tiny speakers from Khan Market for the trip to use with Sanjeev's MP3 player. He's put together an eclectic playlist that includes Nusrat Fateh Ali Khan, Lou Reed, and Mukesh's "Awara Hoon."

"*Awara hoon. Gardish mein hoon, aasmaan ka taara hoon*" ("I'm a wanderer. I'm a star in the sky, but I've fallen on hard times"), Mukesh's jaunty voice bleats from the tinny speakers I've set up on my side of the dashboard.

We decide to break up the trip by stopping midway and take a hotel room in Roorkee, the town where both he and my father attended university. It would be a drab stopover for someone else, but for me it is a perfect amuse-bouche for our trip.

Sanjeev is also eager to stop so that he can watch the World Cup soccer quarterfinals—Germany, the host country, is playing Argentina. That first night, my head is swimming from the long, polluted drive, and I cannot stay awake for the match. I collapse on the hotel bed. Watching television, Sanjeev draws me into his arms as I sleep.

I awake later when the match is nearly ending. I feel much better.

"Your touch is very therapeutic," I say groggily.

Sanjeev smiles his gnomic smile.

"How is the match?" I ask.

Germany has won and will move on to the semifinals. Sanjeev tells me he thinks it was fixed and the Argentinian coach has been bought off. "He took his best players off the field. And since the World Cup is being held in Berlin, it would be upsetting for Germans if their team didn't advance to the semifinals."

I think Sanjeev's assessment is entirely plausible and go back to sleep, amused at his skeptical, "out of the box" thinking.

The next day, Sanjeev drives me around the campus of his and my father's alma mater. Like most Indian universities, little concession has been made to elegant architecture. He points out the fields where he used to play soccer and cricket, the different buildings he lived in, the architecture department where he studied. The only thing that distinguishes this building from those housing the engineering or mathematics departments is the massive modernist iron sculpture sitting next to it.

As we drive around, I recall some of my father's stories about his Roorkee days, like his "drinking" story. My father could outdrink anyone at Roorkee—drinking water, that is. Since engineering students in India weren't big partiers back in the sixties, my father made a bet with his circle of friends that he could drink the most water of anybody. And he did. He guzzled five gallons right on the spot and then collected his earnings. (I guess I'm a chip off the old block.) Being at my father's university four decades later also makes me think of the naïve hopes that imbued his spirit back then—that a good education would secure a good life in India. He would have to leave the country to fulfill those hopes.

Outside the campus, the city of Roorkee boasts the same tumult of blaring horns, motorcycles swerving around cows, dilapidated storefronts, and busy signage that define most north

Indian cities. But Sanjeev is proud to show off his former college town. He takes me to the place that serves the town's best milkshakes. I have a coffee milkshake and he has one made with mango. We try each other's milkshakes. This weekend is perfect, yet, yet . . .

I have bought Sanjeev, the quintessential bookworm, the American cult classic *A Confederacy of Dunces*, and he spends the whole weekend devouring *it*—not me. I try to ignore the fact that we're not having sex, but I can't stop thinking about it. When I bring it up, he says not to worry, that he's having a nice time. I worry. Of course, I know sex tapers off as a relationship continues, but we've just started dating. I've always thought the first weekend you go away with a new boyfriend should be rollicking good fun.

As Sanjeev reads, I leave our cottage and walk down the hill outside to sit on the banks of the Ganges. An hour later, at dusk, he emerges from the room, wearing a long red cotton *kurta* and white pajamas, and finds me. The first thing he does is build a fire. I watch him gather nearby driftwood and twigs and leaves, setting them on fire with a lighter. I have never watched a man build a fire before, having dated men who've grown up in cities and suburbs, and I'm suitably impressed. Wearing his cotton *kurta* and stoking a fire, he presents a picture of spartan Thoreauvian elegance. A damn sexy one to boot.

Sanjeev sits down on a large rock facing the one I'm sitting on, lights a cigarette, and begins telling me the story of his life, his migration from Gorakhpur to Roorkee to Lucknow to Bangalore, and eventually to Delhi. He started out as an architect but found his aesthetic vision too compromised in India. He eventually moved into the booming IT sector. I watch him speak as the light from the fire flickers across his face. My heart aches. Sanjeev is interesting, well-spoken, kind, capable. I don't know why it's not working. I take his hand, kiss his palm, and bring it to my cheek.

On our last day, we drive past Rishikesh further up into the mountains, to a place called Devprayag, a tiny town perched in the hills where the Ganges begins. Two separate rivers, the Bhagirathi and the Alaknanda, meet here to form the country's holiest piece of topography, the Ganges. We walk to the platform set up at the intersection of the two individual rivers. It is the place they flow together to create something much larger than either is alone. A pandit comes forward to extort us. We allow ourselves to be blessed. He asks if we are married.

"*Haan*," Sanjeev says.

I know Sanjeev is saying it to deflect unnecessary questioning. Unmarried couples in India usually do not travel together. But it feels heartening nonetheless. The pandit asks us to recite various Sanskrit incantations. He drips water from the Ganges into our palms and then places marigolds in them. He adorns both of our foreheads with a red *tika*. I look out at the two rivers flowing together, creating something much larger than either is alone. It is the closest I've ever been to being married.

We drive back and spend the night in the same hotel in Roorkee. In the room, we call room service and order *paneer tikka* and *dal makhni*. Sanjeev is also vegetarian, which is actually rarer than you would think in India today. He's the first man I've dated here who is, and somehow I like the idea that we eat the same thing. Food is bonding, after all.

Now, after a shared two days together on this journey, we've achieved a comfort level. We lie in bed and talk easily, swapping stories about our best friends and college days. And we finally have sex. It is the best day of our trip.

*   *   *

Sanjeev and I chug along for another month or so before he has to leave for a three-month work stint in the U.S., his first trip to America. We've been picking at each other as his departure nears. Something is not quite right. Certainly we don't share a great deal of sexual chemistry, and because of his stated preference for women from India's northeast, I feel particularly self-conscious about my body in bed.

Rather uncalled for one day, he describes me as too flamboyant as well as a "loud American."

"Sanjeev, I've long held reserve to be an entirely overrated virtue," I reply.

I take far more umbrage, though, at his second comment, saying, "Why can't I be a loud Indian? Plenty of Indians are loud too."

"The women aren't," he answers.

What we're really doing is circling around something else—a mismatch in our exposure to the world, something that unnerves us both, to our mutual surprise. Sanjeev tastes champagne for the first time on my roof terrace, with the lights of Humayun's Tomb blinking in the background. Though he lived in Nigeria for a few years during his childhood, his only forays out of India as an adult have been to neighboring Bhutan and Nepal. He certainly couldn't afford to travel to Europe or the U.S. without being sent there for work. When I offhandedly mention that I prefer my winter wardrobe to my summer one because I purchased my winter clothing in Paris the previous fall when I met a friend there and my summer attire is from Fab India, a local chain, it sounds pretentious as soon as it comes out of my mouth. Sanjeev responds to the comment with his strange smile.

Having been single for long periods of my adulthood, I have become accustomed to a life of trying out new restaurants and bars; it is the life I have lived. Here in India, however, the price of going out for dinner or drinks is so completely out of proportion to monthly salaries that only the city's moneyed elite—the Delhi businessmen's sons who I find boorish—can afford such a lifestyle. Sanjeev might end up paying a tenth of his salary for dinner out at a restaurant, and it makes him squirm when I pay.

Sanjeev is extremely bright—as bright as they come, really—and has liberal values, and yet we both can't seem to overlook the difference in exposure. Perhaps it intimidates him that I'm more worldly than he is, and it makes me question whether a life together is feasible. Neither of us had thought *that* was something that could come between two people otherwise of the same intellect, and yet it sits between us like the elephant in the room.

He goes off to Baltimore, and I return to the U.S. to visit my parents in California. The separation is the perfect *deus ex machina* for the breakdown of our relationship. We have difficult telephone conversations about whether we should meet somewhere in the U.S. We both know it's not working—we are too different—but I'm loath to call it off. After all, my parents have been asking about him every day. I'm back in the roiling pot of hot water that parental pressure to get married has become for me, and the disconnect between us is a bit too intangible for me to make a considered decision. Not to mention, it's always painful to split with somebody, and after a few months of dating, I've developed feelings for Sanjeev.

So instead I strike out at him for his lack of high-octane enthusiasm for the relationship. Finally, when the arguments escalate, Sanjeev calls it off.

I can't escape the feeling that I pushed him to do it.

I've been in Delhi for a year, the time I'd given myself to find a husband. I am alone. I wonder if my escapades were much different from those in New York. Many of them weren't, as the variegated cultures of the world increasingly collapse into one—urban, homogenous, fast paced, self-interested.

But in this year, amid all the raciness and jadedness I find among Delhi's youth, I know that I also see glimpses of a startling innocence and beauty that are harder to come by in benumbed cities like New York and London. The oddly nude yet chaste night I spent with Vikram in his cot in Gurgaon, with him reciting Urdu couplets into my ear. The day at Tughlakabad Fort with Shekhar as we dangled our feet off a parapet and smoked a spliff. Naveen, the "vernac" guy from Pegs and Pints, taking me on the moonlit motorcycle ride. My nightly rambles with Mustafa as we both lay in bed, he in Kashmir, me in Delhi. Kissing Amarjeet, inaugurating him into a world of intimacy. My earnest chats with Nair on my terrace about his background and his aspirations. Gurpeet's exquisitely planned evening that kicked off with the fortune tellers. The encrypted message from Manoj, which asked nothing of me but to be delighted. My first kiss with Sanjeev in a moving car with two Finns in the backseat, and our two strangely affecting nights in the hotel room in Roorkee.

What I don't know, though, is how much longer that innocence will last.

Epilogue

Farhad was right, you know. Remember the friend who used to tell me to take comfort in cold, hard numbers when I would lament that I would grow old alone? It's true, what he said; few people do end up alone.

It's been a year since Sanjeev and I split up, and I think back to all the men I've spent time with, both in my first year in India and before—the men I flirted with, dated, almost married.

There was, of course, my filmmaker uncle, Arjun. Toward the end of my first year in Delhi, he had managed to track me down through my relatives in Ghaziabad. And one day, while sitting in an autorickshaw, I received a call from an unfamiliar number and picked up to hear a voice I had not heard for nearly fifteen years, since that summer I had left his flat near Connaught Place, dust kicking up in my wake.

"Anita, you've been in India for a year, and you haven't called me," Arjun said in Hindi.

"Hi, Arjun. Yes, I haven't called you. What happened between us was many, many years ago. I didn't feel the need," I said in the formal language of English, shouting to make myself heard above Delhi's traffic commotion.

"I would like to see you," he said in Hindi.

I agreed to meet him, since I too was curious about who this man who had been so instrumental to my introduction to India, or a particular type of India, really was. We made plans to meet for lunch the next day at a restaurant in Asian Games Village.

He came attired in what appeared to be a black tuxedo without the bow tie and shiny, patent-leather shoes. I arrived in a hooded sweatshirt, jeans, and flip-flops. Interestingly, Arjun hadn't aged badly, largely because he had already looked so old when we'd spent those long-ago summers together. He looked more or less the same, his straight hair dyed blue-black.

He studied me. "You've grown thin, Anita. You've lost a lot of weight," he said in Hindi. To say someone is thin in *his* India isn't a compliment. It means you look haggard and peaked.

"Well, it's been a long time. I'm thirty-three years old now," I replied in English, struggling to keep things neutral.

I quickly added, to dispense with any chance of his wanting to resume things, "So, are you married?"

"*Haan, shaadi hogayi hai.* Yes, I married," he said. "I still don't understand why you didn't call me."

"That's wonderful that you're married. How long has it been? Any children?" I said.

"It's been a few years, no children," he said, waving away the question before saying, "I was so hurt when you ran out the way you did."

Arjun and I went on like this, picking over our Indian buffet lunch, for the next hour, him trying to rehash events from fifteen years ago in Hindi, and me trying to rein us back into safe territory, as well as the present, in English.

Mercifully, after the lunch was over, he didn't call again.

Then there's Rahul, my first love, the one who I would spot around campus with the tweed blazer and the Harry Potter glasses—though it's an anachronistic comparison to say so, since Harry Potter didn't exist back then.

Rahul, who was so much like me—Indian-American from California, interested in books, a writer. Rahul, the one I was supposed to marry but didn't because I feared he was incapable of the daily push-and-pull of marriage, the quotidian, on-the-ground business of dishes and bills and everyday affections. I didn't think he was the marrying kind.

Rahul met a woman soon after I turned down his marriage proposal and dated her for a couple of years before marrying her. They have been married for seven years now.

You may wonder, too, about Mustafa, the Sufi saint from Kashmir. Although we've not been in touch, I've heard through mutual friends that Mustafa married a Kashmiri woman who'd grown up outside of India—I assume the one I saw him with that evening in Khan Market—and left the country.

And Sanjeev? The last one from Gorakhpur, who seemed at first so perfect for me—from the same caste, well read, kind, and generous.

One day, a few months after we both returned from our separate sojourns in the U.S., I called him to say hello. We'd been in touch sporadically, and I knew that he'd started dating someone new immediately after he returned to India. Among the first questions I asked was if she was from the northeast, and indeed, she was.

When I called him on this particular day, he picked up after the first or second ring, "Hello?"

"Hi, Sanjeev. It's me, Anita," I said, though I'm sure he already knew from the caller ID. "How are you?"

"I'm good, doing well. Actually I'm at home right now, in Gorakhpur, with my parents," he said. "How are you?"

"Good, good. Same old thing," I replied. "Any special reason you're back in Gorakhpur?"

"Well, I brought my girlfriend with me, to introduce her to my parents."

"Oh," I said, stung by the words. My voice shrank, and in a wavering tone, I said, "I guess it means it's serious then. I guess . . . I guess you'll get married to her."

There was a seconds-long pause. "We just did," he said. "We just got married."

"You . . . just . . . got . . . *married*?"

"Yes, just a few hours ago."

Certainly, not everybody I know except me got married, but a year later, many of my friends were in long, sturdy relationships. Nair, the New Indian archetype, was still going strong with his Australian girlfriend, Genevieve, as were TJ and Lisa.

Nandini, my on-again off-again partner in crime that first year in India, has been living in Gurgaon with Matthew for nearly a year. Despite his Western-sounding name, Matthew isn't a *gora*; he's an Indian Christian from Kerala, seven or eight years her elder and established in his career as a software engineer.

Being wise beyond her age, Nandini has always preferred older men. I have met Matthew now quite a few times, and I think she couldn't have made a better match. The two would like to marry, but she still, of course, has her parents to deal with, and they are dead-set on her marrying a Rajput. She doesn't know what she will do to circumvent them, but she's hoping a few years of her remaining unmarried will soften their stance— in that way Indian parents lower their standards after a daughter is divorced or beyond prime marriageable age.

In this relationship, it's she who tries to rein in his drinking when they go out.

Then, of course, there's Farhad himself. His oh-so-tempting suggestion that we end up together with that bottle of gin (I don't even like gin) no longer seems as preposterous as it did a few years ago—"Who needs a man when you can grow old and bitter with a flaming faggot by your side?" But Farhad, who fornicated his way through London and New York and who'd never had a relationship that lasted beyond a week, met someone when he left New York to live in Johannesburg. He has been involved in a serious relationship for the last three years and says things like "You know, Anita, I just didn't want to be that leering fifty-year-old troll in the gay bar." Even Farhad— Farhad!—is in love.

But I'm sure you're wondering about me. What happened to me, after all?

I decided to remain in Delhi, a city just as anarchic and sweltering as when my father left more than three decades ago, because I had found a sense of home. My immediate family may be in California and my closest friends in New York, but we live in postmodern times, and we are the arbiters of our own destinies. Who's to stop us if we decide to stay in a city for reasons as intangible as the glimpse of a Mughal-era tomb out of the corner of our eye as we sit in a noisy autorickshaw, or Chandra's lovingly made morning *lassis*? Who's to tell us that the moments of grace we encounter in a place are not enough to keep us there—that instead we need a context, a future, a father, a husband?

In New York, I had felt irremediably stuck in my workaday, drink-a-day job in journalism and felt that the city's dating ethos encouraged a type of desperation among its single thirtysome-thing—not to mention fortysomething—women, including me. I didn't like who I'd become in New York. Nearly every night I would join a gaggle of my female friends—poets, professors, corporate lawyers, journalists—to perform forensic science on the e-mail exchanges of various prospects, who would soon disappear, to be replaced by new ones. Intelligent women with wide-ranging interests, we decided to throw over imaginative conversation for the disturbing minutiae of the New York dating life.

Don't get me wrong. I was hardly above it; I was just as eager a participant in these circuitous sessions. Rather, I was like an addict being surrounded by her enablers. At some point, while returning from these evenings, I began experiencing an empty feeling akin to the one we get when we've just binged on junk food, and I was finding it increasingly difficult to spend time with people I genuinely cared about in this dispiriting fashion.

It all seemed so desperately retrograde. In the West, women had made so many advancements—and for what? Our top-notch educations and successful careers all went neglected in the end as we tripped over each other to bag a guy. I had to change my life.

It was different in Delhi. My ideas kept flowing from a pipeline that could not be stanched. I wanted to buy a vineyard in the new wine region in India; I wanted to open a tapas bar with Jose, my Spanish chef ex-boyfriend; I wanted to produce my friend Vincent's film. I saw opportunity in this New India everywhere I looked. Whether or not these ideas came to fruition, I was happy to be having them. The old and new worlds had inverted themselves. India had that full-of-possibility, anything-can-happen feel, while New York felt set in its ways, traditional: This is what happens to thirtysomething single women and there's no way out. I couldn't go back.

In Delhi, I haven't yet found a love so undeniable that it has led to marriage. Perhaps there is something to the age-old wisdom that love is the one thing we can't go looking for in life. That said, I'm not likely to ever stop looking altogether;

romantics are the worst kind of incorrigible, having less self-discipline than on-the-wagon alcoholics or yo-yo dieters. You know what? I think I'll be just fine.

After two years in my swanky—swanky for me, at least—flat in Nizamuddin East, it was time to move on. Having tired of the revelers, many of them male, they saw coming and going up the stairs, my landlords, who had earlier seemed so different from Delhi's other landlords, wanted to reoccupy the flat. Something else, too, had poisoned my relations with them in my last few months in Nizamuddin. After nearly two years of working for me and being treated with dignity, Chandra had developed a taste for self-respect. Can you blame her? She had started to answer back when they railed at her for missing a spot while cleaning or expected her to work backbreaking hours when ill.

The landlords noticed Chandra's growing sense of empowerment, which to them was insolence, plain and simple. And they had a fair idea who was responsible for her burgeoning self-esteem. They no longer greeted me when I ran into them on the stairwell, and our exchanges were no longer punctuated by bouts of informality. I knew I had worn out my welcome.

I didn't mind giving up my flat, because I'd wanted to leave anyway to look for cheaper and more modest accommodations. Though Nizamuddin was one of Delhi's most picturesque neighborhoods, I had tired of it. The city's chaos ended at its staid, family-oriented, manicured border. An English girlfriend of mine was moving out of her flat in Jangpura, a lively neighborhood across the main road from Nizamuddin, and I decided to take her place. Older than my first flat but with more character, it was just as spacious but half the rent. Jangpura was home to the bustling Bhogal market and, as I kept noticing, a much younger population of both expats and locals.

The day I left my flat was not an easy one. I had moved alone by now so many times that it had taken a psychic toll; every time I did it, I had said, "Never again." The first part of the day was the hardest, when five wiry men from the moving company came to box my goods. Watching them pack up my life took five hours and a piece of me. I first lay on my bed, until they took the bed. Then I sat on a chair, then a stool, then finally the floor, each shift downward corresponding to my mood. I was broken at the end, keen to get to my new home.

The day I left, Piyush, his wife, his mother, his sister, and, bizarrely, his eight-year-old son came to inspect the flat to decide how much of the two-month deposit they had of mine should be extorted for "damages." I had put off the inspection to the last few minutes before I vacated, as I knew they were not going to make it easy for me, particularly when it came to money. As expected, they totted up an outrageous charge of $700. For all his Frank Zappa–loving ways, Piyush was just another rapacious Indian landlord.

I didn't argue. Like a zombie, I accepted the small handful of cash they gave me—my eviscerated deposit. A single woman, if she can afford it, does battle with her checkbook. I doubted this would have occurred if I'd had a husband, the stinking irony of it all being that even if you do manage to find a flat as a single woman in Delhi, you'll get shafted some way, somehow, in the end.

My flat was now an empty, bombed-out shell of a place, with scraps of cardboard and bubble wrap lying around. Indeed, it was no longer *my* flat—the one where I'd hosted parties and learned so much about this razzle-dazzle new India and nurtured high hopes for love. After saying a disgusted and stilted thanks and goodbye to my landlord's family, I ran down the stairs. I couldn't get out of there fast enough. I jumped into the first mode of transport I saw. It was . . . a cycle rickshaw. As the driver pedaled toward my new neighborhood, my panic ebbed and my mood lifted with each stroke of his skeletal legs. Ten minutes later, I was in my new flat in Jangpura, which Chandra had already scrubbed, cleaned, and mopped—twice. Chandra was understandably leaving the landlords for good, and I had provided her with her own room in the new flat.

It took far less time to unpack than it did to pack up. Maybe it's intuitive: Shutting the door on an old life takes a painfully long time, but starting a fresh new one can be done rapidly, lightly even. Chandra was indefatigable that day. "Madam, *mein sab kar doongi*. I'll set up the flat tonight, I'll do it all, even if I have to stay up until four in the morning."

Once my bedroom was in an inhabitable state, Chandra and I sat on the cement floor of my bedroom to eat a late dinner of cold *aloo paranthas*, washed down with a Kingfisher beer each. We had not eaten all day long. The day had been difficult and I felt shaky and vulnerable, but ultimately proud that we'd done it together and that I'd survived the day without too much damage to anything but my bank account. I knew I would sleep well that night, ready for the new day, a new beginning, a reinvention. Reincarnation, I would wager, is as necessary for the living as it is for the dead.

Acknowledgments

Unlike most writers, I never expected to write a book. This book chose me rather than the other way around. For this reason, perhaps, this book owes far more to the efforts and inspiration of other people in making it a reality than do most.

Jared Hohlt's offhand suggestion one summer on a midtown rooftop that I write an article for *New York* magazine snowballed into what is arguably my destiny. For that, and his tireless championing of the article as well as his careful reading of my manuscript, I am eternally in his debt.

For the last decade, I have benefited from long discussions with Hema Easley on Indian society and culture. Her graciousness in treating me like a family member has added greatly to my knowledge and understanding of modern India. She was also kind enough to pay particular attention to the book's Hindi transliteration.

I have long relied on the sage counsel, not to mention the tough love, of Houtan Bassiri; it proved especially astute when it came to issues involving this book.

I am indebted to Joseph Johnson and the *Financial Times* for hiring me, which allowed me to live in Delhi, and later, for gently relieving me of my duties. Also, Kishan Negi was particularly helpful to me even after my tenure at the paper ended.

My first few months in Delhi were made bearable by the epistolary friendship of Azadeh Moaveni, who, though I've yet to meet her in person, spent considerable time elucidating the peculiarly hairy quandary of the "ethnic expat."

In Delhi, Pooja Arya and Sudhir Chowdhary exemplified the Indian axiom "the guest is god" with their generous hospitality and friendship. Kiran Bhushi, A. Singh, and Sharif Rangnekar went out of their way to share their experiences, extend their friendship, and welcome me into their social networks. Anand Mahindra offered unfailing technical support. Nicholas Kharkongor was my touchstone on writing matters and India's new social mores. Bobby Mehta, from his perch in San Francisco, and Sushmita Mani were key links to the outside world during the writing of this book. Without the efforts of Chandra and Amma, I imagine I would still be in the early stages of my manuscript.

My agents, the dashing and good-natured Esmond Harmsworth and behind-the-scenes sorceress Lane Zachary, navigated me through the byzantine publishing process and provided invaluable insight into both my proposal and various drafts of the manuscript. Without the perspicacious editing and vision of Gillian Blake at Bloomsbury USA, this book would be in much poorer shape. Arzu Tahsin and Mary Morris of Bloomsbury in the UK also made suggestions that made a lasting impact on the book.

I am profoundly fortunate for the as-of-yet unconditional love and support of my parents, to whom this book is dedicated. I can also, at this juncture, admit to being grateful for their colorful antics that I have reproduced here, without which I fear I would not have had much of a story to tell. In addition to much else, they have taught me the most valuable lesson of all and one I struggle to follow, though not always successfully—that to keep one's dignity one must allow others theirs.

Though Tracy K. Smith has not made an appearance in this book in veiled character form, for me, her presence is felt on every page. In addition to being deputized to read words soon after they emerged on the page, Tracy graciously fielded the panicky phone calls and tolerated the unbearable behavior during the writing of this book that I tried to shield from others, again not always successfully. She encouraged me to write for years, if not decades, before I did and has taught me everything I know. Thank you.

A NOTE ON THE AUTHOR

Anita Jain has worked as a journalist in a number of cities, including Mexico City, London, Singapore, New York, and New Delhi, where she currently lives. She grew up in northern California and graduated from Harvard University.

A NOTE ON THE TYPE

The text of this book is set Adobe Garamond. It is one of several versions of Garamond based on the designs of Claude Garamond. It is thought that Garamond based his font on Bembo, cut in 1495 by Francesco Griffo in collaboration with the Italian printer Aldus Manutius. Garamond types were first used in books printed in Paris around 1532. Many of the present-day versions of this type are based on the *Typi Academiae* of Jean Jannon, cut in Sedan in 1615.

Claude Garamond was born in Paris in 1480. He learned how to cut type from his father and by the age of fifteen he was able to fashion steel punches the size of a pica with great precision. At the age of sixty he was commissioned by King Francis I to design a Greek alphabet; for this he was given the honorable title of royal type founder. He died in 1561.